THE HEBRIDES

ABOUT THE AUTHOR

Since moving to Scotland from the south of England in 2006, Peter has developed a passion for the Hebrides and takes every available opportunity to get out among the islands. He lives in Glasgow with his wife, Fiona, and Dougal the Labrador. Peter also writes about his walking and cycling trips on his blog site at www.writesofway.com.

Other Cicerone guides by the author
Mountain Biking on the North Downs
Mountain Biking on the South Downs
Walking on Jura, Islay and Colonsay
Walking on Rum and the Small Isles

THE HEBRIDES

by

Peter Edwards

2 POLICE SQUARE, MILNTHORPE, CUMBRIA LA7 7PY
www.cicerone.co.uk

© Peter Edwards 2015
First edition 2015
ISBN: 978 1 85284 705 0

Printed by KHL Printing, Singapore

A catalogue record for this book is available from the British Library.
All photographs are by the author unless otherwise stated.

Route mapping by Lovell Johns www.lovelljohns.com
Contains Ordnance Survey data © Crown copyright and database right 2015. NASA relief data courtesy of ESRI.

This book is dedicated to Fiona and Dougal Mòr – islophiles both

ACKNOWLEDGEMENTS

While walking in the Hebrides I have greatly enjoyed the company of Rich Baldwin, Jon Beck, Sarah Blann, Konrad Borkowski, James Boulter, Andy and Jen Dodd, Finlay Finlay, Clare Gilman-Meadows, Garry Glover, Andy Godfrey, Chris Hallworth, Giulia Hetherington, Susan Kemp, Felicity Parsons, Anne-Marie and David Parsons, Alex Rintoul, Marianne Taylor, Dan Twyman, Malcolm Walker, Steve Wilkinson, Dougal Mòr, Reuben and Sol. Thanks are due to Duncan Philips, skipper of the Farsain, who has delivered us safely to many obscure corners of the Southern Hebrides, and to Murdo Macdonald, skipper of the Cuma, for our wonderful trip to St Kilda. Thanks to Glasgow-based photographer, Kerstin Grünling (www.ciorstain-photography.com) for throwing some light on the mechanics of photography. Thanks also to Brett Collins (BEng FGS) for rubber-stamping the geology section. Richard Barrett, Graham Uney and Mike Townsend recommended a number of routes in the Outer Hebrides and provided valuable insights along the way. Thank you to Dave Hoult for correspondence on matters Hebridean. Thanks to the team at Cicerone for transforming my words and pictures into such a fine book. Most of all thanks to my wife, the lovely Fiona Rintoul, who introduced me to the Hebrides and has been my companion on many fine walks since 2001.

UPDATES TO THIS GUIDE

While every effort is made by our authors to ensure the accuracy of guidebooks as they go to print, changes can occur during the lifetime of an edition. Any updates that we know of for this guide will be on the Cicerone website (www.cicerone.co.uk/705/updates), so please check before planning your trip. We also advise that you check information about such things as transport, accommodation and shops locally. Even rights of way can be altered over time. We are always grateful for information about any discrepancies between a guidebook and the facts on the ground, sent by email to info@cicerone.co.uk or by post to Cicerone, 2 Police Square, Milnthorpe LA7 7PY, United Kingdom.

Front cover: Port a' Ghràig, Oronsay, with the Paps of Jura beyond (Walk 9)

CONTENTS

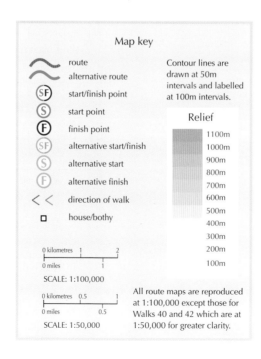

Map key

~ route
~ alternative route

(SF) start/finish point
(S) start point
(F) finish point
(SF) alternative start/finish
(S) alternative start
(F) alternative finish
< < direction of walk
□ house/bothy

Contour lines are drawn at 50m intervals and labelled at 100m intervals.

Relief

1100m
1000m
900m
800m
700m
600m
500m
400m
300m
200m
100m

0 kilometres 1 2
0 miles 1
SCALE: 1:100,000

0 kilometres 0.5 1
0 miles 0.5
SCALE: 1:50,000

All route maps are reproduced at 1:100,000 except those for Walks 40 and 42 which are at 1:50,000 for greater clarity.

PREFACE

*The myriad islands of Scotland's western seaboard cast a spell, some sort of magic.
The people of the Hebrides are part of this charm but the strongest power emanates
from the wide seas, the complicated topography, the very rocks and the lichens
and limpets upon them, the birds and the seals and the island creatures and the
remnants of human cultures little known or dreamed of and the wide, sad skies.*

Roger Redfern, 1934–2011

I first visited the Hebrides more than 25 years ago on a week-long midwinter trip to South Uist, most memorable for the 100mph gales blowing sheep past the windows of our rented cottage. If we ventured outdoors, we were hurled to the ground by violent gusts. This was a disappointment, not least because the journey to and from the south coast of England took two days each way. This is probably why many years passed before my next visit, to Islay and Jura this time, in the company of my future wife.

From the summit of Beinn Shiantaidh – one of the Paps of Jura – we glimpsed Jura's wild northwest coast through fleeting breaks in the fast-moving cloud. A seed was sown. We vowed to return to walk the west coast of Jura the following year, which we duly did, and we have returned several times most years since. From this spectacular coastline the shores and mountains of Mull, Scarba, the Garvellachs, Colonsay and Islay beckoned. From those islands in turn we looked across to Skye, the Small Isles, the Outer Hebrides and beyond, until, on St Kilda, the only way to look was back at where we'd come from.

In the nine years since that first trip we've covered many miles on foot across the Hebrides, often revisiting favourite places many times. This guidebook was born out of a near-obsessive preoccupation with this island domain and it is aimed at adventurous and resourceful walkers who are willing to go the extra mile for something special. Although the islands are a wonderful place to visit on a touring holiday, enjoying the magnificent scenery and the superb beaches, visiting sites of cultural and historical interest and generally soaking up the Hebridean ambience, the best of the Hebrides is often experienced in the course of a journey on foot – with remarkable vistas ranging from rugged mountain ridges to breathtakingly beautiful coastal scenery alive with spectacular wildlife. The Hebrides is a region of great geological, topographical and natural diversity with ten designated National Scenic Areas: although the denomination 'area of outstanding natural beauty', used in the rest of the UK, would be a fair description of the entire archipelago.

If you're prepared to put up with occasional inclement weather, you too may find that walking in the Hebrides is an experience you will want to repeat over and over again.

This book owes a debt to the late Roger Redfern, whose *Rambles in the Hebrides* (1966) was later updated and re-published by Cicerone Press as *Walking in the Hebrides* (1998). Roger's insightful and affectionate accounts of his journeys in the Hebrides provided inspiration for some of my own explorations of these elemental and enchanting islands.

Peter Edwards, 2014

← *Looking across Loch Trolamaraig from the ruined crofts at
Gearraidh Lotaigear on the Reinigeadal path, Lewis (Walk 45)*

9

INTRODUCTION

The Hebridean isles lie scattered like rough gemstones along Scotland's Atlantic seaboard, and some of the finest walking in the British Isles can be found here amid the sublime, elemental beauty of the Hebridean hills and shores. In the islands' rugged hinterlands scree-strewn mountain ridges rise above austere moorlands jewelled with peat-dark lochans, while whisky-hued burns tumble through mighty glens to the sea. Along the wild Hebridean shores towering cliffs and storm-battered headlands give way to silver shell-sand beaches and iridescent blue-green waters.

Against this magnificent backdrop the mercurial Hebridean weather can turn so quickly that at times it's like watching speeded-up film from a time-lapse camera. The sea-reflected Hebridean light is itself a thing of wonder, especially in the wake of stormy weather when sunshine sets the rain-washed air aglow: the play of light on hill and glen animates the landscape, and sun-silvered clouds sail swiftly across the vast Atlantic skies.

The Hebridean archipelago is comprised of two main island groups, the Inner and Outer Hebrides. There are 36 inhabited islands in the Inner Hebrides, with a combined population of around 19,000, and a further 43 uninhabited islands of substantial size. The 15 inhabited islands of the Outer Hebrides have a population of around 26,500, and there are more than 50 substantial uninhabited islands. One of the

Hebrides' most striking aspects is the distinctive topographical character of the islands, which make them so readily distinguishable from one another. These are landscapes wrought by tremendous tectonic upheavals and intense volcanic activity, further shaped by the advance and retreat of glaciers and resultant sea level fluctuations. These geomorphic processes have forged a realm of remarkable contrasts in a relatively compact geographical region; here the formidable volcanic peaks of Skye and Rum, the scree-clad Paps of Jura and the towering basalt cliffs of Eigg are counterpoints to the vast peat bog hinterland of north Lewis, the verdant pasture land of Islay and the pristine sandy beaches of the Uists, Coll and Tiree.

Despite being sparsely populated the Hebrides have a long history of human occupation, and traces of man's tenure – ancient and more recent – are scattered throughout the landscape. Mesolithic hunter–gatherers' shell middens, enigmatic Neolithic standing stones, Bronze Age roundhouses, Iron Age hill forts and early Christian beehive cells are among the ancient vestiges found on hill, moor and coast, while many place names are threaded through with Old Norse after centuries of occupation.

Chapters of more recent Hebridean history are also written in the landscape. The corrugations of crofters' lazy beds, their long-ruined black houses and abandoned villages, testify to life before the

← *Looking down from Aird Uachdarachd to the high cliffs at The Gap, St Kilda (Walk 50)*

↑ *An Cliseam (Clisham) (right) and the Harris Hills seen from Tràigh Rosamul, Harris (Walk 42)*

Looking back to Carsaig nestled between the cliffs, Mull (Walk 14)

Clearances of the 19th century, while the long-forgotten enterprises of entrepreneurial Victorians, the grandiose follies of wealthy Edwardians, shipwrecks, monuments, coastal defences and radar stations chart the ages of industry and global conflict.

The Hebrides provide the adventurous walker with a wide range of fine walks among diverse and magnificent landscapes. From the jagged mountain ridges of the Skye and Rum Cuillin, the majestic glens and summits of Mull and Harris, to the wild shores of Jura and Islay, the vertiginous sea cliffs of St Kilda and the dune-backed bays and machair pastures of the Uists, these islands provide a wealth of possibilities – and no shortage of challenges. The terrain is often rough, rugged and pathless and a degree of navigational competence is essential. The facilities and infrastructure walkers may rely on elsewhere, such as waymarked paths and public transport, are few and far between, so walking here requires a certain amount of self-reliance. This of course only adds to the rewarding nature of walking in the Hebrides for those who like a challenge. While there are plenty

of opportunities for a pleasant stroll on many of the islands, that is the territory of other guidebooks. The routes included here are aimed at experienced walkers with a good degree of fitness.

The Hebridean weather brings its own challenges. Storms battering in off the Atlantic, driving horizontal rain and buffeting winds can make coast and hillwalking ill-advised at times, while dense cloud, persistent rain and poor visibility can put a literal dampener on the experience. However, island weather is changeable, which usually provides some variety over the course of a few days. Such unpredictability is best viewed as stimulating, but you should be prepared for every eventuality when planning walks. High winds and persistent rain are not uncommon, but when the sun shines – as, contrary to popular myth, it frequently does in the Hebrides – the islands really are an earthly paradise. The Hebridean climate, greatly influenced by the North Atlantic Drift, is in fact generally milder than the mainland's, with subtle or significant variations between the islands.

Unsurprisingly, many of the routes included in this guidebook are coastal walks. This is a diverse range of walks over extremely varied terrain, from half-day circular routes along sparkling white sandy beaches to multi-day backpacks traversing some of the wildest, most rugged coastline in the British Isles – and some of the finest. The Hebridean shores teem with wildlife – including white-tailed eagles, otters, seals, waders, dippers and assorted seabirds – and are arrayed with remarkable geological features, including vast raised beaches of storm-scoured, sun-bleached pebbles, glacial cliffs, natural arches, huge submarine caves lifted above the waves after the glaciers' retreat, and imposing basalt dikes exposed by coastal erosion. Many traces of the islands' histories, both ancient and more recent, are also found around their coastlines – from Bronze Age fortifications perched on rocky promontories to abandoned crofting settlements.

From the walker's perspective, however, there is much more to the Hebrides than coastline alone. Several of the finest hillwalking days and mountain ridge traverses in all of Scotland are included here, along with day walks and backpacking routes through remote island hinterlands. What all of these routes have in common is the breathtakingly beautiful landscapes they traverse, with elements of the diverse geology, plants, wildlife and human history of the Hebrides encountered on every walk.

This guidebook brings together 50 fine walks in the Hebrides. Some are well known or established routes while others are off the beaten track. The aim is to provide an overview of the vast array of magnificent walks that the Hebrides have to offer.

GEOLOGY

The Hebrides is a region with a diverse geological composition and a wealth of remarkable geological phenomena, which contribute immeasurably to the profound and dramatic beauty of the islands. A little insight into the geological processes that shaped

Harris Bay with the Bullough Mausoleum and Cuillin backdrop, Rum (Walk 22)

these landscapes can only enhance the experience of visiting the islands.

The basic geology of the Hebrides consists of a basement layer of ancient rock, overlain in many places by more recent rocks. The basement was formed from even older igneous rocks, metamorphosed by intense heat and pressure deep within the Earth's crust around 3000 million years ago. These are the oldest rocks in the British Isles, known as Lewisian gneiss, after the largest island in the Outer Hebrides, where they are extensively exposed. In most of the Inner Hebrides the basement rock is overlain with sedimentary rocks. These include, for example, Torridonian sandstones formed from silts deposited by great rivers rising in the ancient continent of Laurentia, between 1200 and 850 million years ago, and the Dalradian Supergroup – including schists, phyllite, conglomerate, quartzite and limestone – which were originally layers of sediment deposited between 800–500 million years ago on the fringes of the ancient Iapetus Ocean.

Massive tectonic movements caused fissures and fault lines to develop, including the Great Glen Fault and the Moine Thrust – one of the most significant geological features in the Hebrides. The Moine Thrust effectively divided the Hebrides, running northeast to southwest through the Scottish mainland and the Inner Hebrides, cutting through the southern tip of Skye, passing south of the Small Isles, Coll and Tiree and north of Mull and the Southern Hebrides. The basement rock of the islands to the south was overlaid by younger strata while Lewisian gneiss remained the dominant strata in the islands to the north, including the entire Outer Hebrides. Tectonic activity between 490–390 million years ago, known as the Caledonian Orogeny, resulted in a period of strata folding and mountain building following the collision of the ancient continents of Laurentia (of which Scotland was a small part) and Baltica and the Avalonia microcontinent (including most of England and Wales), which closed the ancient Iapetus Ocean. Mountain ranges of Himalayan proportions were

Lewisian gneiss cliffs near Mangarstadh, Lewis

formed and subsequently eroded, principally by water and ice action, to the modest hills seen today.

Around 60 million years ago, during the Paleogene or Lower Tertiary Period, large-scale tectonic movements stretched and thinned the Earth's crust along the western margin of Scotland, precipitating an intense period of volcanic activity. Deep beneath the Earth's surface rocks melted, forming magma, which rose up through fractures in the thinned crust. Volcanoes formed where the magma reached the surface. The extensive lava flows that erupted from these volcanoes can be seen today, notably on Skye, Mull, Rum, Canna, Eigg and Muck. Large volumes of molten rock were also squeezed sideways into layers of sediment laid down on the sea-floor during the Jurassic Period. The magma cooled and crystallised, forming sills – thick, gently sloping sheets of igneous rock. Upwelling magma also filled cracks in the Earth's crust radiating out from centres of eruption on Ardnamurchan, Arran, Mull, Skye and Rum, forming intrusive basalt dike swarms, mainly with a northwest–southeast orientation. In the Inner Hebrides, erosion of the less-resistant rock into which the dikes intruded has left the dikes exposed as natural walls, particularly where subjected to coastal erosion. Conversely, in the Outer Hebrides the relative softness of basalt intrusions compared with the Lewisian gneisses resulted in the erosion of numerous steep-sided inlets or 'geos'.

When volcanic activity ceased along what is now the west coast of Scotland, 50 million years ago, the continental crust west of Scotland split completely as Greenland pulled away from Europe. From deep below the Earth's crust magma rose up and erupted, forming a new ocean floor. The North Atlantic Ocean continued to widen, while the exposed rocks on land were weathered and eroded under warm and humid conditions for over 45 million years, initiating much of the topography and coastline recognisable today. The North Atlantic continues to widen, and recent volcanic eruptions on Iceland are a continuation of the Paleogene volcanic episode that started in Scotland.

The climate of northern Europe cooled from about 7 million years ago, when the Greenland ice sheet began to form. Significant ice sheets first advanced across the mid-latitude continents about 2.6 million years ago, ushering in the Quarternary Ice Age – a period continuing to the present day – which

Weathered Torridonian sandstone outcrop, Rum

has encompassed several very cold glacial episodes interspersed with warmer periods known as interglacials. The present day landscapes of the Hebrides were shaped to a significant extent by the passage of the ice sheets during the last glacial period, which began about 30,000 years ago. Evidence of earlier glaciations, including glacial deposits, was swept away by the Devensian ice.

During the last glacial period, the Inner Hebrides were covered by an ice sheet flowing west from the western Highlands, while the Outer Hebrides were covered by an ice cap flowing radially outwards from the mountainous areas of Harris and Lewis, fending off ice flowing from the mainland. Sea levels dropped as fresh waters were locked up in the advancing ice sheets. Parts of St Kilda remained ice-free, probably the only land area in Scotland that did, apart from some mountaintops, which protruded through the ice like the nunataks found in Greenland today.

The climate warmed rapidly around 14,700 years ago and the ice melted away: then, around 12,500 years ago, the climate cooled again, an ice cap covered the western Highlands once more and glaciers formed in mountainous areas of the Hebrides. The final retreat of the glaciers occurred around 11,500 years ago.

Sea levels rose again as the glaciers melted and the landmass, which sank under the weight of the ice cap, gradually rebounded in a process known as 'glacio-isostatic uplift'. In the Inner Hebrides the land continued to rise beyond the maximum increase in sea level, gradually lifting shore platforms out of the sea, exposing numerous submarine caves, natural arches, rock stacks and raised beaches lying up to 40m above present sea level.

Because the Outer Hebrides are further away from the former centre of ice accumulation in the western Highlands, that landmass has not risen substantially. Nonetheless, the sea level rose sufficiently that the ice-scoured coastline was inundated, resulting in the archipelago of islands, skerries and reefs recognisable today. Glacial meltwaters swept vast quantities of sand and gravel into the sea, spreading debris over much of what is now the continental shelf. As the sea level rose, a mixture of glacial sediment and tiny fragments of crushed mollusc shells was swept ashore by wind and wave action, forming the white sand beaches and sand dunes characteristic of the low-lying areas of the western coastline.

The range of remarkable geomorphological features that can be seen today in the Hebrides date from the Devensian glaciation (the last glacial period of the current Ice Age). In the Inner Hebrides, the passage of the ice cap is evident in the curious oblique striations visible in the exposed rock, notably on Jura and Scarba. There are fine examples of glacial cliffs on northwestern Islay and Jura, and most spectacularly in the sheer 200m basalt wall flanking the Beinn Bhuidhe plateau at Cleadale on Eigg. Mull and Skye are home to some impressive U-shaped glacial valleys, such as Glen Clachaig and Glen Sligachan, while the jagged, basalt and gabbro ridges of the Rum and Skye Cuillin were shaped by repeated episodes of glacial erosion. The quartzite screes cladding the Paps of Jura are the result of frost-shattering during the Loch Lomond Stadial, when these mountains protruded from the ice as nunataks. On Tiree, a large glacial erratic boulder perched on the north coast, known as the Ringing Stone, was carried by the ice from Rum, 56km to the north. The light grey granodiorite boulder is much younger than Tiree's ancient Lewisian gneiss.

In the Outer Hebrides much of the rocky low-lying terrain was heavily scoured by the advancing ice sheet, creating the characteristic 'knock-and-lochan' topography. The knocks are rounded, ice-sculpted mounds which are interspersed with lochans, small lochs filling shallow, scoured depressions. Good examples of mountain glacier landforms and deposits show that the mountainous areas of South Uist and North Harris had their own small glaciers during the Loch Lomond Stadial, with evidence of glacial erosion particularly apparent in the northeastern corrie of Beinn Mhòr on South Uist. In the intense cold, frost shattering created fields of loose, broken rock, pinnacles and tors on these summits. Gleann Bhaltois at Uig in western Lewis is a remarkable example of a glacial meltwater channel: a single narrow gorge some 2.5km long and 45m deep at its maximum, carved out of the bedrock by meltwaters carrying heavy loads of pebbles.

Basalt glacial cliffs flanking the Beinn Bhuidhe plateau at Cleadale, Isle of Eigg

The sheer, overhanging buttress of Sròn Uladail in North Harris is a fine example of a truncated spur, carved by ice flowing down Gleann Uladail, while Loch Seaforth, which separates North Harris from the Pairc region of Lewis, is one of the finest fjords in northwest Scotland.

Where the ice sheets deposited quantities of eroded material or glacial till, including clays, sand, gravel and boulders, the resulting soils were usually highly fertile. However, in much of the Hebrides glaciation exposed the acidic gneiss and quartzite bedrock, such deposits were sparse and the resulting soils were not very fertile. With the retreat of the ice sheets, the climate improved and tundra vegetation gave way to burgeoning forest cover. At its warmest, 6000 years ago, the climate encouraged forestation to a higher altitude than the present day. However Scotland's climate became cooler and damper 3000 years ago, during the Neolithic and early Bronze Ages, and peat and heather moorland expanded at the expense of woodland. A dearth of cultivable land also led to woodland clearance by the early farming communities. Gneiss is non-porous and the low-lying land is often wet; over thousands of years, decomposing vegetation formed thick layers of peat on the bedrock. On the coastal fringes, peaty soil combined with wind-blown shell-sand to form the basis of the fertile, well-drained, flower-rich grassland known as machair, found on the western coastline of the Outer Hebrides, Tiree and Islay. The extensive machair pastures, sand dunes, sandy beaches and inter-tidal sandflats are a particularly outstanding feature of the coastal geomorphology of the area.

HISTORY

Pre-history
Mankind may have first reached parts of Scotland during the mild phases of the last glacial periods of the Quarternary Ice Age, retreating as the climate deteriorated. All traces of Palaeolithic (Old Stone Age) occupation were obliterated by the ice sheets during the subsequent glaciation. Archaeological evidence established the existence of Mesolithic (Middle Stone Age) settlement in some areas of Scotland from around 6500BC, with hunter–gatherers in seasonal occupation as early as 10,500BC on the fringes of the retreating ice sheet. Traces of the earliest known settlement in Scotland, dating to approximately 6600BC, were found at Kinloch on Rum, where concentrations of bloodstone fragments indicated the manufacture of stone tools.

By the early fourth millennium BC the itinerant hunter–gatherers were settling into permanent agriculture-based communities employing new livestock-rearing and crop-growing skills imported from mainland Europe. Evidence of Neolithic (New Stone Age, c4000–2000BC) culture in the Hebrides is quite extensive: perhaps the best-known site is the spectacular megalithic standing stones at Callanish (Calanais) on Lewis, erected around 2000BC. Archaeological sites dating from the Bronze Age (c2500–600BC) are also found throughout the Hebrides, including hut circles, field systems, burial cairns, cists and standing stones. However, many marginal Bronze Age settlements may have been abandoned during a period of harsh climatic conditions in northern Europe following the eruption of the Icelandic volcano, Hekla, around 1150BC. Iron-working skills were introduced to Scotland around 500BC by Celtic people migrating from continental Europe, who also introduced characteristic structures including brochs, duns, wheelhouses, crannogs and souterrains, found at many sites in Scotland.

Romans, Picts and Gaels
The first written references to the early Caledonian people come from the Romans, following Agricola's expedition north in AD81. The Caledonian tribes confronted the Roman forces and were defeated at the battle of Mons Graupius, after which Agricola sent his fleet on a sabre-rattling voyage around the north of Scotland. References to the *Picti* first appeared in Roman accounts around AD300, although the Picts were probably an assortment of racial and cultural groups, including the aboriginal Bronze Age peoples, bound together by the threat of the Romans. The Hebridean populations at this time were likely Pictish in origin.

From early in the third century an Irish Gaelic tribe – the Scotti of Dál Riata – began the colonisation of Argyll and the Inner Hebrides. The process of conquering and colonising the region continued until late in the fifth century when the kingdom of Dalriada established its capital at Dunadd following the decisive invasion of Argyll. To the north of Dalriada, the

Bostadh Iron Age village, Great Bernera, Lewis

Inner and Outer Hebrides were nominally under Pictish control at this time although the historical record is sketchy in this regard. The pre-eminent figure in the history of Dál Riata, St Columba, came from Ireland around AD563 and exiled himself to Iona, where he established a monastery that would become an important centre of learning and spirituality. Columba's followers, the early Celtic Christian missionaries, set about converting the populations of the islands and the mainland, ensuring that the kingdom would be of great importance in the spread of Christianity in northern Britain.

Norse rule

At the end of the eighth century the Vikings first arrived in the Hebrides, raiding and plundering monasteries. In AD794 Iona suffered the first of many raids, which gradually forced the monastery into decline as the Hebrides succumbed to Norse domination. Norse control of the Hebrides was formalised in 1098, when Edgar of Scotland relinquished the islands to Magnus III of Norway. The Norsemen ruled the islands from the Isle of Man until 1156,

when the Norse–Gaelic warlord, Somerled, divided the Norse Kingdom of Man and the Isles by defeating Godred Olaffson, King of the Isles, in a sea battle off Islay. Somerled took control of the Inner Hebrides, while the Outer Hebrides and the Isle of Man remained in Norse hands until the Treaty of Perth of 1266, when they were ceded to the Kingdom of Scotland following the Battle of Largs and the subsequent death of Haakon IV of Norway in 1263.

The Lords of the Isles and Scottish rule

Somerled was killed in 1164 during an invasion of mainland Scotland, but his descendants, Clan Donald – known as the Lords of the Isles – emerged as the most important power in northwestern Scotland by the 14th century. The Lords of the Isles extended their rule to the entire west coast and parts of northern Scotland, which they ruled from Finlaggan on Islay as subjects of the King of Scots. In theory Clan Donald were feudal superiors of the other Gaelic-speaking clan chiefs, including the Macleods of Harris and Lewis and MacNeils of Barra, who had gradually replaced the Norse

Ancient monastic beehive cell on Eileach an Naoimh, Garvellachs

princes, although this transition failed to rid the islands of internecine conflict. The Lordship came to an end in 1493 after John MacDonald II, fourth Lord of the Isles, signed a secret treaty with Edward IV of England against the Scottish Crown, hoping to become King of Scotland in return for his allegiance. Instead, his duplicity led to the confiscation of all MacDonald land and power by James IV.

Scottish control

In 1597, after years of feuding and warfare between local clans, the lands of Clan MacLeod were also forfeited to the crown and in 1598 King James VI awarded the Isle of Lewis to a group of Lowland colonists, known as the 'Fife Adventurers', in an attempt to anglicise the islands. Although initially successful, the putative colonists were driven out by local forces commanded by Murdoch and Neil MacLeod, based on Bearasaigh in Loch Ròg. In 1605 a second attempt was repulsed, and although a third attempt in 1607 was more successful possession eventually passed to the MacKenzies of Kintail in 1609 when Coinneach, Lord MacKenzie, bought out the lowlanders.

With the Treaty of Union in 1707 the Hebrides became part of the new Kingdom of Great Britain, even if loyalty to a distant monarch was not strong among the clans. There was in fact considerable support for the Stuart cause among the island clan chiefs, including Macleod of Dunvegan and MacLea of

Lismore, during the 1715 and 1745 Jacobite rebellions. However, in 1746 the decisive defeat of Charles Edward Stuart's forces by loyalist troops at the Battle of Culloden effectively ended Jacobite hopes of a Stuart restoration, and there were serious repercussions for the highlanders and islanders. The British government broke up the clan system and turned the Hebridean islands into a series of landed estates. This strategy may have ended the internecine feuding rife among the islands, but the islanders would have to pay a heavy price. The descendants of the clan chiefs became English-speaking landlords, alienated from their kinsmen and more concerned with the revenues generated by their estates than the condition of those who lived on them. Rents were increased and demanded in cash rather than kind, Gaelic-speaking was discouraged and the wearing of folk dress was outlawed.

Industry and Clearances

Nonetheless, the early 19th century was a time of improvement and population growth in the Hebrides, largely due to agricultural innovation, the introduction of the potato crop and the development of kelp farming for soda and potash – essential to the soap and glass industries. Furthermore, the construction of infrastructure, including roads, bridges and quays, and engineering projects such as the Crinan and Caledonian canals, improved transport links to and from the islands. However,

by the mid-19th century the price of soda and pot-ash had declined, potato crops failed and crofting communities in many parts of the Hebrides were further devastated by the Clearances. Throughout the Highlands and Islands human populations were evicted – often forcefully – by their landlords and replaced with Blackface sheep and red deer. Large scale emigration followed, some voluntary, some forced, with islanders relocated to the west coast and lowlands of mainland Scotland, as well as to the North American colonies.

The outlook for the depleted island communities remained bleak with high rents, no security of tenure and no land access rights. However, the tide began to turn in the 1870s when crofters and cottars (ten-ant and peasant farmers) on Lewis and in Wester Ross took part in rent strikes and land raids. By the early 1880s agitation had begun on Skye and threatened to spread throughout the Highlands and Islands. Police forces were drafted in to suppress the agitators, but were severely overstretched. In 1882, at the crofting

settlement of Braes on Skye, a demonstration against lack of access to land and the serving of eviction notices turned into a full-scale skirmish between police and demonstrators, which became known as the Battle of the Braes. This event precipitated the creation of the Napier Commission, which reported in 1884 on the situation of crofters and cottars in the Highlands and Islands: nonetheless, disturbances continued until the passing of the 1886 Crofters Act. The act set fair rents and guaranteed security of tenure and the right to bequeath crofts to a successor.

Despite these improvements in the islanders' situation emigration from the Hebrides continued apace, and many communities dwindled through-out the late 19th century and for much of the 20th century. Population decline made some communi-ties untenable and a number of smaller islands were eventually abandoned. For those who remained, however, the economic situation gradually improved with cattle farming, fisheries and tourism providing much of the stimulus. Nonetheless, the fortunes of

Edwardian folly? Kinloch Castle on Rum

Exotic Edwardiana on display in the interior of Kinloch Castle, Rum

many islanders were also influenced to a significant extent by the lairds, landowners and entrepeneurs who between them owned much of the archipelago. The philanthropic entrepeneur, Lord Leverhulme, invested in infrastructure and economic development on Harris and Lewis – with limited success. The fabulously wealthy tycoon George Bullough turned Rum into a private sporting estate – which did at least provide employment for a large retinue of staff – until the family fortunes dwindled.

Absentee landlords failing to maintain their estates and associated infrastructure posed a big problem for some communities. The nadir of mismanagement by absentee landlords was probably endured by the population of Eigg in the latter part of the 20th century. However in 1997, with help from the Highland Council, Eigg was acquired by the Eigg Heritage Trust – a scenario repeated many times since throughout the Highlands and Islands. Today the economy of the islands, which is dependent on farming, crofting, fishing, tourism, the oil industry and renewable energy, is in better health and with the assistance of bodies such as the Highlands and Islands Enterprise, the population decline that has so seriously affected the Hebrides since the mid-19th century has stalled and in some cases reversed for the first time. For the moment the future looks brighter for the Hebrides, but as the islanders are keenly aware, these will always be islands at the edge.

PEOPLE, LANGUAGE AND CULTURE

*Canna and her people – I remember so
many of them. Every day one realises
that it is not scenery but people who
create a world and all its beauty.*

Kathleen Raine, letter to Margaret Fay Shaw

Part of the appeal of walking in the Hebrides lies in the wide expanses of sea and sky and the grandeur of magnificent landscapes largely devoid of other people. Today large areas of many Hebridean islands are uninhabited, or at best sparsely populated, but it is worth remembering that these landscapes, commonly referred to as wild and remote, had often been continuously occupied for 5000 years or more – the traces of man's long tenure scattered far and wide on hill, glen and coast. The Hebrides are a cultural landscape, shaped and influenced by the hand of Man over thousands of years, just as the islanders themselves are shaped by the landscapes and elements of their island domain.

Some parts of the islands – most notably the Outer Hebrides – have a distinctive cultural identity. Common ancestry, culture and language are defining characteristics, as are the small, tight-knit communities where livelihoods are still eked from the land and sea and remain vulnerable to the elements. Through necessity, Hebridean people tend to be capable and pragmatic – competent multi-taskers who look out for each other. As a rule, islanders have a certain quiet reserve about them, but scratch the surface and you will find that they are warm, friendly and hospitable in an understated way, with a wonderfully dry sense of humour.

Christianity has deep roots in the Hebrides and the Church remains an important part of island life, particularly in the Western Isles, where a decline in its influence has been much more gradual than on the mainland. Owing in part to historical clan allegiances, the people of the northern isles of the Outer Hebrides – Lewis, Harris and North Uist – are predominantly Presbyterian while those of the southern islands – South Uist, Eriskay and Barra – are predominantly Roman Catholic. Lying between North Uist and South Uist, Benbecula is a harmonious mixture of both confessions.

Many indigenous islanders are descended from the Gaels and Norsemen who settled the Hebrides between the third and 12th centuries, and their history, cultural traditions and language – Scottish Gaelic – owe much to this shared heritage. However, this is not to imply an ethnic homogeneity. Emigration and immigration have been continual themes in the islands' history and this remains the case. Many young people still leave the islands, not least because of a dearth of employment opportunities, and a gradual influx of incomers keeps many communities viable. The populations of some smaller islands have very few or no families with roots extending for more than a generation or two, and several islands have experienced a high population turnover in recent years. However, the overall picture for the Hebrides is one of a stabilisation of population numbers after years of decline, which began with the mid-19th century Clearances, and some islands are actually experiencing small population increases.

*Tobar Oran, an early Christian statue now
in the grounds of Colonsay House*

'Welcome to the Isle of Eigg': Gaelic sign at Galmisdale (Walk 24)

The distribution of Scottish Gaelic speakers provides some indication of the proportion of indigenous islanders making up the populations throughout the Hebrides. The main stronghold of the language in Scotland remains the Outer Hebrides, with over 75 per cent Gaelic speakers in some parishes, an overall proportion of 60 per cent and all parishes over 50 per cent. The Parish of Kilmuir in Northern Skye is also over the 50 per cent threshold. In the Inner Hebrides the only areas with significant percentages of Gaelic speakers are the islands of Tiree, with 47 per cent, Skye and Raasay with 35 per cent, Lismore with 30 per cent and Islay with 25 per cent. The overwhelming majority of Gaelic speakers are bilingual. The number of Gaelic speakers has declined in recent years, although there have been efforts to revive the language with initiatives to increase the number of younger speakers. The Gaelic higher education college, Sabhal Mòr Ostaig, is based on Skye and has an associate campus on Islay.

Traditional Gaelic music and singing are popular in the Hebrides, and the genre is promoted at a number of annual music festivals throughout the islands, including the raucous Jura Music Festival. Several of the islands – including Islay, Skye and Lewis – have their own pipe bands, which have competed with success at the annual World Pipe Band Championships. Music is an important part of Hebridean life, but there is considerably more to island culture. Fèis Bharraigh began in 1981 on the islands of Barra and Vatersay with the aim of developing the practice and study of the Gaelic language, literature, music and drama. The two-week festival has inspired 43 other *feisean* throughout the islands and mainland Scotland.

WILDLIFE

The Hebrides lack the biodiversity of the mainland: only half the British Isles' mammal species are present, with even less in the Outer Hebrides. Nonetheless, the islands' diverse terrain, including large tracts of undeveloped land, together with sensitive land management, provides an abundance of natural habitats allowing many species to thrive. Opportunities to encounter wildlife at close quarters are plentiful when venturing into the hills and hinterlands or out along the wild Hebridean shores.

Deer are the largest mammals present, with red deer the largest and most numerous variety. Small herds of fallow deer are found on Islay, Scarba, Mull

Startled red deer hind, northwest Islay (Walk 1)

and Skye, and roe deer are also common on Islay and Skye. The red deer population grew exponentially with the expansion of deer forests for commercial sport in the latter half of the 19th century, particularly on Jura and Rum. They graze on the lower ground during the winter and take to the higher ground during the summer months as the grazing improves. The mating season, or 'rut', takes place during late September and October, when the stags engage in antlered combat for their own harem of hinds and the hills are alive with the sound of their throaty barking, or 'belling'.

Wild goats are found on many Inner Hebridean islands. Legend has it that they are descended from animals that swam ashore from Spanish Armada ships wrecked in stormy seas, although they are probably descended from domestic animals abandoned during the mid-19th century Clearances. Wild goats are usually dark brown and sometimes have white patches. They have long, shaggy coats and the billy goats have curving, swept-back horns.

Otters are present throughout the Hebrides and populations are thriving now that they are protected from persecution. Breeding pairs usually have a coastal territory around 5km (3 miles) in length. They tend to hunt on uninhabited or sparsely populated stretches of coastline. They are most often seen when hunting just off shore.

Skye is the only Hebridean island with populations of foxes and badgers, and pine martens are now found there and on Mull. A number of other predatory land mammals are present on some of the other islands including introduced species such as brown and black rats, feral cats, mink, polecats and hedgehogs. Other land mammals variously present throughout the Hebrides include brown hares, rabbits, various shrews, voles, wood, house and field mice, with mountain hares and red and grey squirrels found only on some Inner Hebridean islands.

Pipistrelle bats are found throughout the Inner Hebrides and on Lewis, while long-eared and Natterer's bats are present in parts of the Inner Hebrides. Three amphibians are commonly found in the Hebrides: common frogs, common toads and newts (smooth and palmate). There are three reptiles: the slow worm, common lizard (there is an experimental colony of introduced sand lizards on Coll) and the adder, which is the only snake found in the Inner Hebrides. There are no snakes in the Outer Hebrides. Among the freshwater fish present in the lochs and burns of the Hebrides are brown trout, salmon, grayling, char, European eels and three-spined sticklebacks.

Hebridean invertebrates include earthworms, snails, grasshoppers, flies, spiders and harvestmen, numerous species of damsel fly, dragonfly, beetle, butterfly and moth as well as several species of bumblebee. These thrive because of the low-intensity crofting agriculture and play a vital role in pollinating the myriad flowers on the machair and grasslands. And finally, of course, there are the biting beasties – midges, clegs (horseflies) and ticks.

Atlantic grey and common seals are abundant throughout the Hebrides and are seen basking on offshore rocks and skerries or observing onshore activity from the sea. Grey seals are considerably larger than common seals: adult males weigh up to 300kg and can be two metres long, while females can weigh 180kg and measure 180cm. Adult common seals are roughly a third of the weight and three-quarters the length. Common seals have a more dog-like appearance, while grey seals have a distinctive, long, sloping nose. Around 40 per cent of the world population of grey seals is found around Britain's shores, with 90 per cent of those breeding in Scotland. Grey seals prefer more exposed coasts and islands and are found throughout the Hebrides, while common seals favour more sheltered waters and are present around the east coast of the Outer Hebrides and throughout the Inner Hebrides.

A variety of cetaceans frequent the Hebrides, including minke whales, pilot whales, killer whales, porpoises, and common, bottle-nosed, white-beaked and Risso's dolphins. Basking sharks are summer visitors most frequently seen around Coll, Tiree and Mull, although seasonal distribution is related to availability of zooplankton. The basking shark is the second largest fish in the world – after the whale shark – measuring up to 11m and weighing about 4500kg.

Hebridean bird life is rich, diverse and often spectacular. A number of rare species such as the corncrake, red-necked phalarope and chough are present, as are several of the most impressive and photogenic species including the white-tailed eagle, gannet and puffin. The seabird populations of certain islands are quite breathtaking to witness and in several cases are of international importance, for example Rum's Manx shearwaters and the gannet colonies of the St Kilda archipelago.

Not so cute-looking dog otter on the Sound of Islay

Fulmar at An Campar on Hirta, St Kilda (Walk 50)

Robust populations of various raptors are distributed among the islands, including merlins, kestrels, sparrowhawks, hen harriers, peregrines, buzzards, golden eagles, white-tailed eagles, tawny owls, short-eared owls and barn owls. Ospreys visit on passage, occasional red kites winter or pass through and vagrant goshawks, gyr falcons and marsh harriers are seen infrequently. White-tailed eagles had been persecuted to extinction in Scotland by the early 20th century. A reintroduction programme began on Rum in 1975, and within 10 years 82 young birds from Norway had been released. Today, a successful breeding population is gradually colonising the west coast of Scotland. Mull, Jura, Scarba, Islay, Rum, Canna and Skye are some of the best places to see these magnificent birds, with their three-metre wingspan and tell-tale white tail feathers.

The Hebrides' high cliffs and sea stacks are the domain of nesting seabirds. The remote, uninhabited outposts of North Rona and Sula Sgeir, the Shiants, Flannans, Monachs and both Berneray and Mingulay to the south of Barra are especially propitious breeding grounds. St Kilda is home to the largest gannetry in the world, with over 60,000 pairs, as well as 64,000 pairs of fulmar, 45,000 pairs of

Pensive puffin at An Campar on Hirta, St Kilda (Walk 50)

Leach's petrels and, during the summer months, a huge colony of some 270,000 puffins.

Rum is renowned for its 61,000 pairs of Manx shearwaters – one of the world's largest breeding colonies. These migratory birds return to Rum every summer to breed in underground burrows high in the Rum Cuillin. Trollaval has high densities of nest burrows, which may have been occupied for many centuries. When the birds swap incubation shifts at night they make a fearsome racket, hence the meaning of the mountain's Norse name: 'hill of the trolls'. Guillemots, razorbills, storm petrels, shags, cormorants, kittiwakes, great skuas (or bonxies), arctic skuas, arctic terns, common terns and little terns can also be found on the main seabird islands. Various gulls are present throughout the islands including common, black-headed, great black-backed, herring and Iceland gulls.

Another of the Hebrides' remarkable avian spectacles occurs on Islay, where the approach of winter brings almost 50,000 migrating white-fronted and barnacle geese from Greenland and Canada. From October to April, huge numbers of these birds can be seen roosting around the fields and sand flats at Loch Gruinart and around Bridgend or taking to the air each morning. Canada, Brent and pinkfoot geese also winter on the island. Around 8000 barnacle, greylag and white-fronted geese also overwinter on Tiree.

Waders, divers and ducks populate the sand flats, salt marshes, freshwater and sea lochs, machair and sandy shorelines throughout the islands – particularly the Outer Hebrides, Islay, Coll and Tiree. Species of wader include the sandpiper, lapwing, turnstone, dunlin, oystercatcher, godwit, redshank, snipe and sanderling. Divers include the little, great-crested and scarce Slavonian grebes and the red-throated, black-throated and great northern divers. Ducks include the wigeon, red-breasted merganser, eider, teal, shoveler, shelduck, goldeneye, pochard and scaup. The grey heron, mute and whooper swan also haunt the islands' lochs, coastline and rivers. The elusive corncrake can be heard, if not seen, particularly around farmland. The corncrake's rasping call presages the onset of spring, and it has become something of a Hebridean mascot in recent years. It is one of Britain's rarest birds, with numbers in serious decline during the last 50 years due in large part to industrialised agriculture destroying habitat. Low-intensity farming practices in the Hebrides have given the corncrake a foothold in the islands. Colonsay, Oronsay and Coll are good places to hear, or if you're very lucky see, them. Other bird species endemic to various of the islands include the cuckoo, raven, chough and hooded crow as well as various finches, tits, chats, thrushes, warblers, pipits and wagtails.

PLANTS AND FLOWERS

Several factors influence the nature and distribution of plants and flowers in the Hebrides. Long days and high rainfall during the summer months, allied to the temperate influence of the Gulf Stream in winter, promote rapid growth. However, the hills and high ground are exposed to scouring winds while western coasts in particular are frequently battered by storms and whipped by salt spray: here the soils are often sparse and acidic, preventing many species gaining a foothold. Between autumn and spring these land-scapes can appear almost barren, but spring brings an eruption of vibrant green bracken ferns, followed by a profusion of bluebells, while clusters of sea pinks, primroses and varieties of orchid dot the shoreline.

Dense bracken and heather on the east coast of Colonsay

Greater diversity is found on lower-lying and more sheltered areas, especially where soils are enhanced by glacial till deposits overlaying the bedrock. Islay, for example, benefits from a varied terrain that includes grazed pasture and arable farmland, rugged quartzite uplands and hill country, woodlands, heathland, marshland, moorland, blanket bog, vegetated raised beach deposits, sea cliffs, sand dune systems, grasslands and machair, sand flats and salt-marsh. These diverse habitats are home to a wide range of vegetation including more than 900 flowering plants.

The underlying geology is a key factor in shaping habitats, with Lewisian gneiss, quartzite and other acidic rocks predominating. The combination of high acidity, low mean temperatures and high precipitation means that on many of the islands large areas of the soil layer consist largely of peat, which is prone to bogginess – especially where it overlies the non-porous gneiss bedrock of the Outer Hebrides. Large tracts of the islands' hinterlands consist of peat moor and heathland. Tussocky purple moor grass and mat grass are widespread. Bog myrtle, bog asphodel, rushes and sedges such as bog cotton and deer grass thrive on the wetter ground along with sundews and mosses, while heathland is dominated by bracken ferns, gorse and ericaceous dwarf shrubs such as bell heather and bilberry.

The Hebrides were largely deforested during the Neolithic and Bronze Ages and, excepting non-native plantation, there is very little woodland to be seen today. Furthermore, re-forestation is hindered by browsing deer and sheep decimating shoots and saplings. On those islands where there are still trees, remnants of native woodland are predominantly located to the east and in sheltered glens. On the northeast coast of Colonsay, for example, there are two areas of mixed deciduous woodland at Rubha na Coille Bige and Beinn nam Fitheach reckoned to be among the finest surviving remnants of native Hebridean woodland. Here you will find birch, sessile oak, hazel, willow and rowan, which shelter ferns, mosses, lichens and liverworts. In spring the woodland floor is covered with bluebells, violets, primroses and wood sorrel. There are extensive, non-native coniferous plantations on Mull and Skye, but there have also been a number of native woodland plantation projects in recent years, including Rebel Wood at Orbost on Skye.

The western coastal fringes of the Outer Hebrides, as well as Tiree and Islay in the Inner Hebrides, are garlanded with remarkable, flower-rich machair

↑ *Stand of birch trees on Garbh Eileach, the Garvellachs*

pastures. Machair is the Gaelic name for low-lying, fertile plains; machair sand has a high seashell content and when blown inland it neutralises the acidity of peat soils, propagating fertile grassland. The machair erupts into bloom in May, building to a floral crescendo in July with species including buttercup, bird's foot trefoil, saxifrage, carline thistle, scarlet pimpernel, eyebright, thyme, clover, wild pansy, violet, daisy, harebell, silverweed and hawkbit, mountain everlasting, gentian and orchid. This remarkable floral riot also encourages a range of insects and other invertebrates including high densities of bees that are now scarce on the mainland. Machair is one of the rarest habitats in Europe, found only in the north and west of Britain and Ireland. Almost half of Scotland's machair occurs in the Outer Hebrides, with the best and most extensive in the Uists and Barra.

A number of the islands' estates have elaborate maintained gardens, which often include exotic species and usually benefit from extensive protection from the elements. Jura House on the Ardfin estate at the island's southeast corner has a large walled garden with a collection of ornamental and non-hardy plants, including an Australasian collection, which would struggle to establish themselves in less clement conditions even significantly further south. The wonderful gardens at Colonsay House are protected by a thick belt of shelter trees. Here you will find magnolia, tree ferns, cordylines and one of the best rhododendron gardens in Scotland. The formerly derelict two-acre walled garden of Canna House has recently been brought back to life after a five-year restoration project. The garden has been replanted with herbaceous borders, flower beds and soft fruits to attract bees, butterflies and moths, and fruit trees and ornamental lawns have been resuscitated. There is also a stunning 25-metre Escallonia arch at the entrance.

GETTING TO THE ISLANDS

By ferry
The usual way to get to most of the Hebridean isles is on the Caledonian MacBrayne (CalMac) ferry services. You can check timetables and book online at www.calmac.co.uk or tel 08000 665000.

Outer Hebrides
Sailings to Castlebay on **Barra** depart from Oban: those for Lochboisdale on **South Uist** from Oban

CalMac ferry in the Sound of Islay, with Beinn a' Chaolais towering above

Getting to the islands

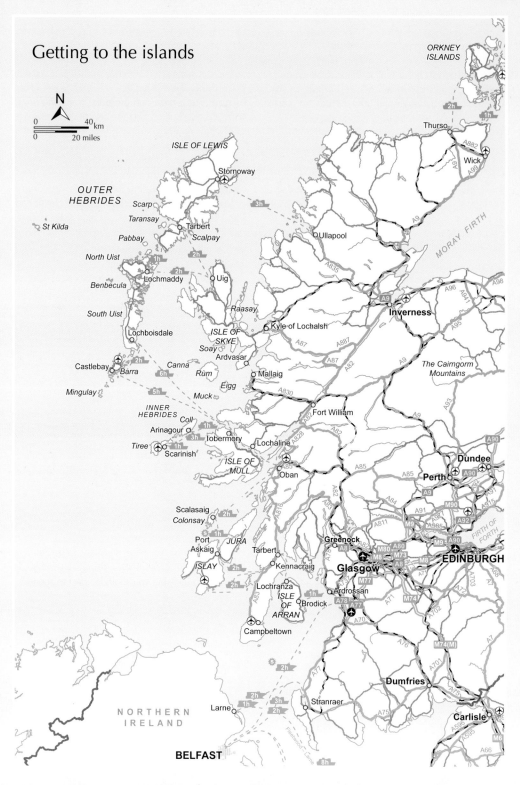

or Mallaig. Lochmaddy on **North Uist** and Tarbert on **Harris** are served from Uig on Skye; Stornoway (**Lewis**) from Ullapool. There are also ferries between the main Outer Hebridean isles that are not linked by causeways: Barra and Eriskay, Berneray and Harris.

Skye, Raasay and the Small Isles
Skye is connected to the mainland by a road bridge, but there is also a ferry service from Mallaig to Armadale. Meanwhile, from Uig (Skye) ferries run to Tarbert (**Harris**) and Lochmaddy (**North Uist**), from Sconser (Skye) to **Raasay**. The **Small Isles** – Rum, Eigg, Muck and Canna – are reached by ferry from Mallaig.

Inner Hebrides
Mull: Craignure from Oban, Fishnish from Lochaline (Morvern), Tobermory from Kilchoan (Ardnamurchan). **Coll** and **Tiree** from Oban.

Southern Hebrides
For **Islay**, Port Ellen and Port Askaig from Kennacraig; Port Askaig from Oban. **Colonsay**: from Oban and Kennacraig (via Port Askaig, Islay).

For **Jura**: a ferry operated on behalf of Argyll and Bute Council runs between Port Askaig (Islay) and Feolin Ferry: www.argyll-bute.gov.uk, tel 01496 840681. A summertime rigid inflatable boat (RIB) ferry runs between Tayvallich and Craighouse: www.jurapassengerferry.com, tel 07768 450000.

GETTING TO ST KILDA

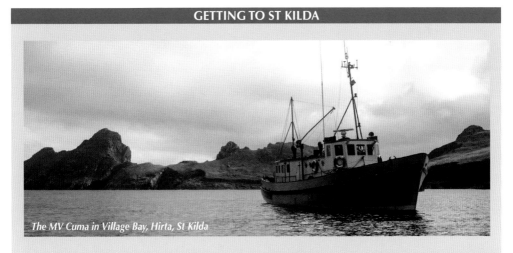

The MV Cuma in Village Bay, Hirta, St Kilda

Other than arriving by helicopter, there is no easy way of getting to St Kilda (Walk 50) – and no inexpensive way either. The small island archipelago lies some 40 miles west of the Outer Hebrides, across often turbulent seas. It is possible to visit St Kilda on a day trip from the Outer Hebrides, but you should expect to spend six hours at sea, with perhaps five hours on Hirta. This may suit people who incorporate such a trip into a holiday in the Outer Hebrides. There are several operators sailing from Leverburgh, Harris, including Sea Harris, www.seaharris.co.uk, tel 01859 502007. If St Kilda really appeals, then it might be worth considering a cruise to the archipelago, which allows more time on Hirta. Murdo Macdonald, skipper of the MV Cuma, operates four- and six-day cruises sailing from Miavaig, Lewis, which also visit other outliers including the Flannan Isles, the Monach Isles and Scarp, www.island-cruising.com, tel 01851 672381.

It is possible to stay at the camping ground on Hirta for up to five nights, although there is limited space: this must be arranged in advance with the National Trust for Scotland (NTS), tel 0844 493 2237. It is also possible to spend two weeks on Hirta as a NTS conservation volunteer: however there is a waiting list, you will need relevant skills and it costs: www.nts.org.uk; www.kilda.org.uk.

By air

Outer Hebrides
Flights to Stornoway (**Lewis**) leave from Inverness, Edinburgh and Glasgow: for details visit www. flybe.com. British Midland fly from Edinburgh to **Stornoway**: www.flybmi.com or tel 0870 6070555.
Flybe also fly daily from Glasgow to **Benbecula** (**Uists**) with connecting weekday flights to **Barra**.

Tiree
Flybe (www.flybe.com) fly to **Tiree** from Glasgow every day except Sunday. Hebridean Airways fly to Tiree from Oban on Monday, Wednesday and some Fridays www.hebrideanair.com or tel 0845 805 7465.

Southern Hebrides
Flybe (www.flybe.com) operates a twice-daily service between Glasgow and **Islay**.
Hebridean Airways (www.hebrideanair.com or tel 0845 805 7465) operates a twice-daily service between Oban and **Colonsay** on Tuesdays and Thursdays.

By rail and coach
There are rail links to the main ferry ports of Oban and Mallaig and there are also coach services to these ports and those not served by rail, including Uig (Skye), Ullapool and Kennacraig (Kintyre). More details of these services may be found at: www.scotrail.co.uk; www.nationalrail.co.uk; www.citylink.co.uk.

GETTING AROUND

Some of the larger islands, such as Skye, Mull, Islay, Harris and Lewis, have relatively extensive road networks and bus services. On other islands roads and bus services are more limited. Public transport options are given in the information box for each walk. Several islands, including, Rum, Canna and Iona, have limited roads and no bus service, and vehicles are not allowed without a permit. If taking a car to the islands, be aware that many roads are single-track with passing places; you should familiarise yourself with the correct use of passing places – including allowing overtaking – preferably in advance of your visit. Bicycles are a good way of getting around most of the islands.

↑ *Heading back up the Loch Coruisk path, Skye, in not untypical weather for the Misty Isle (Walk 31)*

WHEN TO GO

In early spring and autumn you are more likely to benefit from mild weather, although rain can be a feature – and rain results in wet, boggy ground. Another important advantage gained by visiting in these seasons is that in early spring the bracken has not yet sprung up and in the autumn it dies back. Bracken forms a serious natural obstacle in some areas on many of the islands and is often festooned with deer ticks (see 'Biting beasties'). Furthermore, midges and horseflies don't generally appear until mid-spring and disappear again in autumn. There are fewer visitors at these times of year than in summer and there is a reasonable amount of daylight to be getting on with.

In late spring and summer you will have to contend with bracken, ticks, midges and horseflies and you're less likely to have the place to yourself. In hot weather – really, it can happen – walking over the difficult terrain often encountered in the Hebrides can be gruelling, especially when backpacking. On the plus side, the days are long and evenings around a campfire are more viable. The ground is generally less boggy and the colours can be fantastic – the combination of sparkling blue–green seas, silver sands, emerald green bracken ferns and the explosion of wild flowers is wonderful. On several islands, including Skye, Mull and Harris, there is a trade-off between the risk of fine weather breaking out and significant visitor numbers. If you're after getting away from it all it's probably best to avoid the visitor 'hotspots' during the high season.

Winter can be a fantastic time for walking in the Hebrides, but this depends to some extent on the type of walking you aim to do and also how experienced, robust and well-equipped you are. Winter hillwalking in the Hebrides can be wonderful, but you must be a competent navigator and go properly equipped for the conditions. In the hills, winter is defined less by the calendar season so much as conditions on the ground. The temperate maritime climate also means that conditions may change quickly. Short winter days are another important factor to consider. It is doubly important to check the weather, let others know your planned route, allow plenty of time to complete your walk in daylight and be properly equipped before setting out. Stormy weather can be a factor and you will also be vulnerable to the elements when walking in coastal areas. Ferry cancellations are also common in the winter months. However, you're much more likely to have the place to yourself in winter and if you're lucky you might enjoy some days of crystal-sharp, winter sunlight. It can also be surprisingly mild in winter, thanks to the Gulf Stream, although the terrain can be very boggy in places, with December and January being the wettest months on most of the islands.

Deer stalking

On those islands where deer are culled it is advisable to contact the estates where you will be walking during the deer stalking season, which runs from 1 July until 15 February, both for your own safety and as a matter of courtesy. Contact numbers for the relevant estates are included in the information boxes for the routes affected.

ACCESS, CAMPING AND BOTHIES

Scotland enjoys among the most liberal access rights in the world. Public access to the countryside in Scotland is a statutory right, but this right also comes with responsibilities. The Scottish Outdoor Access Code provides guidance both for those exercising their right to roam, and for land managers. Provided walkers act responsibly they may roam over all open land, forests, rivers and lochs at any time of day or night. This does not apply to private gardens, farmyards, industrial sites, paying visitor attractions and crop fields. 'Responsible behaviour' means treating the environment and wildlife with care, respecting the needs and privacy of those living and working in the countryside, not obstructing activities such as farming, crofting and deer stalking, respecting reasonable detours in place during forestry work or stalking and keeping dogs under close control near livestock or ground-nesting birds.

Access rights also extend to wild camping. This type of camping is lightweight, done in small numbers and only for two or three nights in any one place. You can camp in this way wherever access rights apply, but help avoid causing problems for local people and land managers by not camping in enclosed fields of crops or livestock and keeping well away from buildings, roads or historic structures.

↑ *Standing stones at Callanish, Lewis*

← *Pitching a tent in front of Dibidil bothy, Rum (Walk 22)*

Take extra care to avoid disturbing deer stalking or grouse shooting. If you wish to camp close to a house or building, seek the owner's permission. Leave no trace by taking away all your litter and removing all traces of your tent pitch and of any open fire.

The excellent Mountain Bothies Association (MBA) looks after around 100 simple refuges in remote and often mountainous environments throughout Scotland, as well as a few in northern England and Wales. The bothies are mostly owned by landowners who allow the MBA to maintain them as basic shelters for walkers, climbers and others engaged in outdoor pursuits. There are nine MBA bothies throughout the Hebrides, as well as several estate bothies that are open for public use. Maintenance work on MBA bothies is carried out by work parties of volunteers. It is incumbent on those staying at a bothy to ensure that it is left in good order for the next users. Obviously there is no refuse collection service from the bothies, so you are responsible for carrying your own rubbish out with you. Human waste should always be buried well away from bothies and water sources. You can join the MBA at www.mountainbothies.org.uk.

SAFETY AND EMERGENCIES

In fine weather the Hebrides seem like an earthly paradise: however, the onset of high winds and driving rain can rapidly make the place feel quite hellish, especially if you are exposed to the elements. Becoming cold and wet rapidly drains body heat, which can lead to hypothermia. It is very important that you are properly equipped and are able to navigate proficiently in poor visibility. Check weather forecasts before setting out (see 'Mountain weather' below) and allow yourself plenty of time to complete your route. Be aware of the available daylight hours. Always let someone know your intended route and estimated time of completion. Ensure you have the correct equipment in case something goes wrong: for more details see 'What to take' below.

In case of injury or other incident, try to stay calm and assess your situation. If anyone is injured remember to check ABC – airway, breathing, circulation. Make any casualties warm and comfortable and place any unconscious casualties in the recovery position. Try to ascertain your exact position on the map and consider your options for walking to safety, finding shelter, staying put or seeking help. (Remember that it may take an emergency team some hours to reach you, especially in poor conditions in a remote area.)

If you decide to call for help, telephone 999 and ask for the Police and Mountain Rescue. Be ready to give the location of the incident (grid references, map sheet number, name of the area and description of the terrain), number and names of people in the party and their condition, any injuries and names of casualties. Be prepared to: supply the numbers of any phones carried by the party; describe the nature and time of the incident; describe the weather conditions, including wind conditions and visibility at the incident site; mention equipment on site, including warm clothing and shelter; and mention distinguishing features and markers at the site, as well as the location you are phoning from if this is different from the incident site.

Looking south along the Trotternish ridge from the Quiraing path, Skye (Walk 34)

WHAT TO TAKE

OS Explorer 1:25,000 maps are indispensable, as is a compass. Take a robust rucksack with a comfortable harness and a waterproof liner: for day walks a 30+ litre pack should be sufficient; for backpacking trips a 60+ litre pack may be required for carrying camping gear and several days' food. Effective waterproofs are essential when undertaking a walk of any length in the Hebrides. Weather can change quickly on the islands and doesn't always obey the forecasts.

Lightweight, wickable, quick-drying clothing is a must when walking the often strenuous routes in this guide. Be sure to have adequate warm clothing and extra layers. The terrain on many of the walks requires robust walking boots with a Vibram sole: trail shoes may be sufficient on less rugged ground. Gaiters are indispensable on wet and boggy terrain and tele-scopic walking poles can be very useful, especially in the hills or when carrying a heavy pack. A warm hat and gloves should always find a place in your ruck-sack. Sun cream, a sun hat and sunglasses should be carried from spring through to autumn.

Always carry plenty of food, including high-energy snacks and some water. There are usually frequent opportunities to fill up from the islands' numerous burns: the water is generally safe to drink, but water-purifying tablets can be carried if you are worried about contamination. When hillwalking or walking in remote areas, you should carry a basic first aid kit and a survival bag: a mobile phone is also useful in case of misadventure, but is not to be relied upon as coverage is patchy in remoter areas. A head torch is invaluable if you are benighted and it can help to attract attention in an emergency: carrying a whistle is useful for the same purpose. Lightweight binoculars are worth their weight for admiring the islands' splendid wildlife. A Lifesystems Tick Remover may also prove invaluable.

Consider carrying Crocs or trainers if you intend river or stream crossings; if there is more than a dust-ing of snow on the mountains you may need to carry an ice axe and crampons.

What to take backpacking

In addition to the items listed above, you should carry a robust lightweight tent (even if intending to stay in bothies), a good quality sleeping bag and a camping mat, camping stove, fuel, lighters and plenty of food. Take extra pairs of socks for boggy conditions and a down jacket for chilly evenings. Carry a few candles for evenings in a bothy.

MAPS AND ROUTE-FINDING

It is essential that you carry the relevant maps and a compass (even if you have a GPS (Global Positioning System)) in addition to the route maps shown in this guidebook: for more information see 'Using this guide' below. A wristwatch altimeter is also useful for navigation, especially in the hills. There are few waymarkers, signposts or even paths of any kind on many of the walks included here, making accurate route-finding all the more important: this is particu-larly the case in the Hebridean hills, which are more prone to mist and cloud than mainland mountains. It's not quite so easy to get lost when walking along the coastline, but it is always worth knowing exactly where you are, particularly in poor weather and low visibility especially if for any reason you need to head inland or seek shelter.

MOUNTAIN WEATHER

The views from Hebridean mountaintops combine land, sea and sky to dramatic effect – handsomely rewarding the effort of climbing. However, proximity to the sea predisposes island hills to mist and cloud cover, making route-finding diffi-cult – especially where paths are vague or non-existent. Furthermore, high winds and driving rain can blow in off the sea with little warning. The Hebridean hills

Be prepared for mountain weather: dense cloud descending near the summit of Beinn Talaidh, Mull (Walk 13)

Weathered rock near Port Snoig, Tiree (Walk 20) →

tend not to get as much snow as the mainland, but the same rules apply in winter conditions (which can also occur in autumn and spring). If there is more than a dusting of snow on the mountains you may need to carry an ice axe and crampons with you (and know how to use them). Be aware of avalanche risk – slopes between 25° and 45° are most at risk – and snow cornices on ridge crests. *Avalanche!* by Roberto Bolognesi (Cicerone, 2007) is a useful guide to assessing risk and reducing danger.

The Mountain Weather Information Service (MWIS) provides forecasts for Scotland's mountain areas at www.mwis.org.uk. The Scotland Avalanche Information Service (SAIS) does what the name suggests: www.sais.gov.uk.

Walking poles are useful for river crossings, such as the Allt nam Bà on Rum (Walk 22)

RIVER CROSSING

Heavy rain and snow melt make many burns and rivers run very high with a terrific volume of fast-moving water. This is especially the case on the mountainous islands. Do not attempt to cross rivers in spate – if you are swept away your chances of survival are very small. If you're successful in crossing one river in such conditions you may come up against an impassable torrent further on; if you then attempt to recross the river you previously crossed, you may find that it is running higher and faster than before.

Fast-flowing water deeper than knee depth is dangerous. Never cross upstream of waterfalls or boulders that you might be swept onto. Ensure that essential items – including dry clothes – are sealed in a waterproof bag. Undo your rucksack's hip and chest straps for quick release should you fall in. Do not attempt to cross barefoot – if you want to avoid wet boots consider carrying Crocs or trainers for this purpose. If you're not confident of your ability to get across a river safely turn around and live to complete the walk another day.

BITING BEASTIES

The vast majority of Hebridean wildlife is entirely benign, but there are a few exceptions. On those islands where there are deer, ticks (most commonly *Ioxides risinus*) are often picked up when walking through bracken and long grass from early spring through to late autumn. Wearing shorts increases your chances of picking them up. These miniscule beasties burrow their heads into your flesh and are best removed with tweezers, but you must ensure that you remove the head when extracting them. Some ticks carry Lyme disease, which can become seriously debilitating if left undiagnosed. However, removing infected ticks within 36 hours greatly reduces the risk of contracting Lyme disease. To date, the Lifesystems Tick Remover is the best tool for the job.

The hugely irritating midge (*Culicoides impunctatus*), a small biting gnat, is the stormtrooper of the small-winged invertebrate world, matched only by the New Zealand sandfly in its tenacity and pathological aggression. Midges are abundant on many of the islands between late spring and autumn, and can seriously detract from the enjoyment of a visit, so be prepared if walking during this period. It is worth carrying some powerful insect repellent and a midge net for your head. The cleg (*Haematopota pluvialis*) – an aggressive horse fly – tends to hang around in gangs during the spring and summer months and can deliver a painful bite, which can swell up.

Adders (*Vipera berus*) are common on some islands, although they are unlikely to bother you unless you bother them first. Be aware, however, as a bite can cause dizziness, vomiting, painful swelling and immobility of an affected limb – which can be a serious problem if you're a long and difficult walk away from treatment. Jellyfish are common in summer so be vigilant when enjoying a swim in one of the islands' beautiful bays.

USING THIS GUIDE

The routes are grouped by island into 22 chapters each with an introduction covering the local geology, history, wildlife, transport and amenities, including information on the local access situation and estate contacts. At the back of the book, four appendices provide a route summary table, glossary, a list of useful contacts and some suggestions for further reading.

The degree of difficulty (in terms of distance, ascent and terrain) of each walk is made clear in these information boxes at the beginning of each route. Some of the walks in this guidebook are demanding and best not attempted alone – these walks should only be undertaken by fit and experienced walkers and are not suitable for the very elderly, very young or anyone carrying an injury.

Maps

This guide uses 1:100,000 mapping (1:50,000 for Walks 40 and 42) to show for the route maps; these should be used in conjunction with OS Explorer (1:25,000) or Landranger (1:50,000) maps – and Harvey Superwalker (1:25,000) maps in several instances – because of the greater topographic detail. Do not rely solely on the maps in this guidebook. It is vital that you can work out where you are in the wider context should you need to abandon your walk and make for the nearest road or settlement. The relevant printed maps are given in the information box for each route.

Route descriptions

Most of the routes in this book are without waymarkers of any kind; in some instances paths are vague or even non-existent at times. Therefore, each of the walks is described in sufficient detail to enable the user to follow the route with relative ease. Natural and man-made features are regularly referenced in the route descriptions. Grid references are also given where deemed useful or necessary in most of the route descriptions; a grid reference for the start/finish points is also given in the information box for each route. Altitudes are given in metres, abbreviated to m, for example '750m'. Distances along the ground are given in metres, fully spelled out, for example '100 metres'.

Information boxes

The information boxes included at the beginning of each route description list the maps covering the route and the start/finish points (with grid references). The total distance (including any variants) of each walk is given in kilometres and miles. A rough timing is given for each route, which is estimated for walkers with a good level of fitness and does not include stopping for breaks – the weather and ground conditions will also affect progress on a walk. Total ascents are given in metres and feet and are worth familiarising yourself with before you set out. The nature of the terrain is also briefly described in the information boxes with any potential difficulties flagged up these are covered in more detail in the route introductions (see below). Public transport to and from the routes is included where such services exist. Other important points to note, such as estate contact details for use during deer stalking, are also included.

Route introductions

Each route starts with a brief overview of the walk and what to expect including access, the terrain encountered, the degree of strenuousness and any potential difficulties or obstacles – including river crossings and areas of navigational difficulty. Highlights and points of interest are also covered, including sites of historical, geological or botanical interest as well as wildlife that might be encountered en route.

ISLAY

Islay (Scottish Gaelic: Ìle), pronounced 'eye-la', is the southernmost of the Inner Hebrides, lying 40km (25 miles) north of the Irish coast and 20km (12½ miles) west of Kintyre. Jura lies 1km to the east across the Sound of Islay. There is a marked contrast between Islay and her rugged, mountainous neighbour; much of the former island is low-lying and fertile, hence agriculture and land management are major influences on the landscape. However, Islay has a varied terrain that also includes rugged quartzite uplands – moorland, hills (the highest being Beinn Bheigeir at 491m) and high sea cliffs – as well as extensive areas of heathland, blanket bog, marshland, sand flats, dunes, machair and some of the most fabulous beaches in all of Scotland. The island is 40km (25 miles) in length from north to south and 25km (15½ miles) from east to west at its widest point. Two sea lochs, Loch Gruinart and Loch Indaal, all but separate the western Rinns of

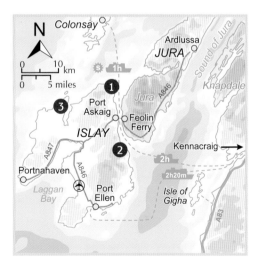

Islay from the rest of the island – and probably once did. If walking, birdwatching and single malt whisky appeal to you then Islay really is paradise.

↑ Southwest of Ardnave at sunset (Walk 3)

WALK 1

Rhuvaal and the northwest coast

ROUTE INFORMATION

Start/Finish	Small parking area at Bunnahabhain (NR 418 734)
Distance	20km (12½ miles)
Total ascent	648m (2126ft)
Time	7–8hrs
Terrain	Boggy moorland, rugged coastline, sand and pebble beaches, springy turf
Maps	OS Explorer 353, OS Landranger 60
Note	The walk out to Rhuvaal from Bunnahabhain can be very boggy

*T*his challenging route around the remote northern tip of Islay covers some difficult terrain. However, this is a truly spectacular walk, which takes in some coastal scenery every bit as remarkable as that of the fabled west coast of Jura. This section of Islay's coastline consists of shore platforms replete with raised beaches, sea caves, rock stacks, basalt dikes and natural arches.

Looking southwest across Port a' Chotain with its caves and raised shore platform

From the car park, which is situated just before the road bends and descends to the **Bunnahabhain** distillery buildings, follow the track west and after 100 metres turn right past some livestock pens and make for a gate in a deer fence. Go through and follow the track down through a small copse, crossing the Margadale River on a footbridge before continuing north along the track. For the next 6km follow the ATV tracks where you can. (This part of the walk can be very boggy.)

As you progress along the coast, there are **fine views of two of Jura's Paps** across the Sound of Islay – Beinn a' Chaolais and Beinn an Oir. The Sgriob na Caillich can be seen descending west to the coast from the flank of Beinn an Oir. The 'old woman's slide' is a 3.5km long belt of boulders deposited between convergent streams of the ice sheet that swept through the Paps from the east during the last glacial period.

Continuing north, the ATV tracks drop into the mouth of **Gleann Dubh**, cross the Allt an Achaidh then climb out again. As the tracks near Rhub' a' Mhàil, the slender white form of **Rhuvaal Lighthouse** comes into view (NR 425 792).

Make for the lighthouse, where there are fine views east to Loch Tarbert and Ruantallain on Jura: to the north lie Oronsay and Colonsay. Leaving the lighthouse behind, continue west along the coast, skirting above several steep-sided inlets and small bays. At A' Bhriogais a fine basalt dike drops towards the sea like a massive rock groyne. Continue along the cliff-top, following deer paths through the heather to arrive above the eastern end of Bàgh an Dà Dhoruis. Look out for a telegraph pole near the cliff edge where a path leads down to the beach (NR 415 788).

This is **a fine beach** even by Islay's high standards and its glory is crowned by a magnificent water-fall descending from the glacial cliffs high above.

Once down on the beach it is possible to walk along the shore for much of the way, although there are several points where tide and terrain make the shoreline impassable. Indeed, 1km beyond Bàgh an Dà Dhoruis an impressively proportioned dike bars the way. In these instances it is easy enough to take to higher ground above the shore. Keep to the shore where you can, however, as the undercliff route is full of interest and great natural beauty. A short way beyond the impassable dike, descend into Port a' Chotain where you will find the remains of an old stone sheiling and several caves including the cavernous Uamh Mhor or 'big cave' (NR 398 784). The entrance to the cave is protected by a dry stone wall and enclosure. Continue along the shore for 1.5km to an impass-able stretch of coastline at Rubha Bolsa. Climb on to the low cliffs and continue west, skirting around the

43

Heading across country with Mala Bholsa and the coast behind

whale-backed flank of **Mala Bholsa** (127m) to the southwest, staying above a large gully (NR 377 777).

A little further on, descend into the amphitheatre of Aonan na Mala. Make for the rock arch on the far side (NR 374 775), pass through and emerge at the foot of a gully. Climb the gully towards a low rock arch, which frames a remarkable view into the next bay. Pass through the arch and descend a gully to arrive at a burn, which can be tricky to cross or impassable when in spate. Once across, continue for a short way to arrive at **Stellaire Mòr** natural arch (NR 372 771). A waterfall drops straight over a rock shelf above the far side of the arch – quite a spectacle after wet weather.

Pass by the waterfall and find an easy route on to the low cliffs. Head southeast inland, following deer tracks where you can, and climb gradually to the Allt na Caillich (NR 375 768). Cross the burn where the ground steepens and continue climbing southeast. Clearing the first steep rise you will see two hillocks just above 200m separated by a shallow gap, about 1km to the southeast. Climb towards the gap (NR 386 762) and turn to the east around the shoulder of the northerly of the two hillocks (219m). Cross a shallow, boggy gully and contour around a spur. From here, in good visibility, you will have views on to the western flank of **Sgarbh Breac** (364m).

Continue south of east making for the pass between Sgarbh Breac and **Shun Bheinn** to its south. Keep north of Loch Mhurchaidh (NR 397 758) without losing too much height, try to pick as firm and dry a course across this boggy and tussocky stretch as you can. When you arrive at the Allt Bhachlaig (NR 405 758), cross the burn and pick up the ATV track running alongside it through the pass.

If you still have some energy, the **summit of Sgarbh Breac** (364m) offers some fine views of the Paps of Jura and much of Islay's hinterland.

Otherwise, continue southeast along the track as it descends to the Sound of Islay and then back to **Bunnahabhain**.

← Waterfall seen through Stellaire Mòr natural arch

WALK 2

An Cladach and Beinn Bheigier

ROUTE INFORMATION	
Start/Finish	Ballygrant (NR 396 663)
Distance	Ballygrant to An Cladach: 8km (5 miles); Beinn Bheigier circuit: 16km (10 miles)
Total ascent	1035m (3400ft)
Time	Ballygrant to An Cladach: 2–2½hrs each way; Beinn Bheigier circuit 5–6hrs
Terrain	Minor roads and farm tracks between Ballygrant and the Sound of Islay. Some boggy and uneven ground along the shore of the Sound: a little scrambling may be necessary when the tide is high. On the hill: some vague stalkers' paths and deer tracks through rocky terrain and dense heather cover. Dense bracken cover on the lower flanks of Beinn Bheigier in summer.
Maps	OS Explorer 352, OS Landranger 60
Public transport	Bus services 450/451/196 to Ballygrant from Bowmore, Portnahaven and Port Askaig
Note	During the deer stalking season (1 July–15 February) contact the Dunlossit Estate office (01496 840232) in advance to notify them of your intended route

*A*t 491m, Beinn Bheigier, Islay's highest peak is dwarfed by the Paps looming across the water on neighbouring Jura. However, a circular walk from An Cladach bothy on the Sound of Islay, taking in Beinn Bheigier and several hills to its north, involves over 1035m (3400ft) of ascent. The walk in to An Cladach from Ballygrant adds 8km and 2hrs to the route. You can avoid adding a further 2hrs to the day's walk – the return to Ballygrant – by spending a night or two at the bothy, using it as a base for walking and enjoying the sublime environs and plentiful wildlife.

↑ *Beinn na Caillich and Gleann Choireadail seen from An Cladach*

BALLYGRANT TO AN CLADACH BOTHY

Opposite the Post Office/shop, take the minor road (NR 396 663) heading southeast. At a fork after 500 metres, keep left and follow a single-track road for 1.5km to Lossit Farm. Go through the farmyard, pass the house and outbuildings, and go through a metal gate onto a track heading east. The track climbs gently then descends past woodland; it then bends south, levels out and climbs a little, passing a stone byre and crossing a burn as it bends east again. After crossing the burn, the path is less distinct and may be churned up by cattle; it soon bends south then northeast before descending steadily and turning south again. The path crosses a burn just before a gate in a deer fence; go through and walk down to the shore by an underwater cable indicator post at **Tràigh Bhàn** (NR 429 654).

Head south along the **Sound of Islay**. The rocky shore and pebble beaches can be awkward underfoot so follow the vague, boggy path through the bracken fringing the beach. Continue along the shore for 3km to An Cladach. There are no real difficulties except at high tide or in rough weather when the narrowed stretches of shoreline either side of **Glen Logain** require a little scrambling to get around.

In the summer months it is usually possible to cross the outflow of the Abhainn Gleann Logain (NR 436 629) at the beach, at other times or when the river is in spate, you may have to cross further upstream. (A bridge that washed away in 2010 has not been replaced at the time of writing (2014)).

An Cladach bothy, with Sgorr nam Faoileann rising above Gleann Ghàireasdail

At the shoreline, **keep an eye open** for patrolling otters and curious seals. Great northern and red-throated divers hunt in the shallows, whooper swans cruise close to shore and oystercatchers dot around on the beach. Hen harriers and golden eagles often hunt around the sound and adders are frequently found basking in the bracken.

Climbing the northern ridge of Glas Bheinn, with Sgorr nam Faoileann behind

An Cladach bothy (NR 439 623) occupies a splendid position just above the beach, with fine views along the Sound of Islay. It is a wonderful place to linger if you have time; happy hours can be spent watching the wildlife from the bench in front of the bothy. The bothy itself, once a derelict croft, was rebuilt by an MBA work party during the summer of 1999.

AN CLADACH – BEINN BHEIGIER CIRCUIT
Walk 100 metres northwest from the bothy, then head southwest up the flank of **Beinn Bhreac**, making for the ridge at the earliest opportunity: the rocky spine makes for firmer, easier going underfoot. Climb southwest for almost 2km, following the ridge as it curves east onto the summit ridge of **Sgorr nam Faoileann**; the summit (429m) is reached after a further 500 metres (NR 434 606).

> The length of the **Sound of Islay** and the curve of Jura's southwestern coastline are visible to the northeast, Rhuvaal lighthouse marks Islay's northeastern extremity, with Colonsay visible beyond. To the northwest, the expanse of Loch Indaal is bordered by the Rinns of Islay.

Descend the southern flank of Sgorr nam Faoileann for 180m, picking a route through patches of scree and heather. Make for the dry stone wall at the eastern side of the saddle and climb northeast to southwest up the rocky northeastern flank of **Glas Bheinn**. From the summit (472m) there are views down to the bay at Proaig on the east coast and over to the humpbacked ridge of Beinn Bheigier 3km to the south. Descend from the summit via the gently gradiented south ridge for 2km, to the bealach at 270m (NR 427 571) beneath the northern flank

of **Beinn Bheigier**. Climb south to gain a second bealach on the west side of the mountain at 350m (NR 425 567). Climb the remaining 140m southeast to the summit following vague paths through the heather and scree. There is an OS trig pillar on the summit with a small shelter wall. Having enjoyed the views, head southeast along the summit ridge with cairns at intervals along the way.

After 1.2km, the ridge begins to drop away. Descend initially eastwards, gradually bearing northeast towards the coast between Rubh' an Aonain Luachraich and Rubha Biorach (NR 459 565). The descent can be difficult going – boggy, tussocky and pathless – but on reaching the shore life immediately becomes easier.

Head north, following the vague path fringing the beach to reach the outflow of the Abhainn Phroaig after 1km. Cross the river on two iron girders a short way upstream to arrive at the former shepherd's cottage, sheepfold and outbuildings at **Proaig**. Continue north along the shore for 1km to the foot of **Beinn na Caillich Beag**, on the far side of a white sand beach. A vague path climbs north following an exposed rock staircase. The path climbs to 100m and continues north before dropping down to **McArthur's Head** lighthouse – built by David and Thomas Stevenson in 1861. From the lighthouse, steps descend to the shore; **An Cladach** is a further 3km along the coast. There are a couple of burns to cross and a section that requires climbing above the shore for a short way, but there are no real difficulties. From the bothy, retrace your outward route to return to **Ballygrant**.

Ardnave Point

*T*his is an undemanding and uplifting walk that suits all weathers – so long as you're prepared for them! Ardnave Point has an understated beauty while benefiting from splendid views east across Loch Gruinart to the coastline of northwest Islay, north to Oronsay and Colonsay and over to Nave Island just off the point. Seals and seabirds can be seen along the way while the sand flats of Loch Gruinart are popular with waders and wildfowl.

In the autumn, tens of thousands of white-fronted and barnacle geese arrive from Greenland. If you are a keen birder, there is an RSPB visitor centre and a couple of hides at Gruinart at the head of the loch.

Looking over to northwest Islay from the western shore of Loch Gruinart

ROUTE INFORMATION

Start/Finish	Parking area by Ardnave Loch (NR 287 728)
Distance	7.25km (4½ miles)
Total ascent	80m (260ft)
Time	2½–3hrs
Terrain	Sandy beaches, rocky coastline, springy turf and some boggy ground: some tracks and paths along the way. There are several livestock fences to be crossed.
Maps	OS Explorer 353, OS Landranger 60
Note	Livestock are grazed around Ardnave – be sure to close all gates

From the parking area, head northeast along the track signposted for 'Tayvullin and the Beach'. After 100 metres the track bends east then sharply northeast after a further 100 metres. Continue for 150 metres then leave the track, heading east down through the dunes to arrive on the shore of **Loch Gruinart**. (If the tide isn't high the shore makes for the most enjoyable route to Ardnave Point, but you can always take to the dunes if necessary.) After crossing an awkward fence the going is easy along the sandy shore with magnificent views and expansive skies to enhance your walk.

Where the shoreline becomes rocky near **Ardnave Point**, continue along the springy turf above the shore with fine views of **Nave Island**. Seals can be seen on the offshore skerries and gannets often dive for fish in this area. Carry on around the point and you will eventually arrive on the sandy beach of Tràigh nam Fuaran (NR 288 747). Head southwest along the sandy shore, before

negotiating a short rocky stretch, which can be slippery when wet, then cross a fence to arrive on the fine, dune-backed beach at **Tràigh Nòstaig**. Carry on along the shore to Port na Muic at the far end of Tràigh Nòstaig, where you will find a curious structure – apparently a disused lobster farm. Follow the obvious track up a slight incline towards a gate (NR 277 736) and go through it, continuing southwest a short way. Follow the track that initially heads northeast then bends around to the southeast before passing through Ardnave Farm. Turn right through the farmyard and continue to a fork in the track by Ardnave Loch; turn left and follow the track back to the parking area.

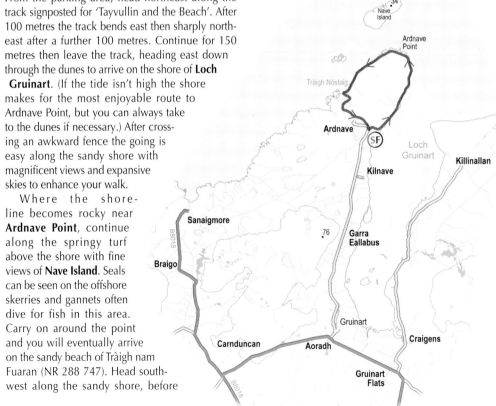

JURA

The wildest of the Southern Hebrides, Jura (Scottish Gaelic: *Diùra*) lies tucked away off the Argyll coast some 80km (50 miles) west of Glasgow as the crow flies. The island is approximately 50km (30 miles) long and 13km (9 miles) across at its widest point. The north and south parts are almost completely bisected by Loch Tarbert, a 1km-wide isthmus separating the sea loch from the Sound of Jura. The island's most famous and striking physical feature is the Paps of Jura – three breast-shaped, quartzite scree-clad mountains. The island's sublime coastal landscapes of crenellated quartzite rock, white sandy bays and sparkling teal waters teem with wildlife and a profusion of breathtaking geological phenomena. A real sense of remoteness is found among the hills and along the shores of this magnificent island, not least because you are more likely to encounter eagles, otters, seals, wild goats and red deer than other people.

↑ *The Paps of Jura seen from Oronsay*

WALK 4

The west coast of Jura

*T*he west coast of Jura is arguably the wildest and most spectacular stretch of coastline in Scotland. There are no roads, no permanent habitations and no livestock management. The shores and glens teem with wildlife and the ruggedly beautiful coastline of quartzite cliffs and white sand bays is adorned with remarkable geological features. The route described here explores the length of Jura's northwest coast in a tough three–four-day, 51–64km walk, which makes for a very challenging and hugely rewarding endeavour – it is one of the British Isles' last great wilderness walks. (A five day, 77km route around the entire west coast of Jura is included in Walking on Jura, Islay and Colonsay.)

Ardlussa is the northernmost stop for the Jura Bus (tel 01436 810200, www.garelochhead coaches.co.uk). There is a small parking area 5.5km beyond Ardlussa at Road End (NR 670 927) if you have your own transport or can arrange a lift. To start the walk from Kinuachdrachd, charter a water taxi from the mainland: contact Duncan Philips of Farsain Cruises at Croabh Haven on 07880 714165 (at the time of writing this cost £80 one way for a group of up to 12 people). At the end of the walk, the Jura Bus stops 300 metres southeast of where the path meets the A846.

ROUTE INFORMATION

Start	Ardlussa (NR 650 880) or Kinuachdrachd Harbour (NR 705 982)
Finish	Tarbert (NR 607 823)
Total distance	51–64km (31½–39¾ miles)
Total ascent	1966–1616m (6450–5302ft)
Total time	3–4 days
Terrain	Begins on a metalled track; thereafter, more varied and challenging terrain, often difficult underfoot, even more so with a backpack. Further details are given day by day below.
Maps	OS Explorer 355, Landranger 61

← Forging a route round to Glentrosdale Bay (Day 1)　　　*↑ The head of Loch Tarbert at dawn (Day 4)*　　　53

DAY 1

Ardlussa or Kinuachdrachd to Glengarrisdale

ROUTE INFORMATION	
Start	Ardlussa (NR 650 880) or Kinuachdrachd Harbour (NR 705 982)
Finish	Glengarrisdale Bothy (NR 644 969)
Distance	26km (16 miles) or 13km (8 miles)
Ascent	845m (2772ft) or 525m (1722ft)
Time	8–9½hrs or 5–6hrs
Terrain	Varied and challenging terrain: the going underfoot is often difficult, even more so with a backpack. Once the 'path' runs out above the Gulf of Corryvreckan you will need to exercise caution and judgement in reading the terrain.
Maps	OS Explorer 355, Landranger 61
Note	During deer stalking season – 1 July–15 February – contact the head stalkers at Barnhill (01496 820327), Ardlussa (01496 820323) and Ruantallain (01496 820331) to notify them of your intended route

*A*fter the track road runs out at Kinuachdrachd Farmhouse the going underfoot is sometimes difficult, the more so with a heavy pack. However, there is a distinct path as far as the island's northern extremity and there are fine views to be enjoyed across north Jura's vast, empty hinterland and the Sound of Jura en route. Once at the north end the views across the Gulf of Corryvreckan to the isle of Scarba are quite magnificent. Here the real challenge begins as paths become vague and forging a route down to and along the west coast involves negotiating some very rugged, often boggy terrain. The considerable efforts involved are amply rewarded by spectacular coastal landscapes, abundant wildlife and the bothy at journey's end, set amid the splendour of Glen Garrisdale.

If you can arrange transport to Road End 5.5km north of Ardlussa, this will save you around 1½hrs.

From **Ardlussa** follow the road through the collection of estate buildings, pass Ardlussa House and continue winding your way northeastwards along the track road for 13km (3hrs). There are a few minor ups and downs and **Barnhill** (where George Orwell wrote *Nineteen Eighty-Four*) is passed 2km before Kinuachdrachd.

From **Kinuachdrachd Harbour** (NR 705 982) continue northwards, following the track skirting the small bay, before climbing a little to **Kinuachdrachd**, where there is a lone farmhouse. Just before the farmhouse a footpath climbs to the left (NR 704 987). A small wooden sign indicates the route to Corryvreckan, 3km to the north. The path, which is boggy in places, climbs through heather and bracken before levelling out and passing through a deer fence by means of a stile and a gate. Also to the north, the mountainous isle of Scarba looms beyond the Gulf of Corryvreckan.

White-tailed eagles can be seen in this area. They are easily identifiable by their size (they boast a wingspan of up to three metres) and characteristic white tail feathers.

From An Cruachan, contour west for 200 metres on a vague track that soon drops into the mouth of a wide gully. From here, make for a rock-walled gully below and a few hundred metres to the northwest. (A burn runs down the gully, making it a little tricky to negotiate, but it provides a good point of access to the lower shore platform and the west coast.)

Once you've arrived **on the west coast** you will find yourself in a landscape that is very different from the eastern side of Jura. There are few trees and the vegetation is largely comprised of bracken, heather, bog myrtle and tussocky purple moor grass: species able to withstand exposure and adapted to the acidic rock and soil.

The countenance of the west coast is altogether craggier than the east: the exposed features of the formerly submarine landscape are subjected to regular scouring by wind, rain and sea.

From the foot of An Cruachan, steer round to the south on relatively level boggy ground until you arrive at the first of two coves forming **Bàgh Gleann nam Muc**. Pick your way around the fringe of the cove and descend to the sandy beach. Cross the beach and work your way through rocky terrain and bracken around an outcrop to reach another sandy beach. Continue around the bay to the western end of the beach, follow a vague path above the shoreline and through rocky outcrops around the Aird Bhreacain promontory. There are several caves and rock arches along this stretch of the coastline including Uamh Bhreacain – Breacan's Cave.

From **Glentrosdale Bay**, continue around the next promontory through rocky, bracken-covered terrain. After 400 metres follow an obvious deer path up a gully, which levels as it crosses the foot of Beinn nan Capull, before descending to Bàgh Uamh Mhór. (The bay is dominated by the craggy triumvirate of Beinn nan Capull, Cruach na Seilcheig and Sgorr Mhór, with twin steep-sided gullies running precipitously down to the shore.) Continue around

After 2km the path passes through another deer fence then drops a little, crossing a small gully and stream (NM 701 007). Here the path splits, but either route leads to an obvious vantage point on the northern flank of **An Cruachan**, with superlative views of Scarba and the **Gulf of Corryvreckan** – the narrow strait between the two islands and the often turbulent confluence of the Firth of Lorn and the Sound of Jura.

The tidal convergence of conflicting **currents in the Gulf** is catalysed by a submerged pyramidal rock, known as Caillich, 'The Hag', which generates an infamous whirlpool of considerable power.

Glengarrisdale Bay, with the bothy at the foot of Ben Garrisdale

the next, smaller promontory into Bàgh Uamh nan Giall and pick your way carefully over some large, often slippery boulders before crossing a beach of large cobbles. Once across, continue round to a small and lovely sandy beach.

Cut across the neck of Garbh Aird and soon take to the higher ground along the seaward flank of Druim nan Cliabh to avoid a tricky stretch of slippery rocks, awkward slopes and boggy ground. After 1km, descend alongside a burn (NR 659 978) feeding into the aptly named Feith a' Chaorainn (bog of the rowan). Once clear of the boggy ground, work your way through the rocky terrain above the shore; look out for some splendid quartz-veined cliff-faces along the way. Eventually the white walls and red roof of Glengarrisdale Bothy will come into view on the far side of **Glengarrisdale Bay**. On reaching the bay, cross the beach to the outflow of the Glengarrisdale River, which fans out where it meets the beach, and ford it here, at its shallowest point.

Glengarrisdale Bothy is an old crofting cottage that was inhabited until after the Second World War. The bothy is on the Ardlussa estate, but it is now maintained by the excellent Mountain Bothies Association.

Glengarrisdale Bay is a wonderful place. There are fine views across to Iona, Mull, the Garvellachs and Scarba. Around the glen you may spot merlins, short-eared owls, hen harriers, golden and white-tailed eagles. Common and Atlantic grey seals bob around in the bay and otters patrol close to the shore. Deer and goats come down to the shore at dusk to graze on the kelp.

DAY 2

Glengarrisdale to Shian Bay

ROUTE INFORMATION	
Start	Glengarrisdale Bothy (NR 644 969)
Finish	Shian Bay (NR 531 875)
Distance	17.5km (10¾ miles)
Ascent	663m (2175ft)
Time	7–9hrs
Terrain	Tough, pathless walking over rough ground, which is boggy and tussocky in places. Along the shore the terrain alternates between broken rocky ground, large pebbles and springy turf.
Maps	OS Explorer 355, Landranger 61

This is a big day's walk: the distance is not especially great, but the terrain is very demanding. A fit walker could manage the 24km (15 miles) to the bothy at Ruantallain in a day (8–10hrs, assuming you take the inland route to Ruantallain from Shian Bay). There are fine opportunities for a bivouac en route, including Corpach Bay and Tràigh a' Mhiadair.

Rugged coastline north of Shian Bay

Head southwest between the bothy and the neighbouring ruin, following the vague path up and across the neck of Aird Rachdaig. There are a number of old peat cuttings and the ground can be very boggy. Continue west, soon dropping down to **Bàgh Gleann Speireig**. From the bay climb through Gleann Speireig, keeping right of the Allt Gleann Speireig.

Map labels:

Glengarrisdale Bay
Glengarrisdale
85 · Bothy
Clachaig Bheag
Bàgh Gleann Speireig
Glendebadel Bay
Grianan Mòr
Cnoc na h-Uamha
365 ·
Ben Garrisdale 373 ·
219 ·
Stac Dearg
Rubha Lag Losguinn
325 ·
Garbh uisge nan Cad
300
Cnoc na Corpaich
Corpach Bay
Cnoc Leac
Beinn Bhreac 467 ·
Tràigh a' Mhiadair
Ceann Garbh na Beinne Brice
158 ·
Cruaidh Gleann
Binnein Liath
Sliabh Allt an Tairbh
Gleann Challuim-chille
Dubh Bheinn 485 ·
Allt an Tairbh
Shian Bay
63 ·
(SF)

southwest through rocky, bracken-infested terrain above the shore for 1km then, after clonking across a beach of large pebbles, emerge on to magnificent **Corpach Bay**. Cross the sandy beach and the outflow of the Abhainn Corpaich and continue for 1km along the shore platform to arrive at **Tràigh a' Mhiadair**, with its gorgeous beaches, rock stacks, arches, caves and sand dunes.

This is a wonderful **bivouac site**; there is plenty of shelter, a burn, flat grassy areas for pitching a tent and usually plenty of driftwood.

If the weather is rough and you don't have the energy or inclination to walk as far as Ruantallain bothy, **Tràigh a' Mhiadair** makes a better bivouac site than Shian Bay.

The tide may force you onto higher ground for the next 2.5km, although it is worthwhile working your way along the shore beneath the cliffs if you can. You will eventually come to the fine, stepped waterfall at Sliabh Allt an Tairbh (NR 543 890). It can be tricky crossing the outflow of the waterfall, which runs out through a narrow rock channel to the sea; in which case cross the Eas Allt an Tairbh upstream of the waterfall and find a route down to the shore further on. Continue along the coast for 2.5km to arrive at **Shian Bay**.

Shian Bay is a beautiful white sand crescent backed by a flat grassy area and protected to the north by Shian Island. The Shian River flows out into the middle of the bay and to the rear the terrain opens out, before rising to the hills in the interior. This is a wonderful spot for camping, if somewhat exposed. Ruantallain bothy is 5.25km (3¼ miles) and 1½–2hrs further on.

From the head of the glen descend towards steep-sided Glen Debadel; make for the point where the Glendebadel Burn reaches the beach at **Glendebadel Bay** (NR 623 951) to find an easy way down.

Once across the burn, continue along the shore platform, weaving a route through the broken, rocky terrain. After 750 metres, skirt around a rocky spur and arrive at another spur soon after. Follow deer tracks up the spur (NR 614 950) and climb to higher ground above the cliffs. Continue southwest, contouring along at 100m for 1km, then cross a burn before gaining **Cnoc na h-Uamha** (110m, NR 608 941). Descend to cross another burn, climb again to 100m then contour for 1km before climbing to the landward side of **Stac Dearg** (130m, NR 594 935). Skirt a lochan then trend southwest, soon descending to cross the **Garbh uisge nan Cad** burn at the obvious point before it drops into a steep-sided gorge (NR 590 930).

Climb westwards to reach level ground crossed by a small burn. Cross the burn and continue southwest for 300 metres to arrive at a natural amphitheatre, then descend springy peat-turfed slopes towards the shore at **Rubha Lag Losguinn**. Follow goat tracks

← *Waterfall at Sliabh Allt an Tairbh*

DAY 3

Shian Bay to Cruib Lodge

ROUTE INFORMATION	
Start	Shian Bay (NR 531 875)
Finish	Cruib Lodge bothy (NR 567 829)
Distance	13km (8¼ miles)
Ascent	294m (964ft)
Time	5–6hrs
Terrain	Rough, boggy and tussocky ground, raised beaches of large pebbles and ATV tracks to Ruantallain. Rugged coastline, pebble beaches and boggy ATV tracks to Cruib Lodge.
Maps	OS Explorer 355, Landranger 61

If you can, take a few hours to explore the environs of Ruantallain. This is an area of such outstanding natural beauty that it is worth factoring an extra day into your itinerary and spending the night here. A good option is to walk from Shian Bay to Runtallain bothy above the shore, deposit your rucksack, then head back beneath the cliffs to explore the realm of caves, stacks, arches and raised beaches.

The route between Ruantallain and Cruib Lodge follows the rugged coastline for much of the way, which is full of interesting geology, wildlife and superb views – not least those of the Paps, rising above the southern shore of Loch Tarbert. Cruib Lodge can also be reached by following ATV tracks inland from the coast; this is a little quicker than the coastal route but not so interesting. It can also be boggy and there is no shelter in wet and windy conditions. The 'inland' route is marked on the route map.

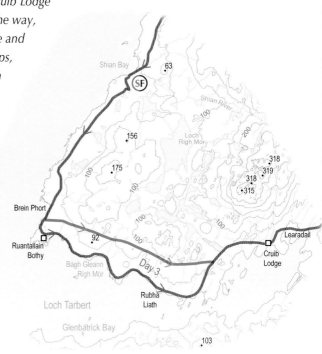

Rain closing in at Ruantallain →

Cross the outflow of the Shian River. Follow the obvious ATV tracks exiting the beach to the east, then after 200 metres turn southwest off the tracks and continue across country. Above Shian Bay the land opens out beneath the mountainous hinterland. Consequently the next 5km make for some of the easiest walking along the entire west coast: the going underfoot is generally good and the terrain is relatively level.

> Avoid crossing the **many raised beaches** in this area, as they make for hard work. Deer also find the cobbles tricky underfoot, so follow their tracks between the swathes of large pebbles, along their edges and across their narrowest points. There are also numerous lochans of varying sizes along the way.

An ATV track soon makes for easier going and steers a course southwest towards Ruantallain. Just north of **Breinn Phort** the track turns sharply southeast for 350 metres before turning southwest again along the clifftop above the bay. The track continues across a raised beach then turns southeast. From this bend in the track (NR 508 835) follow a faint path southwest past a large dry stone walled enclosure, then descend through rocky outcrops to arrive at **Ruantallain Bothy**.

> The **bothy** is at the eastern end of a long corrugated iron-roofed house belonging to the Ruantallain Estate. The main part of the house is private and locked when not in use. The bothy is a single room with a fireplace. A dry stone wall in front of the bothy encloses a level grassy area, which is ideal for pitching tents. Fresh water can be collected from a lochan a short way south of the enclosure or from a burn 500 metres to the southeast around An Sàilean bay.

From the bothy head southeast to An Sàilean bay, avoiding the boggy ground immediately to the east of the lochan. Continue along the coast following deer tracks, which skirt or cross the pebble beaches

Raised beaches at Bàgh Gleann Righ Mòr

and pick routes through the bracken. An enormous, spectacular raised beach sits above Rubha Buidhe, the rocky point that flanks the bay to the east. Around 300 metres beyond Rubha Buidhe the rocky shore platform beneath Creag nan Seabhag is gained. The next 1km involves some enjoyable weaving through rocky terrain and slipping through gaps in numerous natural dikes. The cliffs here are dotted with caves, including Uamh Righ – the King's Cave (NR 515 827) – which is found just before the coastline bends northeast into Bàgh Gleann Righ Mòr.

Continue into **Bàgh Gleann Righ Mòr**, crossing sandy beaches, rocky outcrops and raised pebble beaches. Follow deer paths through the rugged terrain of the Aird Reamhar promontory, with its impressive dikes, and around into the next bay. Pick your way around a rocky outcrop above the shore (taking care as the rocks are slippery when wet and pitched steeply enough to be hazardous). Carry on around the pebble-beached bay as the coastline turns to the southeast. At **Rubha Liath**, with its series of obliquely-angled dikes, there are good views southeast across the loch to the impressive raised beach forming a natural dam between Lochan Maol an t-Sornaich and Loch Tarbert.

Beyond Rubha Liath, work your way around the bay of Port Falaich a' Chumhainn Mhòir, looking out for some navigation pillars (metre-high obelisks, white-painted on their seaward faces) above Rubha Gille nan Ordag at the eastern end of the bay (NR 543 814). Beyond here the shoreline becomes estuarine, relatively uninteresting and very difficult to walk around, so leave the shore here and make for higher ground. Continue northeast along a ridge running parallel to the shoreline of **Loch Tarbert**, which also turns sharply northeast. Keep your height to avoid boggy ground where possible. After 1km or so you should intersect an ATV track that continues northeast into the glen through which the Garbh Uisge burn flows. Descend, cross Garbh Uisge – you may need to walk upstream to find a safe crossing point – before gaining height again and follow the ATV track northeast on a winding course to arrive at a point (NR 563 832) northwest of Cruib Lodge bothy, which remains out of view. Head southeast across country, descend towards the corner of a deer-fenced woodland enclosure then follow the burn around to the bothy. **Cruib Lodge** bothy is on the Ruantallain Estate. It was renovated in the spring of 2012 and is maintained by the MBA.

DAY 4

Cruib Lodge to Tarbert

This is a shorter day's walk than the previous days, but the terrain can be difficult to read in places and as the route is largely away from the shore route-finding is more challenging.

ROUTE INFORMATION	
Start	Cruib Lodge bothy (NR 567 829)
Finish	Tarbert (NR 607 823)
Distance	6.5km (4 miles)
Ascent	172m (564ft)
Time	2–2½hrs
Terrain	Although this section is short the going underfoot is often boggy and tussocky
Maps	OS Explorer 355, Landranger 61

From the bothy, cross the burn and skirt around to the east of the deer-fenced enclosure following an ATV track bearing northeast. Follow the track along a ridge for 500 metres, before turning east and descending through an obvious gap (NR 570 834) to the mud and sand flats of **Learadail**. Cross the outflow of the burn where shallowest and head southeast to cut across the neck of the promontory on the eastern side of Learadail. Cross the mud flats of Sàilean nam Màireach, making for a tumbling burn, which is the outflow of **Loch na Pearaich**. Climb next to the burn for 500 metres to reach the loch, then skirt around to its northern end. At the northern tip of the loch follow an ATV track southeast, up a slight rise then down a slope onto a small, very boggy plateau. Having crossed this area, turn northeast, following a vague path, and continue without losing any height for 500 metres. Contour along the hillside, with the mud and sand flats at the head of Loch Tarbert below to the right. Look out for a rough path descending diagonally northeast to a small

salient of land bulging out into the estuary's mud flats (NR 593 835).

Skirt around the edge of the mud flats to the northeast for 800 metres, making for a weir and dam. Just beyond, stepping stones ford the river (NR 598 843) where a rickety footbridge once stood. Once across, follow the obvious path – marked with white-painted stones – to the point where it divides after 600 metres. The white-painted stones continue on the left-hand branch, which climbs a short way and makes for the A846, 1.5km further on.

Whether you're heading north to Ardlussa, Road End or Kinuachdrachd, or south to Craighouse or Feolin (for the Islay ferry) the Jura Bus can be flagged down on the A846 at the point where the track from the settlement at **Tarbert** joins the road. This is 300 metres southeast of where the path meets the road. Check times with the bus company – www.gareloch headcoaches.co.uk, tel 01436 810200.

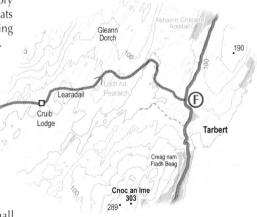

WALK 5

The Paps of Jura

	ROUTE INFORMATION
Start/Finish	A846 just over 1km northeast of Three Arch Bridge (NR 550 732)
Alternative finish	Three Arch Bridge (NR 544 720)
Distance	17km (11 miles)
Total ascent	1500m (5000ft)
Time	8–9hrs
Terrain	Pathless in places, often boggy and tussocky; the scree-flanked mountainsides are very tough going at times – rugged, exposed and best avoided in rough weather and poor visibility
Maps	OS Explorer 355, Landranger 61
Public transport	456 bus from Feolin Ferry or Craighouse – ask the driver to let you down by the start of Evans' Walk (the scheduled stop is Three Arch Bridge)
Note	From 1 July–15 February contact the head stalker at the Tarbert Estate, 01496 820207

*A*round of all three Paps – Beinn Shiantaidh (pronounced 'Ben-a-Hinta'), Beinn an Oir ('Ben-an-Ore') and Beinn a' Chaolais ('Ben-a-Hoolish') – makes for a big day's walk, which should only be attempted by fit, properly equipped walkers, who are also competent navigators. Each of these mountains has marvellous views in fine weather, with Beinn an Oir benefiting from the most extensive. On a clear day, a 360° panorama takes in Scarba, Mull, the Garvellachs, Iona, Tiree and the Skye Cuillin to the north, Colonsay and Oronsay to the northwest, Islay to the southwest, with Northern Ireland's Mountains of Morne far beyond, and the hills of Arran visible to the southeast.

The route described here follows the Evans' Walk path as far as the flank of Corra Bheinn. This route starts on the left-hand side of the A846. There is a lay-by on the opposite side of the road and a signpost, which points into the bog and indicates that this, as a concept at least, is Evans' Walk. The path is actually well-defined for much of its length, but it can be difficult to follow in its early stages. An alternative, signposted 'Paps Walk', starts from Three Arch Bridge: this route has ATV tracks for some of the way, but can be horrendously boggy at times, and is a route for after dry weather only.

From the signpost, climb initially north on a steady gradient; the path can be vague along this first section, depending on usage and just how boggy the ground is. Don't follow the ATV tracks too far north but bear northwest after 250 metres and you'll have a good chance of joining Evans' Walk proper. Climb to 150m then contour for 500 metres, crossing several burns in succession. (The Allt Bràigh an Fheadain can be difficult to cross in spate, in which case follow the burn 500 metres or so upstream to cross safely.) Continue northwest, crossing another burn and climbing to a rocky outcrop at around 200m (NR 540 747). Leave Evans' Walk as it bends to the north (look for a small cairn marking a narrow path) and continue northwest for 350 metres, climbing to 300m. Bear west, gradually climbing to 350m, with Beinn Shiantaidh looming ever closer. Now contour around to the saddle between **Corra Bheinn** and Beinn Shiantaidh, with its speckling of lochans known as the Lochanan Tana.

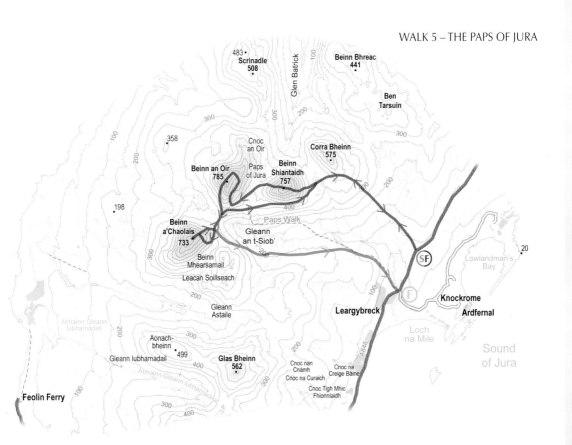

Beinn Shiantaidh from the start of Evans' Walk

Beinn Shiantaidh is the toughest Pap to climb because of its very steep scree slopes composed of large quartzite stones. A path starts up the southeast flank (NR 520 745), but soon fades; patches of heather offer some respite from the ankle-jarring scree. A false summit is reached at 700m, with the summit cairn a few hundred metres further west at 757m. From the top there is a clearer path down to the west and a steep gully just north of west makes for a good way down the mountain's rocky western flank. Once below the rocky terrain, head down to the saddle, making for the southeastern flank of Beinn an Oir and the obvious path climbing south–north (NR 503 745 – this path makes for a surprisingly easy climb on an even gradient).

After 750 metres a narrower path heads more steeply northwest up on to the summit ridge. On gaining the ridge, swing southwest and continue along the last stretch to the summit on a broad track levelled into the rocky terrain by Ordnance Survey mapmakers at the end of the 19th century. At 785m (2576ft) **Beinn an Oir** is the highest of the Paps and qualifies as a Corbett – Scottish mountains between 2500 and 3000ft (there are 220). From the summit trig point descend 400m, initially south, then southwest to the saddle between Beinn an Oir and Beinn a' Chaolais along the south ridge, avoiding the very steep ground to your right. There are reasonable paths on the descent, which becomes a scree slope in its lower reaches: enjoy the great views onto Beinn a' Chaolais, with Islay and its eponymous sound beyond.

The saddle is gained at 370m, above the uppermost of the Na Garbh-lochanan (NR 495 741). Skirt around the head of **Gleann an t-Siob'** to the saddle between the eastern flank of Beinn a' Chaolais and **Beinn Mhearsamail**, gaining around 30m. Climb west up the eastern ridge for 330m to reach the summit of **Beinn a' Chaolais** (733m). Descend initially by the same route, but look out for tracks descending the steep scree slopes northeast back to the saddle at the head of Gleann an t-Siob'. From the saddle, contour beneath the southern flanks of Beinn an Oir and Beinn Shiantaidh at around 350m and retrace your steps to the Evans' Walk path back to the A846.

Alternative finish from
Beinn a' Chaolais
An alternative return route from Beinn a' Chaolais involves contouring around the southern side of **Gleann an t-Siob** above Loch an t-Siob, and then following the Corran River to Three Arch Bridge; this benefits from ATV tracks for some of the way, but it can be horrendously boggy at times. This is a route recommend only after dry weather.

↑ *Beinn an Oir from Beinn a' Chaolais*

WALK 6

Ardlussa to Corpach Bay and Tràigh a' Mhiadair

ROUTE INFORMATION

Start/Finish	Parking area at Ardlussa (NR 646 879)
Distance	24km (15 miles) return
Total ascent	1050m (3444ft)
Time	6–7hrs
Terrain	There are ATV tracks for much of the way, traversing some rough terrain, including some boggy sections; the terrain is complex in places and in poor visibility navigation can be challenging
Maps	OS Explorer 355, Landranger 61
Public transport	456 bus from Feolin Ferry or Craighouse: Ardlussa is the northern terminus
Parking	Park on the hard standing a short way along the Lussa River track: let the estate know if you're leaving a car there overnight (phone the number below)
Note	In the deer stalking season (1 July–15 February) contact the head keeper at Ardlussa Estate on 01496 820323 in advance of your walk

*T*his fine out-and-return route crosses the north of Jura from Ardlussa on the east coast, climbing up and over the island's mountainous spine before descending to Corpach Bay on the wild west coast. When the ground is dry the ATV tracks followed for much of the way make this one of the least-challenging cross-island routes on Jura: after wet weather, however, you may find yourself traversing a soggy morass. The reward comes in the splendid views en route and the opportunity to explore a sublime stretch of Jura's magnificent western coastline.

This is a splendid place to spend a night or two if you can – the coast to northeast and southwest is well worth exploration – at the very least you should factor in a few extra hours if walking out and back the same day. Corpach Bay and Tràigh a' Mhiadair are wonderful places to camp: the timings, distance and ascent given above are roughly half each way. Carrying camping gear will slow progress a bit.

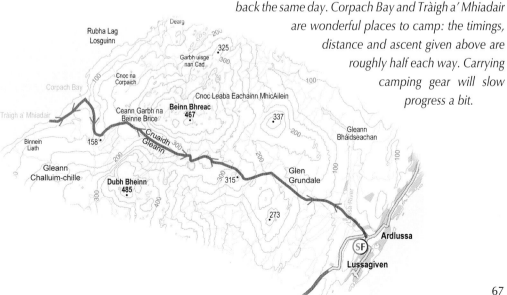

67

On the north side of the bridge across the **Lussa River**, take the track road leading to the Fishing Loch. Walk along the track to the loch, cross a footbridge then the dam at the southern end of the loch. Follow the ATV track climbing the rise straight ahead. Keep left where the track forks – it can be sketchy in places – soon descending to cross the Allt Grundale via a wooden ATV bridge. Climb steadily for 500 metres before the track levels and swings northwest, contouring above **Glen Grundale**. After 800 metres cross a small burn, turn left and climb steadily. After 500 metres the track turns northwest again, winding a sinuous up-and-down route through the rugged landscape. (To the north the view opens up towards Ben Garrisdale, with the Garvellachs and Mull visible beyond.)

Pass a pair of lochans, climb a little and continue along the track through a boggy area to the Bealach a' Chruaidh-ghlinn between Cnoc Tigh-sealga and Beinn Bhreac. Begin the well-earned descent into **Cruaidh Ghleann**.

There are **views** southwest to Dubh Bheinn, south to Loch Tigh-sealga nestled above the head of the glen and west to Loch Aird a' Chruaidh-ghlinn sitting in the bowl of the glen. As you descend, the low-lying length of Colonsay, 20km to the west, is framed perfectly by the flanks of Beinn Bhreac and Dubh Bheinn.

Continue down into the glen, following the ATV track, which bottoms out by the burn running down to Loch Aird a' Chruaidh-ghlinn. The track contours along above the loch, bearing northwestwards, with a few minor ups and downs over the next 2km. The north end of Loch lochdarach a' Chruaidh-ghlinn appears beneath Creag Mhòr na Dubh Bheinn, and the west coast soon comes into view.

There are several ways down into **Gleann Challuim-chille**, but probably the easiest option is to trend southwest above Loch lochdarach a' Chruaidh-ghlinn for several hundred metres then head northwestwards through rocky outcrops and

In Cruaidh Gleann beneath Creag Mhòr na Dubh-bheinn

Tràigh a' Mhiadair and Corpach Bay from the south

down the steep slope into the glen, following deer paths. (The view down Gleann Challuim-chille, with the Abhainn na Corpaich winding its way to Corpach Bay, is quite lovely.) Follow deer paths through the bracken on the right-hand (east) side of the burn and cross it where it bends sharply right beneath a raised beach. Skirt right around the raised beach and follow the burn down to the shore at **Corpach Bay**.

'**Corpach**' is from the Gaelic meaning 'body' or 'corpse': long ago, deceased notables were carried here across the island to await transportation to Iona or Oronsay, which were important ecclesiastical centres. Coffins were often kept in a cave here, known as Corpach Challuim-chille.

Corpach Bay possesses a beautiful sandy beach and makes for a wonderful bivouacking site. There is a burn, flat grassy areas for pitching a tent and usually plenty of driftwood to be gleaned.

Continuing southwest for 1km, following deer paths along the shore platform, brings you to the fine beaches, rock stacks, natural arches, caves and sand dunes of **Tràigh a' Mhiadair**, which is also a fine, sheltered spot for pitching a tent. The magnificent coastline hereabouts deserves exploration before you retrace your outward route to Ardlussa.

WALK 7

Evans' Walk to Glenbatrick Bay (and return)

ROUTE INFORMATION

Start/Finish	Left-hand side of the A846, just over 1km northeast of Three Arch Bridge (NR 550 732)
Distance	18km (11 miles)
Total ascent	525m (1722ft)
Time	6–7hrs
Terrain	A good path for much of the route; this may be lost in the boggy ground at either end of the walk, and after heavy rain several burns can be impassable
Maps	OS Explorer 355, Landranger 61
Public transport	456 bus from Feolin Ferry or Craighouse – ask the driver to let you down by the start of Evans' Walk (the scheduled stop is Three Arch Bridge)
Note	During the deer stalking season contact the head keeper of the Tarbert Estate in advance on 01496 820207

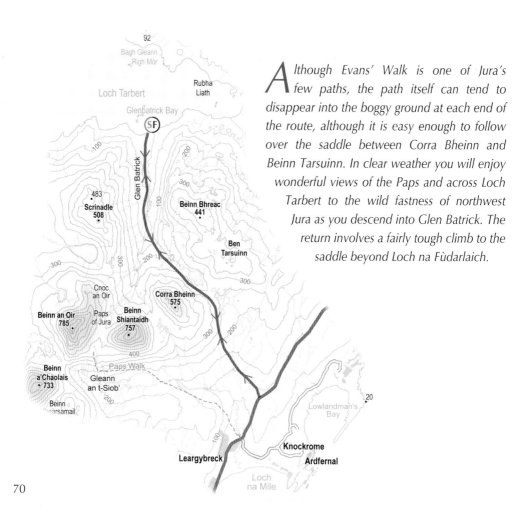

*A*lthough Evans' Walk is one of Jura's few paths, the path itself can tend to disappear into the boggy ground at each end of the route, although it is easy enough to follow over the saddle between Corra Bheinn and Beinn Tarsuinn. In clear weather you will enjoy wonderful views of the Paps and across Loch Tarbert to the wild fastness of northwest Jura as you descend into Glen Batrick. The return involves a fairly tough climb to the saddle beyond Loch na Fùdarlaich.

Looking along the Glenbatrick River to Loch Tarbert

From the signpost, climb initially north on a steady gradient, taking care as the path can be vague along this first section, depending on usage and just how boggy the ground is. Don't follow the ATV tracks too far north but bear northwest after 250 metres and you'll have a good chance of joining Evans' Walk proper. Climb to 150m then contour for 500 metres, crossing several burns in succession (the Allt Bràigh an Fheadain can be difficult to cross in spate, in which case follow the burn 500 metres or so upstream to cross safely). Continue northwest, crossing another burn and climbing to a rocky outcrop at around 200m (NR 540 747). The path soon bends north and continues to climb to the saddle between **Corra Bheinn** and **Beinn Tarsuinn**. Soon after reaching 250m the path contours to the west of Loch na Cloiche and two other sizeable lochans, then bears northwest again, following the shore of Loch na Fùdarlaich.

The path soon begins its descent into **Glen Batrick** alongside the Abhainn Loch na Fùdarlaich, which tumbles into the glen in a series of whisky-hued cascades. The path keeps to the left bank of the river except for a couple fords in its lower reaches. Further down the glen the river is fed by several burns flowing off the surrounding hills, and at its confluence with the Allt Teanga nan Abhainn it becomes the Glenbatrick River. In reasonable

Walking by the Abhainn Loch na Fùdarlaich

weather conditions these burns can be stepped across, however, after heavy rain they can become raging, un-fordable torrents. The lower reaches of the glen can be very boggy.

Approaching **Glenbatrick Bay**, the path leads down through the ramparts of an extinct cliff to the rear of Glenbatrick Lodge – a finer location for a 'summer house' is hard to imagine. If the weather is clement, a swim – for the robust – and picnic on the beautiful beach can be enjoyed.

Before heading back the way you came, it is worth having a look at the massive **raised beach** lying above the western end of the bay – just follow the obvious ATV tracks to the end of the bay and up a short incline.

SCARBA

The mountainous isle of Scarba (Scottish Gaelic: *Sgarba*) lies a kilometre to the north of Jura across the infamous Gulf of Corryvreckan, the narrow strait that is home to the northern hemisphere's second largest whirlpool, after Norway's Maelstrom. To the north of the island another notorious tidal race, the Bealach a' Choin Ghlais – 'the Grey Dog' – runs through the narrow channel between Scarba and Lunga, the southernmost of the Slate Islands. The island's name is probably of Norse origin, from *skarpoe* (sharp, stony, hilly terrain) or *skarf-øy* ('cormorant island').

Scarba is roughly square, measuring 5km east to west and 4.5km north to south with an area of around 15 square kilometres. Inhospitable and rugged, Scarba is dominated by its mountainous summit, Cruach Scarba (Gaelic *cruach*, 'stack' or 'heap'), which reaches 449m. The southern and western flanks of the mountain rise steeply from sea level and here the coastline is adorned with caves, natural arches and raised beaches. The island is uninhabited for much of the year. The only habitations are Kilmory Lodge, used mainly as a lodge during the deer stalking season, and Gleann a' Mhaoil bothy.

Sunrise at Gleann a' Mhaoil bothy

↑ *Cruach Scarba from Rubha nam Faoileann*

WALK 8

Cruach Scarba

ROUTE INFORMATION

Start/Finish	Jetty at Poll na h-Ealaidh (NM 720 060)
Distance	9.7km (6 miles) or 10.5km (6½ miles)
Total ascent	589m (1932ft) or 585m (1920ft)
Time	4–5hrs
Terrain	Rough and boggy moorland and hillwalking, although the pony path greatly assists progress
Maps	OS Explorer 355, Landranger 55
Note	There are no ferries to Scarba and, aside from the bothy at Gleann a' Mhaoil, there are no amenities whatsoever: for access see below.

*U*nless you sail or kayak yourself, private boat charter is the only means of access. Duncan Philips operates Farsain Cruises from Craobh Haven Marina, north of Lochgilphead on the Argyll coast. The 45-minute crossing costs £60 one way or £10 per head for more than six people (as at 2014, max 12 people), tel 07880 714165.

The main attraction for walkers on Scarba is Cruach Scarba, which qualifies as a Marilyn for those who collect the 'relative hills' of Britain. The route follows an old pony path contouring much of the way around the island, taking in spectacular views of Jura to the south, before striking up the ridge to the summit of Cruach Scarba then descending to rejoin a path around the island's north side.

Climbing along the pony path

From the jetty, follow the track as it climbs towards white-painted **Kilmory Lodge**. Pass to the rear of the lodge, continue along the track for 350 metres to a junction.

Alternative via Gleann a' Mhaoil bothy

To reach the Gleann a' Mhaoil bothy (NM 714 036), keep straight ahead along the contouring track. Turn right where it forks after 1km and continue along the track, which soon begins a winding descent into **Gleann a' Mhaoil**. The roof of the bothy soon comes into view.

To join the pony path from the bothy, head directly northwest, climbing steeply on rough, boggy ground with heather and myrtle cover – deer paths greatly aid progress. After 500 metres reach a small boggy plateau above a steep-sided glen immediately to the west. Continue northwest to cross the burn flowing down the glen at the obvious point near two small oak trees. Climb west, steeply at first, to reach the inflow of **Loch Airigh a' Chruidh** after 750 metres. The pony path passes just above and along the western edge of the loch: join it here, continuing southwest.

To skip the bothy, turn right at the junction along the intersecting path heading west away from the main track. After 250m turn left onto another track heading southwest. The track – an old pony path that is well-defined for much of its course – climbs gradually, passing to the west of **Loch Airigh a' Chruidh** after 1.5km. (A short way beyond the loch the view onto northwest Jura opens up magnificently across the Gulf of Corryvreckan.)

The path swings west and contours along around 280m on the southern flank of Cruach Scarba for 1km, gaining and losing a little height here and there. The path is mostly well-defined, if sketchy in places.

Around NM 688 035, the path becomes vaguer and descends to the northwest. Leave the path here and climb steadily northeast, soon arriving at a bealach atop two gullies descending to northwest and southeast. The summit of **Cruach Scarba** lies almost 1km directly to the north – a further 135m climb, which presents no difficulties.

> The **summit** is marked by a 'Vanessa' triangulation pillar, protected on three sides by a shelter wall. The views from the summit encompass Jura, Lunga, Luing, the 'Slate Isles', the Garvellachs, Mull and Colonsay.

From the summit, pass to the left of a small lochan and descend northeast along the ridge. Make for a large lochan perched on the ridge at around 410m and skirt around its left-hand side before crossing slippery rocks damming the outflow. Continue descending northeast, although not along the course of the burn flowing down from the lochan as this is steep and slippery. Pick your way through initially rocky and boggy terrain: continue descending

northeast, making for a rocky cnoc overlooking Scarba's north and the island vista beyond. Before reaching the cnoc, turn east and descend into the glen running northeast down the mountain's flank. Don't continue down the glen, but cross the burn flowing through it then climb a short way above its eastern side.

Now continue downhill with another burn over to your right (east) and a fine cascade soon coming into view below to your right. Where the terrain steepens, drop down to recross the burn and then continue downhill to join the path contouring around the island's northern flank. Turn right along the path, soon crossing a burn tumbling through a wooded gully. Continue on your way and the path soon begins following the course of a stock fence. Go through a gateway with an old iron gate post on your left and descend boggy ground, following the course of a dry stone wall and fence. Cross a boggy burn then climb a short way to join a metalled track. Turn right and follow the track for 600 metres to rejoin the Kilmory track to return to either the jetty or bothy.

The Grey Dog tidal race

COLONSAY

Colonsay (Scottish Gaelic: *Colbhasa*) and its tide-separated sister island of Oronsay (Scottish Gaelic: *Orasaigh*) have a combined length of 15km (9½ miles) and are 5km (3 miles) across the widest point. They lie 15km west of Jura, some 40km west of the Argyll mainland, 9km north of Islay and 25km south of Mull. Westwards is the Atlantic, with only Dubh Artach Lighthouse standing between Colonsay and Canada.

However, the wild and rugged terrain one might expect in such an exposed situation forms only part of the picture. Although small these islands possess great scenic variety: the moorland, hills and rocky outcrops of their interiors overlook some remarkably verdant terrain, including tracts of indigenous woodland and exotic plantation, and a coastline garlanded with magnificent sandy bays, small coves, raised beaches, towering cliffs and outlying skerries.

Annual rainfall is half that of mainland Argyll and summer sunshine hours are on a par with Tiree – the sunniest place in Scotland. In winter the temperature rarely drops below two or three degrees; the mild climate provides suitable conditions for a wide range of plants, flowers and trees that flourish, most notably in the exotic woodland and gardens of Colonsay House at Kiloran.

↑ Tràigh an Eacail on Colonsay's southeast coast (Walk 9)

WALK 9

South Colonsay Coast and Oronsay

ROUTE INFORMATION

Start/Finish	Junction of B8086 and B8087 at Scalasaig (NR 395 941)
Distance	27.5km (17 miles); shortcut to Scalasaig: 23km (14¼ miles)
Total ascent	368m (1207ft)
Time	6½–7½hrs
Terrain	Some dense heather and myrtle cover, sandy beaches, some boggy ground between The Strand and Machrins Bay. Access to Oronsay is tidal (see below).
Maps	OS Explorer 354, Landranger 061

*T*his route is circular, returning to Scalasaig along a narrow country lane: alternatively it can be terminated at Kilchattan.

Oronsay is accessible between one and three hours either side of low tide: ask at Colonsay Post Office for tide tables. Crossing The Strand may involve paddling – a pair of Crocs or flip-flops may be useful. Oronsay is an RSPB nature reserve so dogs must be kept under close control at all times.

At the road junction in **Scalasaig**, follow signs for The Pantry café. Pass in front of the café and go through a metal gate. Turn left behind the café and follow the vague path cutting across the point of Rubha Dubh. Head towards the shore south of **Rubha Dubh**, but keep to the ground above the rocky coastline as you continue southwest towards a sandy bay frequented by seals and otters. Cross the beach and at the far side step up on to rocks, clamber through a livestock fence and climb the slope onto level ground. (For the next 1km or so bracken, heather and boggy ground are a feature.)

Continue around **Rubha Eilean Mhàrtain** through rocky terrain, pass inside a long dry stone wall above the shore before reaching another sandy beach. Go through a gateway after 100 metres and cross the beach before clambering over bracken covered rocks around **Rubha Dubh**. Carry on round to Port a' Chrochaire, go through a stock gate and follow a fence for 300 metres, exiting through another stock gate. Pass around or cross the sandy inlet at Port na Bèiste, as the tide allows, and climb over the sand dunes on the far side. Drop down to the beautiful sandy beach of Tràigh an Eacail, which frames splendid views southeast to Islay and Jura. Cross the bay and climb the dunes at the far end before

continuing around the coastline to Port a' Chapuill. If the tide is out, walk along the lovely sandy strand then over dunes and rocks to emerge at the large bay between Colonsay and Oronsay.

At times other than exceptional spring tides, it is not possible to cross between the islands along the eastern shore, so head west across the sandy shore and then over the promontory of Rubha Bàgh nan Capull to the tidal sand flats of **The Strand**. If you've planned to coincide with the tidal 'window', follow the tyre tracks that emerge from the shoreline below the houses at Poll Gorm and head southwest across the flats to **Oronsay**. After 500 metres pick up a track road skirting the coast of Oronsay for 500 metres before coming ashore by Eilean Fhionnlaidh. Follow the track road for 1km as it climbs a little then turns south. Where the track bends west to follow the course of a dry stone wall, go through a gate and head south, passing through a gateway in another dry stone wall, before turning southeast and making for **Seal Cottage**, sitting among the dunes above the shore.

Seal Cottage is owned by the Oronsay Estate and is really worth a look. Although the cottage is not open to the public, the large, arched, window to the seaward side allows views into the beautiful sitting room – a maritime fantasia adorned with a scallop shell-framed mirror, glass float and wrought iron chandelier, whale bones and driftwood.

From Seal Cottage, continue southwest by the shore for 2km until the coastline turns north from **Rubha Caol**. A Landrover track covers the 2km from Rubha Caol to Oronsay Farm and the ruins of the Augustinian priory, but the magnificent dunes and beaches along Oronsay's west coast make the better walking route. Around 1km north of Rubha Caol a steep drop over a rocky outcrop blocks the shoreline route, so follow a dry stone wall inland and go through a gateway before heading back to the shore. Continue along a glorious stretch of dune-backed beach facing the vast Atlantic. Near its northern end follow the right bank of a small burn away from the shore and take the track through a gate in a livestock fence. Go through a gateway in a dry stone wall a little further on and continue along a walled track, which emerges on the main track from The Strand to Oronsay Farm. Turn left for the farm and the ruins of **Oronsay Priory**.

> **Oronsay Priory** dates from the mid-14th century. The site retains traces of an ancient monastic settlement dating from the sixth century. The earlier monastic community here links the site to Saint Columba, who is said to have landed on Oronsay on his way from Ireland to Iona.

Alternative route via Beinn Oronsay

It is worth scaling **Beinn Oronsay**, which looms immediately northeast of Oronsay Farm, rises to 93m and commands views south and east to Jura and Islay and north over The Strand to Colonsay.

Ascend its flank from the main track 200 metres east of the priory. From the top of the hill either descend east along its rocky slopes to rejoin the main track or simply descend by the route you climbed.

Return along the main track to The Strand and cross the 1.5km of sand flats, not the way you came, but northeast towards the southern end of the B8085, following the tyre tracks.

Shortcut via B8085

You can shorten the walk by continuing to the parking area at the north side of The Strand and then returning the 4.5km to Scalasaig by road. Simply follow the B8085 north for 3km to the junction with the B8086, then turn right and walk the remaining 1.5km to Scalasaig.

Seal Cottage, Oronsay, looking on to the Paps of Jura

Sandy bay on the Ardskenish peninsula

Before reaching the parking area at the road end, turn northwest off the main route and make for the track 400 metres distant coming ashore southeast of **Garvard** (NR 368 910). Follow the track through a gate, turn left by a stone byre, go through another gate and continue along the track for 1km to arrive at **Tràigh nam Bàrc**. Head west across the flat, sandy expanse to the dunes of the Ardskenish peninsula on the far side. (Between low and high tides the sea comes in 700 metres at Tràigh nam Bàrc; at high tide follow the shore around to the northwest, although if you have just crossed The Strand the tide will also be low here.)

Cross a stock fence, head into the sand dunes and look for a distinct track winding northwards to exit the dunes by the rocky outcrops of Carn Glas. The track becomes rocky, climbs then descends a little through boggy ground before turning north. Take the path that peels off the main track to the left and follow it around the beach at Port Lobh, crossing a burn and passing by the perimeter fence around the western end of Colonsay's tiny airstrip. Head across country towards the sandy beach at Machrins Bay (Tràigh an Tobair Fhuair), taking care to avoid boggy ground en route. From the beach, head northeast following a grassy track up onto the B8086. Turn right onto the B8086 and continue for 4km back to Scalasaig.

Alternative finish at Lower Kilchattan
Turning left along the B8086 brings you, in 1km, past **Port Mòr** to Lower Kilchattan.

WALK 10

Lower Kilchattan to Kiloran Bay

ROUTE INFORMATION	
Start	B8086 opposite the Colonsay and Oransay Heritage Trust (NR 362 948)
Finish	Kiloran Bay (NR 397 977)
Distance	7.75km (4¾ miles); including Carnan Eoin: 10.75km (6½ miles)
Total ascent	604m (1980ft); including Carnan Eoin: 744m (2440ft)
Time	2½–3hrs; including Carnan Eoin: 3–3½hrs
Terrain	Rugged cliff tops, some boggy ground, minor roads
Maps	OS Explorer 354, OS Landranger 61

*T*his varied walk takes in some clifftop scenery and also visits Kiloran Bay, famed for its beautiful broad sandy beach, which in clement conditions is an excellent beach for swimming and picnicking. The beach is framed to the north by Carnan Eoin – Colonsay's highest peak at 143m – which may be visited as an extension to the main route.

Much of this walk is along or near high cliffs and care should be exercised at all times, especially in windy conditions.

From the B8086, take the track heading northwest opposite the small Colonsay and Oransay Heritage Trust building (NR 362 948). Don't go through a gate after 100 metres, but follow the fence towards the shore and pass around it. Follow the vague path by the shore on the outside of the fence then cross a stile just past a gate. Continue by the rocky shore, gain a little height following the paths nearest the cliffs, initially keeping to the seaward side of the western flank of **Binnein Riabhach**, which dominates this section of the coast. There are good views of the cliff face below and the many seabirds nesting here, including fulmars, guillemots, razorbills, cormorants, shags and kittiwakes.

When the clifftop route becomes impassable, find a route up to the summit of Binnein Riabhach (120m), crossing a livestock fence once or twice. Descend northeast on a gentle gradient for around 500 metres along Aoineadh an t-Sruth until you are looking on to the broad V-shaped gully leading to Meall Lamalum ('lamb's holm promontory'). Head inland along the edge of the gully until you can safely descend into it, then follow the vague

The Arandora Star memorial cairn at Lamalum

path on the far side that soon steers around the flank of Lamalum. Stay high up on the grassy slope, soon crossing a narrow rocky ledge, hard against the rock face. Follow the path around the flank then up and over a rocky high point before descending towards Meall Lamalum. It is worth looking round

Cliffs covered by nesting seabirds at Aoineadh nam Muc – Pig's Paradise →

this promontory and the small bay at Leum a' Bhriair as there are good views on to cliffs swarming with sea birds.

On the clifftop above Leum a' Bhriair a cairn and plaque commemorates **Giuseppe Delgrosso**, who was found washed ashore here by islanders during the last war. Delgrosso was an Italian civilian among more than 800 victims drowned when the Arandora Star was torpedoed by a German U-boat off Ireland while transporting internees to Canada on 2 July 1940. There were 1673 passengers and crew aboard the Arandora Star, including a 200-man military escort, 479 German internees, 86 German POWs and 734 Italians, many of whom had been resident in Scotland and were rounded-up after Italy joined the Axis powers in June 1940.

The magnficent Tràigh Bàn – or 'white strand' – fringing Kiloran Bay, with Carnan Eoin rising above the north end

Continue around the clifftop from Meall Lamalum to arrive above Port Bàn, beneath the seabird-infested cliffs of **Aoineadh nam Muc** ('Pig's Paradise'). A path leads down to the beach, which is worth exploring. Head southwest back inland beneath a steep escarpment and find a way up the hillside where the incline is gentler; a path leads northeast, crossing a dry stone wall on a step stile (NR 374 968) before reaching the top of **Beinn Bhreac**, from where peregrines, merlins and choughs may be seen. Descend gently along the cliff top, which is boggy in places. When the descent steepens look for a vague path descending to the left of a burn (NR 376 974). After dropping 50m, follow the path that weaves its way along the cliff tops, giving grand views on to the promontory at Uragaig. Cross a dry stone wall and fence (NR 383 977) and follow a path down through rocky outcrops to the beach at Port nam Fliuchan – a fine sheltered inlet, ideal for swimming.

Follow the track at the top of the beach (NR 384 981) northeast past houses at Duntealtaig before turning southeast and passing through **Uragaig** then northeast again through Creagan, where the track becomes a road. After 500 metres you will arrive at a small parking area above **Kiloran Bay**, with a gate leading down to the beach.

> **Kiloran Bay** is famed for its beautiful broad sandy beach, framed to the north by **Carnan Eoin** – Colonsay's highest peak at 143m. In clement conditions it is an excellent beach for swimming and picnicking.

Extension to Carnan Eoin

To include Carnan Eoin in your walk, head northeast along the sublime sandy sweep of **Kiloran Bay**. At its northern extremity, make for a stile across a low fence (NR 404 984). Head up a boggy gully opposite to reach the Balnahard track road beneath some overhead power lines (NR 406 985). Cross the track and head northeast up a grassy slope to the bealach between Beinn Bheag and Carnan Eoin. Turn right (west) and follow a path marked with small cairns winding its way to the summit.

Atop Carnan Eoin is a very large stone cairn – a splendid **vantage point** for views over Kiloran Bay as well as Islay, Jura and Mull. Looking northwest to Port Sgibinis, 1km distant, lies the curious **Balnahard Whale**, a 160m-long 'sculpture' made of pebbles from a raised beach, which remains a work in progress and is not easily recognisable at ground level.

From here there are several options. For the fit and determined it is possible to continue north around the coast to Balnahard Bay, then south to Scalasaig as described in *Walking on Jura, Islay and Colonsay*. Alternatively, you can return to Lower Kilchattan by retracing your steps back along the coast or by following the B8086 southwest for 5km.

Alternative finish
If you retrace your steps it is possible to pick up a well-defined track above **Aoineadh nam Muc** that leads south to the road at Lower Kilchattan, passing by **Gortain** Cottage en route.

COLONSAY HOUSE

While in the area, it would be remiss not to visit Colonsay House and gardens, 1.5km back along the B8086 from Kiloran Bay. Colonsay House was built in 1722 on the site of Kiloran Abbey by the MacNeills, who were lairds of Colonsay until 1905. The private inner gardens are open to the public on Wednesdays and Fridays. Highlights include a Monterey cypress tree equipped with a swing in front of the house, a fine pond with curious benches and gigantic gunnera plants, and the lighthouse garden, which has the old lens from Rhuvaal Lighthouse on Islay as its centrepiece. An early Christian statue stands by a well, known as Tobar Oran, dedicated to Saint Oran. The statue, dating from the seventh or eighth century, was removed from the burial ground at Riasg Buidhe on the east coast and brought to Colonsay House in 1870.

Monterey cypress tree, Colonsay House gardens

THE GARVELLACHS

The Garvellachs (Scottish Gaelic: *An Garbh Eileaichan*), the 'rough islands' or 'Isles of the Sea' are a chain of four small islands lying north of the Isle of Jura and southeast of Mull, about 6.5km west of the Isle of Luing, at the entrance to the Firth of Lorn. Eileach an Naoimh (meaning 'Isle of the Saints') is home to the ruins of an ancient Celtic monastery and the best-preserved example of a monastic 'beehive cell' in Scotland. The site is in the care of Historic Scotland.

The private bothy near Rubha Mòr

↑ Above the Bealach an Tarabairt, Garbh Eileach

Garbh Eileach

ROUTE INFORMATION	
Start/Finish	Landing jetty at NM 669 117
Distance	5.75km (3½ miles)
Total ascent	256m (840ft)
Time	2–2½hrs
Terrain	Grassy, tussocky and pathless moorland; high cliffs and rugged, rocky coastline; some dwarf birch woodland
Maps	OS Explorer 359, OS Landranger 55

*O*ther than arriving in your own boat or kayak, the only way to reach the Garvellachs is to charter a water taxi. Farsain Cruises operates from Croabh Haven Marina on the Argyll coast, contact Duncan Philips on 07880 714165. The wonderful journey itself is enough to justify the expense. It is worth camping overnight on Garbh Eileach if you possibly can to allow time to explore. Although this will make a charter more expensive you could also include a visit to Eileach an Naiomh.

The best walking on the Garvellachs is to be had on Garbh Eileach – the largest of these small islands, at a mere 2km long and 1km wide. Along the north coast steep cliffs rise almost vertically from the sea, cleft by the Bealach an Tarabairt, while the ground slopes down to the low-lying southern shores as if the whole island is on a tilt, which in fact it is – the result of glacio-isostatic uplift after the ice cap retreated during the last glacial period. A small herd of red deer live on the island: keep your distance and give them space and time to get away from you.

From the jetty walk around to the estate **bothy** (which is private and locked; there are good spots to pitch a tent in the immediate environs, although if the bothy is occupied it is best to ask before doing so). From the right-hand side of the bothy head north-northwest across the island, following a vague path through the small glen, making for the cleft of **Bealach an Tarabairt**. Bear left to stay above the scrubby woodland nestled in the middle of the glen, soon gaining the bealach, which gives access to the rocky northern coast. It is worth exploring the coastline here, not least for the fine views

Looking southwest along Garbh Eileach to Eileach an Naoimh

north to the Isle of Mull. Returning to the bealach, climb northeastwards onto the high ground and continue along the cliff tops. The cliffs are steep and airy in places, so proceed with care and stay back from the edge.

The terrain rises to a high point of 110m near the island's northeastern end, where dwarf birch woodland thrives.

From here there are **fine views** east to Dùn Chonnuill, the smallest of the island chain. It is possible to descend the wooded slopes to Garbh Eileach's easternmost point, but do so with caution as the ground is steep and loose in places.

Bear south then southwest to descend more gradual slopes and arrive on the south coast. Continue along the rugged south shore, passing in front of the **bothy** again and continuing as far as the island's western end. After a short way the north coast is not navigable, so the high ground must be regained to continue back to the **Bealach an Tarabairt** to complete a circuit of Garbh Eileach.

Climbing to the high ground on Garbh Eileach

MULL

The Isle of Mull (Scottish Gaelic: *Muile*) is the largest island of the Southern Hebrides. With an area of 875 square kilometres (338 square miles) Mull is the fourth largest Scottish island and has a permanent resident population of nearly 3000. Numerous islands lie off the west coast of Mull, including Erraid, Inch Kenneth, Iona, Ulva and Gometra. Smaller uninhabited islands include Eorsa, Little Colonsay, the Treshnish Isles and Staffa – home to the remarkable basalt-pillared Fingal's Cave.

Mull, Iona and Staffa have long been among the most popular destinations for people visiting Scotland, and while much interest has centred on the historical and religious significance of Iona, the islands' spectacular landscapes and famous geological sites are also a considerable part of their appeal. The main attraction for walkers is Mull's splendidly mountainous south, crowned by the 966m summit of Ben More – the only island Munro outwith Skye. However, the island also has some magnificent,

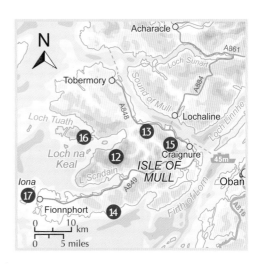

rugged coastline and the close-by isles of Ulva and Iona are well worth exploring. The islands are a haven for wildlife, and boast among the largest populations of golden and white-tailed eagles in the British Isles.

↑ *Towering cliffs seen from Carsaig (Walk 14)*   89

WALK 12

Ben More

ROUTE INFORMATION

Start/Finish	Parking area on the shore side of the B8035 just north of the bridge over the Scarisdale river (NM 517 376)
Alternative start/finish	Parking area on grass on the shore side of the A8035, opposite the track for Dhiseig (NM 494 359)
Distance	14.5km (9 miles) or 9.25km (5¾ miles)
Total ascent	1255m (4118ft) or 962m (3155ft)
Time	7–8hrs or 3½–5hrs
Terrain	Boggy ground at the start. Rocky ridges with some exposed easy scrambling. Care is needed on the final climb to the summit of Ben More on a very steep ridge with loose scree and rocks.
Maps	OS Explorer 375, Landranger 48

*T*he route described here is a horseshoe that starts by ascending Beinn Fhada before tackling A' Chioch and Ben More then descending along the 'easy' up-and-down route from Dhiseig – altogether making a demanding day in the hills. The alternative up-and-down Ben More route is not to be sniffed at either; however, it will suit those with less time, energy or enthusiasm for airy ridges – it also makes a more viable option in winter conditions.

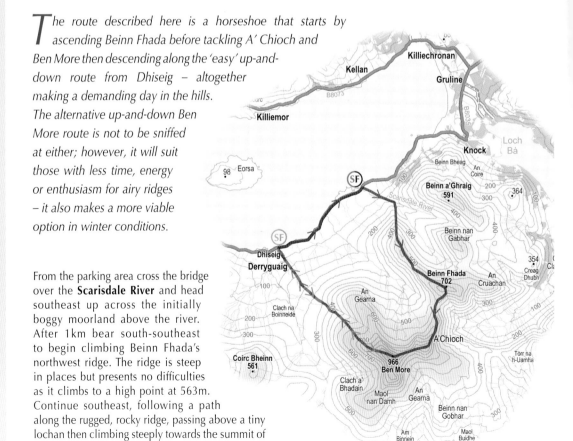

From the parking area cross the bridge over the **Scarisdale River** and head southeast up across the initially boggy moorland above the river. After 1km bear south-southeast to begin climbing Beinn Fhada's northwest ridge. The ridge is steep in places but presents no difficulties as it climbs to a high point at 563m. Continue southeast, following a path along the rugged, rocky ridge, passing above a tiny lochan then climbing steeply towards the summit of

On the summit of A' Chioch looking onto Ben More and its rugged northeast ridge

Beinn Fhada. The ascent is rocky at first before the ridge becomes broader and grassy for a while. Pass to the left (north) of a small lochan and make the final climb to the cairn-marked summit of **Beinn Fhada** (702m).

From the top it is best to retrace your steps initially to avoid craggy slopes, then make for the eastern side of the small lochan: from here the descent south-southwest towards the bealach is more straightforward, initially on a broad grassy slope. Further down the ridge a rocky section presents an obstacle, but this can be easily bypassed to the left. Continue down to the bealach, with grand views of A' Chioch and Ben More looming ahead. From the bealach continue southwards up the initially broad ridge towards **A' Chioch**: higher up the ridge narrows dramatically, requiring some straightforward, easy scrambling before the summit (867m) is gained. (From here the view of Ben More is magnificent and the route to it along the narrow, rugged northeast ridge with its steep final ascent looks formidable.)

Descend initially westwards, soon trending southwestwards on a clear path down the final rocky section to the bealach. There are steep cliffs on the right (west) side of the bealach and here a path cuts across the left (east) flank of the ridge before regaining the crest as the ridge climbs more steeply south-southwest. The ascent becomes very steep and airy, but paths on the left side of the ridge aid progress up through the loose, rocky ground. Route-finding requires care as various tracks lead further south, petering out on the hillside: keep gaining height to stay with the ridge and eventually emerge at the summit of **Ben More** (966m), with its low shelter wall.

The climb is spectacular and exhilarating and the views on a clear day are superb – a magnificent panorama of mountains, sea and islands. From the summit, continue along the northwest ridge following the stony path and numerous cairns marking the up-and-down route from Dhiseig, initially through scree and a few rock bands. The path descends to the left

Looking back down Ben More's northeast ridge to A' Chioch

of Coire nam Fuaran before approaching the Abhainn Dhiseig then crossing to the opposite bank. Lower down the ground is boggier and the path is sometimes indistinct. Join a track to the left of the cottage at **Dhiseig** and follow this down to the road. To return to the start turn right along the road for 3km, enjoying the views of Ben More and A' Chioch along the way.

Ben More from Dhiseig
The 'up-and-down' route also makes a fine walk with some fabulous views. Head up the track and keep straight ahead past the entrance to the house at Dhiseig, following the sign indicating 'up'. Go through a gate and follow a path alongside the Abhainn Dhiseig. At a fence go through a gate on the left then bear right to follow the burn once more.

Cross a stream at the obvious point and continue alongside the Abhainn Dhiseig, soon crossing the burn to gain the northwest ridge of Ben More where the ground begins to rise more steeply. Follow the eroded path, which becomes increasingly stony as you climb. (As the ridge becomes more defined a series of cairns show the way; higher up the ground is stonier with areas of scree.) Where the ground steepens the path climbs in small zig zags until the gradient eases on the summit ridge. Follow the ridge southeast to reach the summit of **Ben More** at 966m, with an OS trigpoint and low shelter wall. Retrace your steps to return to Dhiseig.

Descending the northwest ridge of Ben More, looking on to Loch na Keal and the island of Ulva →

WALK 13

Beinn Talaidh via Glen Forsa

ROUTE INFORMATION

Start/Finish	Parking area at the foot of Glen Forsa (NM 596 426)
Distance	18km (11¼ miles)
Total ascent	748m (2454ft)
Time	5–6hrs
Terrain	Metalled track through Glen Forsa. Rough, pathless moorland beyond Tomslèibhe bothy. Beinn Talaidh's lower reaches are very steep and grassy, giving way to scree higher up.
Maps	OS Explorer 375, OS Landranger 49
Public transport	The 495 bus between Craignure and Salen passes the entrance of Glen Forsa by Pennygown: ask to be let off here
Note	The turning for Glen Forsa is off the A849, 2km east of Salen on a section where the two carriageways separate. A small sign indicates 'Glen Forsa Estate only', but there is a place and invitation to park a short way along the lane by a house called Pennygown. Access further up the glen is on foot or by bicycle only. Glen Forsa is used for livestock grazing – including Highland cattle – something for bovinophobes and walkers with dogs to be aware of. Access to this walk may be limited during deer stalking.

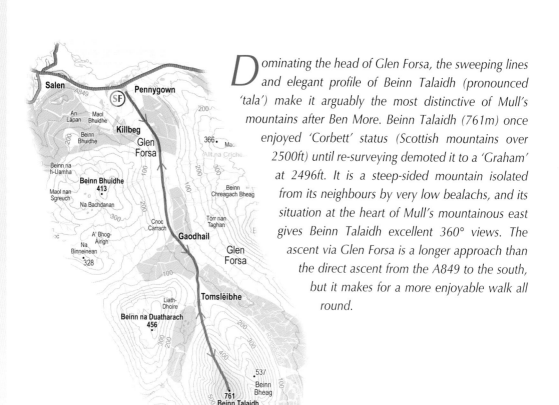

*D*ominating the head of Glen Forsa, the sweeping lines and elegant profile of Beinn Talaidh (pronounced 'tala') make it arguably the most distinctive of Mull's mountains after Ben More. Beinn Talaidh (761m) once enjoyed 'Corbett' status (Scottish mountains over 2500ft) until re-surveying demoted it to a 'Graham' at 2496ft. It is a steep-sided mountain isolated from its neighbours by very low bealachs, and its situation at the heart of Mull's mountainous east gives Beinn Talaidh excellent 360° views. The ascent via Glen Forsa is a longer approach than the direct ascent from the A849 to the south, but it makes for a more enjoyable walk all round.

Go through a gate and continue along the gravel track, with the River Forsa and a large forestry plantation to the left and Beinn Talaidh and its subsidiary summit, Beinn Bheag, dominating the view ahead. Follow the track past **Killbeg** cottage and the ruins of a chapel and burial ground, then go through another gate.

> In the past as many as ten families lived in the glen, but most were evicted from their homes to make way for blackface sheep farming during the **Clearances**.

Once the forestry plantation is left behind the middle reaches of the glen open out for a while before the track moves closer to the river and more forestry plantations. Cross a wooden bridge over a tributary, then keep right at a fork on the main track, staying to the right of the river.

The track swings around to a gate, beyond which a ford crosses another tributary (the footbridge marked on the OS 1:25k map does not exist); this is generally shallow and is the best option for crossing the burn even after heavy rain. Bear right at a fork by a striking memorial.

> This **buckled propeller** comes from a wartime plane crash on Beinn Talaidh in 1945. Three of eight crew and passengers aboard the Dakota transport plane were killed in the crash: one of the survivors alerted rescuers from the farmsteads in the glen.

Climbing the track towards Tomslèibhe and Beinn Talaidh

*Descending the northwest ridge of Beinn Talaidh with Beinn na Duatharach
across the glen and Cruachan Dearg beyond*

One of these was Bentalla Cottage, 500 metres further along the path from the memorial, which is now **Tomslèibhe bothy** – maintained by the Mountain Bothies Association – a fine base from which to tackle the mountain.

Beyond the bothy the path becomes fainter and very boggy, soon dropping slightly to cross the Allt na Clàr burn at the mouth of Gleann Lèan before fading out altogether. Head south towards the foot of the steep grassy ridge of Beinn Talaidh and go through a gate in the deer fence. Cross more boggy ground before beginning to climb very steeply. Higher up the north ridge – at around 500m – the gradient eases and efforts are rewarded by fine views back down Glen Forsa, with Loch Bà over to the west and Ben More rising above the surrounding peaks. The final climb crosses stony ground before the grassy summit plateau is reached. There is a trig point and a large cairn just beyond – the latter marking the highest point. Retrace your steps and enjoy the long walk out through **Glen Forsa**.

Carsaig Arches

ROUTE INFORMATION

Start/Finish	Parking area just above Carsaig pier (NM 545 213)
Distance	13.25km (8¼ miles)
Total ascent	85m (279ft)
Time	5½–6hrs
Terrain	Rocky coastal path beneath cliffs
Maps	OS Explorer 373, Landranger 48
Note	The coastal path is very rocky; the climb to reach the second arch is very exposed and requires great care.

*T*his magnificent walk along the coastline of the Ross of Mull to Malcolm's Point and the remarkable Carsaig Arches is one of the finest on Mull. However, it is a much more demanding walk than a glance at the OS map suggests. This is a tough route over very rocky ground with several sections of narrow, unstable path – although these can mostly be avoided by following the rocky shore. The spectacular coastal landscape is in large part the result of erosion of the sedimentary rock underlying the layers of basalt lava flows laid down during a period of volcanic activity between 50–60 million years ago, when the North Atlantic was forming. The arches are impressive formations, wrought by the elements from the eroded sea cliffs.

While walking through this geologically stimulating landscape you will likely encounter some of the wild goats that haunt this stretch of coastline: there is also a good chance of spotting white-tailed eagles, peregrine falcons and, in season, breeding fulmars and kittiwakes.

From the parking area by the pier, head a short way back up the road and turn left along a track with a No Through Road sign. Follow the track above the shoreline of Carsaig Bay, passing a static caravan, and at a fork bear left round an old iron gate and continue towards the shore. Follow the path on the shore side of the wall; at a fence turn left towards the beach. Follow the trodden path around the bay, crossing the outflows of a couple of burns on the beach where easiest. Rejoin the path above the shore, soon

Waterfall near Malcolm's Point

Natural arch with columnar basalt pillars

passing through a kissing gate in a stone wall. Cross a boggy area and where the path can be seen rising steeply ahead (this is dangerously eroded with a steep drop to seaward) head left to follow the rocky shore, picking up the path again on the far side of the landslip. Continue along the coast, taking care on narrow sections of path.

> The **Nun's Pass** or **Nun's Cave** is soon reached – a wide, shallow sandstone cave capped with basalt, which was reputedly used as a refuge by nuns exiled from Iona during the Reformation. Crosses carved into the sandstone on the left at the rear of the cave may date from the sixth century.

Continue along the coast, soon passing beneath a high waterfall. The going becomes easier for a while providing the opportunity to admire the huge, phantasmagorically eroded cliffs towering dramatically above, while across the Firth of Lorn, the Garvellachs, Scarba, Jura, Colonsay and Islay can all be seen.

Continue beneath the cliffs of **Aoineadh Mòr**, following a grassy sward or crossing rocks and pebbles along the beach. The path eventually passes a ruin at **Malcolm's Point** and, after a bouldery stretch, the first arch – a huge tunnel through the rock – comes into view. Cross the beach towards the arch and climb on to a basalt outcrop: a deep inlet separates you from the first arch, so backtrack a little to a small burn, looking out for a goat track that leads precariously above the inlet and out along the brow of the arch. (A good head for heights, good weather and great care are required here as any slip would be fatal.) The path traverses the cliff above the first arch and descends to the beach by the second arch, which is narrower but taller than the first arch, topped by a chimney-like rock stack and linked to the cliff by a rocky causeway. When you've finished marvelling at these splendid geological phenomena, retrace your steps to return to Carsaig.

WALK 15

Dùn da Ghaoithe

ROUTE INFORMATION

Start/Finish	Lane off the A849 leading to Upper Achnacroish (NM 727 350) ; or ferry terminal at Craignure (NM 718 371); or Pennygown (parking area at the head of Glen Forsa) (NM 596 426)
Distance	15km (9¼ miles); from Craignure: 20km (12½ miles); from Pennygown: 27.5km (17 miles)
Total ascent	843m (2766ft); from Craignure: 898m (2945ft); from Pennygown: 1070m (3510ft)
Time	4–5hrs; from Craignure: 5–6hrs; from Pennygown: 7–8½hrs
Terrain	An excellent track leads up to the two masts. From the second mast the walk is pathless hillwalking on mostly grassy ridges
Maps	OS Explorer 375, Landranger 49
Note	If travelling by car, head south along the A849 from Craignure, pass the (left) turn to Torosay Castle then take the next lane on the right, 250m further on. The lane swings sharply right and climbs steeply through woodland; where it levels by a row of large oak trees there is some room to park carefully on the grassy verge.

*T*he second highest summit on Mull, Dùn da Ghaoithe (pronounced: Doon da Goo-ee), the rugged yet elegant 'hill of the two winds' rises above Craignure, dominating the view of visitors arriving on the Oban ferry.

The usual route from Achnacroish, described here, follows an access track up to Maol nan Uan (546m), beyond which the walk along the summit ridge is superb. It is possible to make the route into a circular walk or a linear walk taking in the whole ridge northwest to the Sound of Mull, but these options involve traversing rough, boggy terrain: much effort for little reward. A challenging alternative, however, climbing the west ridge from Glen Forsa, is briefly described at the end of the main route description.

Alternative start from Craignure

Walk south from the ferry terminal, passing the Craignure Inn, and continue along the A849 heading out of Craignure. At Torosay North Lodge turn left and follow the track (signed: Forest Walk to Torosay Castle) until it swings round towards the castle. Continue past the castle to rejoin the road, turning left (with care) before turning right after 200 metres onto the lane leading to **Achnacroish**.

Starting from **Achnacroish** head along the lane, which becomes a track after passing the farm at Upper Achnacroish, soon reaching a locked gate

with a ladder stile. Climb over and continue along the track as it swings right and then left, climbing gently. The track continues climbing, steeply in places, as the views open up. (The twin summits of Ben Cruachan rise to the east of Oban; to the northeast the mainland mountains gather towards Ben Nevis, some 60km distant.) After another zig-zag the track climbs and passes to the rear (right) of the masts and buildings perched on the east side of the ridge at 403m. Here there is a first view across the vast bowl of Coire Mòr to your objective – Dùn da Ghaoithe is the northernmost of the two visible summits.

Looking northwest along the ridge to Dùn da Ghoaithe's higher, cairn-marked summit from the lower summit's trig pillar

Where the track divides take the right-hand fork and continue, winding steeply up on to the ridge; the gradient eases near the summit of **Maol nan Uan**, (546m) where there is another mast sheltered by a low bluff. Pass to the right of the fence and climb up onto the bluff; from here onwards the route is pathless and the short-cropped turf is a joy to walk on. Continue along the ridge passing a couple of tiny lochans with

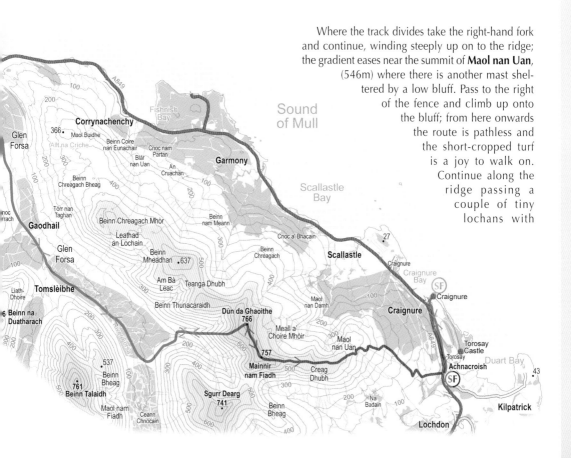

Beginning the long climb up Dùn da Ghaoithe's west ridge from Glen Forsa

the prominent summit of Mainnir nam Fiadh ahead. Climb westwards over a succession of easy rises; an increasingly distinct path runs parallel with the cliff edge dropping into the corrie. The ridge rises more steeply then narrows as the the ground falls away on either side. Continue climbing to reach the summit of **Mainnir nam Fiadh**; the trig pillar stands at the edge of the drop into Coire Mòr a short way from the highest point, marked by an enormous cairn: Dùn da Ghaoithe lies 1km further along the ridge to the northwest.

Descend northwards a little before the ridge broadens as it leads on to the bealach. Climb the stony slope, which levels off before reaching the summit of **Dùn da Ghaoithe** (766m).

> **The summit** has a large cairn and sublime views. Morvern lies to the north across the Sound of Mull while a swathe of Argyll and the Isles is laid out to east and south: westwards Beinn Talaidh, A' Chioch and Ben More are resplendent amid the undulating mountain landscape of eastern Mull.

Retrace your outward route.

Dùn da Ghaoithe via Glen Forsa

Climbing the mountain via its west ridge arguably makes the better, although tougher, route: however access might be a problem due to ongoing forestry work. This route is not Sunday stroll material; navigational competence and willingness to tackle rough, boggy ground are required. Furthermore, it is best to cycle in along the Glen Forsa track or overnight at Tomslèibhe bothy, otherwise the route is a bit long (27.5km).

From Pennygown

Follow the route description in Walk 13 as far as the Dakota crash memorial, then fork left to follow a metalled track into the forestry plantation. After 2km the metalled track peters out, but continue following the often boggy path straight ahead for 1km. If the going is difficult follow the outside edge of the forestry instead.

Once clear of the trees, follow the edge of the plantation roughly east, crossing a burn on a footbridge. Following paths where possible, cross the foot of **Sgurr Dearg**'s northern spur, Beinn Bhearnach, and descend to cross the Abhainn an t-Sratha Bhàin to the west side of the Allt Coire nam Fuaran. Follow the latter burn uphill, passing some ruined sheilings before crossing over to gain the west ridge of **Dùn da Ghaoithe**. (The climb is long and steady, steepening at around 450m before easing off towards the summit.) At the top of the ridge, bear northeast to arrive at the cairn marked summit (766m). Continue southeast along the summit ridge, descending a short way then gaining a little height to arrive at the lower summit of **Mainnir nam Fiadh** (757m), furnished with a trig pillar and cairn. Enjoy the views before retracing your outward route (skirt northwest beneath the higher summit to regain the west ridge).

ULVA

The islands of Ulva (Scottish gaelic: Ulbha) and its sibling, Gometra, project westwards into the Atlantic accompanied by a flotilla of small islands, including Staffa and the Treshnish Isles. At its narrowest the Sound of Ulva, which separates the island from Mull, is a mere 200 metres across, and yet Ulva feels like a place apart with an atmosphere all its own. Ulva is a peaceful, fertile island with a rugged moorland interior – a haven for wildlife, including white-tailed eagles.

The Boathouse on the Sound of Ulva

Once home to a thriving community of some 600 souls, the population of Ulva today numbers fewer than 15. In 1837, at the height of the kelp boom, the population was at its peak, with 16 townships or settlements around the island, still vividly apparent in the abandoned houses and corrugations of lazy bed cultivation at Ormaig and Cragaig. However, potato blight and the collapse of the kelp market precipitated migration en masse. The remaining crofters were eventually cleared from the land, often violently, by the landowner's factors and resettled in mainland Scotland, North America and Australia.

↑ On the South Side path with cloud shrouding the Ardmeanach peninsula across Loch na Keal

WALK 16

Ormaig and the south side

ROUTE INFORMATION

Start/Finish	The Boathouse, Ulva (NM 444 398)
Distance	11km (7 miles)
Total ascent	311m (1020ft)
Time	3½–4½hrs
Terrain	Rocky heather moorland, woodland and rugged coastline benefiting from good tracks and paths most of the way, although these can hold big puddles after wet weather. High bracken in summer.
Maps	OS Explorer 374, OS Landranger 48
Note	Ferry from Ulva Ferry on demand 9am–5pm weekdays (not Saturdays) from Easter until the end of September and on Sundays, June–August: tel 01688 500226 (mobile 07919 902407)

*T*his walk along the south side of Ulva is full of interest, so allow plenty of time for exploration. *If you have a surfeit of time, energy and enthusiasm, you may consider the rough, heather and bracken festooned climb to the summit of Beinn Chreagach, the island's highest point (313m), a worthwhile endeavour for the splendid views.*

The Boathouse licensed tea room provides top quality meals and refreshments between 9am–5pm from Easter until the end of September. More information on the island is available at www.isleofulva.com.

On the South Side path en route to Ormaig

From **The Boathouse** follow the track past the thatched Sheila's Cottage (now a museum). Keep straight ahead at the first track junction, signed for Ormaig. Continue along the winding track for 500 metres then take the left-hand turning by a wall, signposted South Side and Livingstone's Croft. Keep straight ahead, ignoring a track joining from the right before reaching some farm buildings. Turn right along a track for the South Side, climbing through mossy, deciduous woodland past a small reservoir. Pass through a deer gate, soon emerging from the woodland onto heathland. Follow the track over open moorland as views open up southwestwards to the Ross of Mull.

Continue to NM 429 392, where the main track to Gometra swings right, and turn left for South Side and Ormaig, soon entering a shallow, heathery valley. The track climbs a little and turns sharply left

where a ladder stile crosses a fence straight ahead; ignore this and stay with the main path. At a high point at just over 100m a path signed 'To the summit' leads off to the right.

Variant to Beinn Chreagach summit
Here is the first option to leave the main route and climb **Beinn Chreagach**, Ulva's highest point. If this is your main objective you should leave the South Side route here, at NM 423 391, to join the route signposted 'To the summit'. There isn't a path all the way, requiring a degree of route-finding and a lot of bashing through heather and bracken in the summer months.

Continue along the main path, soon descending towards Ormaig. The view opens out spectacularly across Loch na Keal and the bay, where myriad tiny islets lead out towards Little Colonsay with Staffa beyond. A cairn bearing a poetic inscription in French (dated 2008) provides a prime viewpoint.

Continue down past the abandoned crofts of **Ormaig**, passing beneath the Ormaig memorial, which tells of the township's Macquarie clan and the Norse origin of the placename. A little further on, at a bend in the track at the foot of Glen Glass, several trees stand by the old **Cragaig** mill where a stream is crossed. Continue across another stream, soon arriving at a fork. The main path, which can be overgrown with bracken in summer, continues to the right and can be followed for a further 1km to the ruined church and burial ground at **Cille Mhic Eoghiann** (Kilvekewen).

ONWARD COASTAL ROUTE

The onward path becomes less distinct, but it is possible to forge a route around the coast to join the cross-island Ulva–Gometra track for the return to the ferry, thus circling the island. However, you would need an early start and good progress in order to make the last ferry.

Variant: Beinn Chreagach (via Ormaig)

If you want to append a climb of **Beinn Chreagach** to a visit to Ormaig then it's as well to climb alongside the burn descending the gully running down from the eastern side of the summit; leave the path at NM 407 391. This is rough going and very overgrown in summer and involves improvisation. Not for the faint-hearted.

The left-hand path continues along the shore to the estate bothy, which is private and locked. There are benches at the front of the bothy and, if it is unoccupied, this makes a grand spot for a lunch break. Seals frequent the skerries and white-tailed eagles can also be seen here. Retrace your outward route to return to The Boathouse and the ferry.

Among the ruins of Ormaig beneath Beinn Chreagach

IONA

Iona (Scottish Gaelic: *Ì Chaluim Chille*) is a small, beautiful island, with great historical and religious significance, lying just to the west of the Ross of Mull. Iona is roughly 5.5km (3½ miles) long and 3km (1¾ miles) across at its widest point; the island's highest point is Dùn I, which rises to 100m near the north end. The island can be comfortably walked around in a day. Iona has a permanent population of 125.

Lewisian gneiss rock along Iona's west coast

↑ *Sandy beach near Goirtean Beag*   107

WALK 17

Around Iona

*T*his fine walk, around the north of the most-visited of small Hebridean islands, passes through the settlement of Baile Mòr, with Iona Nunnery and the world-famous ruins of Iona Abbey, before heading out to the northernmost point of the island, then continuing around the beautiful northwest coastline to arrive at the idyllic beach of Camas Cùil an t-Saimh ('The bay at the back of the Ocean'). Heading directly east back across the island on a single-track road soon brings you back to Baile Mòr and the ferry pier.

Iona can be very busy in the summer months: most visitors, however, will be visiting the Abbey, and once you are out along the coast, normal Hebridean tranquility will be restored.

ROUTE INFORMATION

Start/Finish	Iona ferry pier (NM 286 240)
Distance	13km (8 miles) or 9km (5½ miles)
Total ascent	345m (1130ft) or 180m (590ft)
Time	4½–5½hrs or 3½–4½hrs
Terrain	Minor road, sandy beaches and machair, some rough, boggy ground
Maps	OS Explorer 373, Landranger 48
Public transport	96 and 496 bus to Fionnphort, ferry to Iona
Note	Sheep and cattle graze all over the island: keep dogs under close control.

From the pier head straight up the street, passing shops on your left and following signs for the Abbey. On the right are the ruins of Iona Nunnery, the best-preserved medieval nunnery in Scotland. Either go through the Nunnery grounds or follow the road round past the primary school, soon passing MacLean's Cross, a tall, elegant 15th-century carved Celtic cross. Follow the road through the settlement, past allotment gardens and the hotel before passing **Iona Abbey**.

The original 13th-century Benedictine **Iona Abbey**, which was built on the foundations of the earlier Columban monastery, has been extensively rebuilt and restored over the centuries. Columba came to Iona from Ireland and founded the monastery, which became an influential centre for the spread of Christianity among the Picts and Scots, in AD563. Such was Iona's importance that Scottish kings were crowned and buried here. *The Book of Kells*, a famous illuminated manuscript, is believed to have been the work of Iona's monks. In 806 Viking raiders massacred 68 monks at Martyrs' Bay, and in 825 the Abbey was torched during another Viking raid.

Continue north along the road, passing houses and crofting land, with Iona's highest point, **Dùn I** (pronounced 'doon-ee'), rising to 100m on the left. (The signposted climb of Dùn I is steep but straightforward and leads to a fine viewpoint marked with a cairn and a trig pillar.)

Where the road turns left for the Iona **Scottish Youth Hostels Association (SYHA) hostel**, continue straight ahead through a gate and follow a path between fences. Continue along a track, eventually bearing left and passing through a stock gate to reach the shore at **Tràigh an t-Suidhe**.

Head initially west then southwestwards along a series of white sand beaches studded with beautifully banded Lewisian gneiss rocks. Cross a shingle beach and follow a vague path onto higher ground, crossing a stock fence. For the next 1.5km, wend your way through a landscape of low hillocks and shallow declivities. Stay as close to the coast as you can, taking advantage of the trodden paths weaving a route through the often boggy terrain.

Iona Abbey on the site of Saint Columba's Celtic Christian monastery

Cross a low wall beneath the rocky eminence of Goirtean Beag and walk down through a grassy valley to the lovely sandy beach at **Port a' Ghoirtein Bhig**, with its fine view onto Corr Eilean; an excellent spot for a break. Retrace your steps a short way, passing beneath Goirtean Beag before returning to the shore at the next opportunity. Continue along a stretch of small sandy beaches and sand dunes. Go through a gate in a stock fence and walk down to the beautiful expanse of beach fringing **Camas Cùil an t-Saimh** – a fine place to contemplate the vast Atlantic Ocean.

Shortcut avoiding Port na Curaich

To return to Baile Mòr and the ferry pier, pick up the obvious track heading east across the machair to join the single track road cutting across the island's middle, passing houses and crofts. The road eventually turns sharply left and continues north to arrive in **Baile Mòr**.

To continue to Port na Curaich, head south following a track across the springy turf of A' Mhachair, which doubles as grazing land and

a golf course. Where the track bends towards the house at Culdamh, continue southwards on a fainter track to the far end of the golf course, crossing a bank of sand beside a fence. A clear track continues

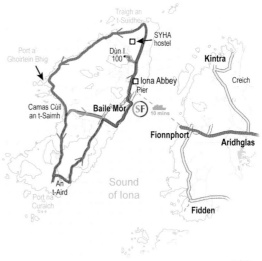

uphill, giving fine views back across the beaches and machair. Continuing through rocky moorland terrain with heather and bracken cover the track soon reaches Loch Staoineig; leave the track and follow the often boggy path passing to the left of the loch. Continue across the moor before descending to the twin bays of Port an Fhir-Bhrèige and **Port na Curaich**, divided by a large rock outcrop. (The curious piles of stones found here were reputedly the work of monks serving penance for their sins.)

Head back across the grassy sward, looking out for a narrow path climbing eastwards (right) through the rocky terrain of **An t-Aird**. The path soon becomes more distinct and trends northeastwards across the moorland, eventually leading to a metal stockgate at NM 276 232. Go through and continue along the fenced-in track, which eventually emerges at the cross-island road. Turn right and follow the road, which soon bends sharply left, to arrive back at **Baile Mòr**.

Rugged coastline, northwest Iona

Approaching Port a' Ghoirtein Bhig

COLL

Coll (Scottish Gaelic: *Cola*) and its neighbour, Tiree are often referred to as the 'Hebridean Twins'. The islands lie 12km (7½ miles) west of Mull. Coll is about 30km (13 miles) long by 5km (3 miles) wide, and its highest point is Ben Hogh, which rises to 106m at the island's southwest. The southern part of Coll is fringed with magnificent dune-backed sandy beaches, while the north of the island is a wild and rugged landscape of rock and heather, scattered with myriad tiny lochans. Coll's main village, Arinagour, lies on the west side of Loch Eatharna, and is home to about half the island's population of 200. The island's north is sparsely populated, and beyond Sorisdale at the far northeast it is entirely uninhabited.

The pier at Arinagour is the landing point for the ferry linking Coll with Tiree and the west coast port of Oban, some 75km distant. Aside from its wonderful beaches, Coll is best known for its birdlife – particuarly its population of corncrakes – and for the 15th-century Breachacha Castle, formerly a stronghold of the MacLeans, with its four storey rectangular tower-house.

Looking across Feall Bay to Ben Feall

↑ *Tràigh Halum, contender for most perfect small beach in the Hebrides*

WALK 18

Coll's western tip

ROUTE INFORMATION

Start/Finish	Coll RSPB Nature Reserve car park (NM 151 538)
Distance	14.5km (9 miles)
Total ascent	205m (670ft)
Time	4–5hrs
Terrain	Shell sand beaches, springy machair and marram grass-matted sand dunes; some rocky and boggy ground
Maps	OS Explorer 372, OS Landranger 46

*T*his circular route around Coll Nature Reserve traverses the entire low-lying coastline of Coll's western tip, visiting several sublime dune-backed beaches, the vantage point of Ben Feall and the exposed, often windy western-most extremity of Calgary Point, with fine views across Caolas Bàn to Gunna and Tiree. This is a route for taking your time over: there are abundant birds and wild flowers to admire, beautiful white sand bays with sparkling blue-green waters and magnificent views in every direction.

From the RSPB Nature Reserve car park, follow the grassy track north, passing an enormous boulder after 600 metres. The track soon bends northwest then forks at the foot of **Ben Feall** after 1km. Take the right-hand path to climb the hill.

> The summit of **Ben Feall** (66m) gives wonderful views across the western end of Coll, with the magnificent white sand crescent of Tràigh Feall fringing Feall Bay below to the southwest.

Head back down the hill, turn right along the track to the eastern end of **Feall Bay** and continue along the 1.5km sweep of Tràigh Feall. At the western end of the bay climb a little above the beach, go through a gate and follow a vague path a short way northwest. A signpost indicates 'Calgary Point 4½ km' to the southwest. Follow the path – there are occasional marker posts – southwest along the coast for 2km before arriving at a signpost with one arrow pointing northwest, indicating 'Calgary Point 2½km', the other indicating 'Crossapol Bay 2km' to the southeast.

Carry on northwest for Calgary Bay, go through a stock gate and continue, shortly crossing a stile over a stock fence. Turn to follow the coast south-west, soon arriving above the next beach, lovely Tràigh Halum, a beautiful white sand arc terminating in the rocky outcrop of Eilean Halum. A marker post above the bay points southwest, but descend to walk around the bay before climbing above the

← Footprints in the sand, Tràigh Feall (photo: Giulia Hetherington)

113

shore again. Follow the coastline southwest for 1km to arrive at the trig pillar on **Calgary Point**.

> This can be a windy spot indeed, but the **view** southwest across Caolas Bàn and Gunna Sound to Gunna and Tiree is sublime and occasionally dramatic when the tide comes roaring through the narrow strait. To the south the coastline extends away in a series of dune-backed, white sand beaches fringed by sparkling jade-green waters.

Continue initially southeast for 1.5km, either along the beach (Tràigh nan Sìolag) or the edge of the dunes, to arrive at the southernmost tip of the peninsula. Come above the shore and continue northeast along the coast on easy ground. Pass around Port a' Mhùrain and cut across the neck of **Rubha nan Faochag**; the terrain becomes rockier as you continue northeast, passing the inlets of Port Bàn and Port an Duine, crossing several stock fences en route. Keep to seaward of a stock fence running parallel to the shore as you approach Walker's Cottage. Pass around the rocky inlet in front of the cottage and continue to the cemetery in front of Crossapol House. Join the track in front of the house and follow it around to the western extremity of Tràigh Garbh. Continue along the beach or dune edge for 700 metres before passing the rocky outcrop of Sgeir Dubh to arrive on the white sand arc of Tràigh Crossapol: the beach at **Crossapol Bay** is 1.5km long and can seem much longer – in a good way. Near the southeastern extremity of the bay take the sandy track up through the low dunes and follow it for 1km back to the Nature Reserve car park.

At Calgary Point with the small island of Gunna across Caolas Bàn

TIREE

Tiree (Scottish Gaelic: *Tir Iodh*) lies southwest of Coll, west of Mull and is the most westerly of the Inner Hebrides – 35km (22 miles) west of Ardnamurchan on the mainland. It is relatively small – just over 16km (10 miles) at its longest, 8km (5 miles) at its widest, and a kilometre at its narrowest – and very flat. Tiree's highest point is Ben Hynish (141m), rising above the island's southwestern end. Much of the 74km (46-mile) coastline is fringed with glorious white shell sand beaches.

Tiree has a population of around 800 and the main settlement and harbour is at Scarinish, where ferries sail to and from Coll and Oban. The island enjoys a mild climate and records among the highest total hours of sunshine anywhere in the British Isles during late spring and early summer. Owing to its exposed situation Tiree is an exceptionally windy island, with gales on average 34 days a year, the fiercest in December and January. A happy consequence of Tiree's windy disposition is that midges are almost non-existent. Tiree is also a magnet for windsurfers.

The long sweep of Tràigh Mhòr fringing Gott Bay

↑ *Along the coast on Gunna Sound (Walk 19)*

WALK 19

Around the coast of east Tiree

ROUTE INFORMATION

Start/Finish	Balephetrish Farm (NM 013 474)
Distance	22.5km (14 miles); shorter variant: 13km (8 miles)
Total ascent	166m (545ft)
Time	5½–6hrs; shorter variant: 3–4hrs
Terrain	Shell sand beaches, springy machair turf and marram grass-thatched sand dunes; some rocky and boggy ground
Maps	OS Explorer 372, Landranger 46
Public transport	497 dial-a-ride bus service: tel 01879 220419 – must be booked in advance

*T*his route is well-suited to the sunny, windy conditions prevailing on Tiree from late spring to late summer, but also makes for a bracing walk in less clement conditions. Be aware, however, that the low-lying terrain affords no protection whatsoever from the elements – hence this is not a walk for stormy weather.

The longer main route traverses much of the coastline of east Tiree, taking in sweeping white sand bays, flower-strewn machair and ancient monuments. The shorter variant includes many of the highlights and can be tackled in a half day's walk.

Tràigh Bhalla and houses at Vaul

Follow the track road signposted for 'Balephetrish' that turns right off the B8068. Continue towards the farm and turn left where a signpost indicates 'Path to Ringing Stone'. Follow the track past houses adorned with buoys and fishing floats and turn right through a stock gate with a white arrow marker. Continue along the coast through more gates and with emerging views of Rum and Eigg. Pass to the south of Loch Aulaig – in truth a small lochan – through two more gates: the second, above a small beach, has a waymarker indicating 'Ringing Stone 300m'. The **Ringing Stone** perches near the shore.

The Ringing Stone, perched by the shore on Tiree's north coast

The **Ringing Stone** (Gaelic: Clach a' Choire) is an erratic boulder carried from Rum, 56km (35 miles) to the north, by the ice during the last glacial period. It emits a range of resonant metallic tones when struck with stones. The grey granodiorite boulder is much younger than Tiree's Lewisian gneiss.

The stone is decorated with 53 cup marks, dating back 4000 years, which are believed to have religious significance, but their precise purpose and meaning is unknown. Tradition has it that the stone was thrown by a giant from Mull – and should it ever be removed from Tiree the island will sink below the waves.

Continue along the coastal machair on the meandering path, watching out for boggy patches. Walk around the beach at Am Beannan Ruadh and cross a fence-topped wall where it abuts a rocky outcrop. Continue past the rocky outcrop and head east across open ground to pick up a track heading northeast below a fence-topped wall. As the track descends gently, an area of raised ground to the left is topped by the remains of **Dùn Mor** broch, an Iron Age fortification. Continue along the track and cross a fence on a stile next to a gate. The track bears right and climbs a little, but it is worth carrying straight on 200 metres to the site of Dùn Beag for fantastic views onto Vaul and Salum bays. Rejoin the path, climb a little past a couple of houses and just before the track swings right through a gateway, turn left on a grassy track that descends toward the shore.

Shortcut

To follow the shorter variant, continue through the gateway and follow the track road southeast for 1.5km to join the B8069 Gott–Caolas road. At the junction continue straight over on to the beach at **Gott Bay**

Kitesurfers in Gott Bay

and turn right (west) and continue for 2km along **Tràigh Mhòr**. Walk along this endless sandy fringe to the southwestern end of the beach. Go through a wooden gate near a large shed to reach the B8068.

Pass a house, go through a stone gateway, follow the track down to the beach and continue along the sandy shore of **Vaul Bay**. At the eastern end of the bay, climb over a rocky outcrop to Salum Bay. Continue around the bay, climbing over a stock fence on the way. At the bay's eastern end, pass to the left of the farmhouse above the shore. Go through a wooden fence next to a stock gate and continue along the track for 1.5km, passing through stock gates en route. On reaching the farmhouse at Miodar, leave the track and go through an old gate in a fence to your left. Continue around the headland at **Urvaig**, with fine views over the sound to Gunna and the dunes of southwest Coll beyond.

Continue along the coast, passing a few houses then go through a gate and descend to the beach at An Tràigh-lochain by houses at Dunbeg. Just before the beach ends at Port Ruadh (NM 086 491), head southwest inland picking up a track and continuing straight ahead to join the B8069 at **Caolas**. Keep straight ahead along the minor road for 2km then turn left (signposted 'Ruaig ¼') along a minor road for 1km, passing between houses, before descending to the shore at **Tràigh Crionaig**. Turn right, continue along the beach and pass around Rubh a' Phuirt Bhig onto the 4km-long sandy expanse of **Tràigh Mhòr**, which curves in a huge ellipse around **Gott Bay**. Walk along this endless sandy fringe to the southwestern end of the beach. Go through a wooden gate near a large shed to reach the B8068. To return to Balephetrish, continue northwest along the B8068 for 3.5km. Otherwise Scarinish is 1km southwest along the road.

Tiree's west coast and three highest points

	ROUTE INFORMATION
Start/Finish	Hynish (NL 985 393)
Alternative start/finish	Balephuil (NL 959 404)
Distance	30km (18¾ miles); Carnan Mòr/Ben Hynish only: 9.25km (5¾ miles); from Balephuil: 21km (13 miles)
Total ascent	736m (2415ft); Carnan Mòr/Ben Hynish only: 335m (1100ft); Beinn Ceann a' Mhara and Beinn Hough only: 401m (1315ft)
Time	7½–8½hrs; Carnan Mòr/Ben Hynish only: 3–3½hrs; from Balephuil: 4½–5hrs
Terrain	Mostly shell sand beaches, springy machair and marram grass-thatched sand dunes, some rocky and boggy ground
Maps	OS Explorer 372, OS Landranger 46
Public transport	497 'dial-a-ride' bus service: tel 01879 220419 – must be booked in advance (daytime only)

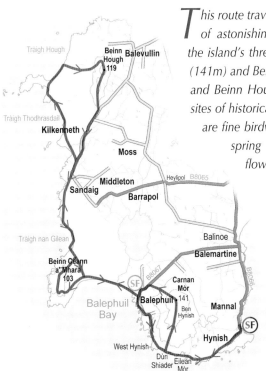

*T*his route traverses much of Tiree's west coast, visiting an array of astonishingly beautiful dune-backed beaches as well as the island's three highest points – the twin tops of Carnan Mòr (141m) and Ben Hynish (126m), Beinn Ceann a' Mhara (119m) and Beinn Hough (103m). The route also passes a number of sites of historical interest – ancient and more recent – and there are fine birdwatching opportunities along the way. From late spring to late summer, the machair is awash with wild flowers.

There are options for shortening the route. After climbing Carnan Mòr/Ben Hynish it is straightforward to return to Hynish from Balephuil. Likewise, the western part of the route can be started and finished at Balephuil. Another alternative is to end the walk on returning to Sandaig – if you can arrange transport or book the Tiree 'dial-a-ride' bus service.

From Hynish follow the B8066 southwest to its end just beyond the old signalling tower, now home to the Skerryvore Lighthouse Museum. Follow the track road through Hynish Farm, pass through several gates before arriving at Millport House and cross a fence on a stile. Continue southwest, cross a small burn and follow a track through boggy ground to arrive at a grassy declivity, known locally as Happy Valley, descending gently southwest between rugged Lewisian gneiss outcrops to the fine little beach at Clèit Mhòr. Head northwest, climbing a little and following a vague path contouring around the coast, soon passing above Port Snoig and then past **Dùn Shiader**, atop its rocky promontory.

Climb a little to meet a dry stone wall then follow it northeast up through heathery, boggy ground onto **Ben Hynish**, soon arriving at the summit (126m) with the 'golf ball' radar station atop **Carnan Mòr** – Tiree's highest point – a short way north. Continue following the wall, descending a little then climbing briefly on the radar station access road to the summit trig pillar (141m), with grand views across the island.

Descend west-northwest across rocky, heathery and boggy terrain, making for some houses with a red telephone box where the B8067 passes through Balephuil. Go through a stock gate near the bottom of the hill, cross a field and go through another gate to the road (NL 959 404).

Direct return to Hynish
From here you can return to the start by turning left to continue along the B8067, which soon becomes a minor road, and then following the last paragraph of the main route description below.

Turn left, walk over a road junction, go through a gate and continue southwest across the machair, soon descending gently to a gate at the eastern end of Balephuil Bay.

Walk along the fine beach, framed at its western end by the headland of Ceann a' Mhara. Cross

Looking across Port Snoig from Tiree's southern cliffs

Beinn Ceann a' Mhara from Tràigh nan Gilean

the outflow of the Abhainn a' Bhèidhe and continue along the shore or the edge of the dunes to the far end of the bay. Follow a track onto the greensward beneath the headland. After 250 metres climb west to the spine of the headland at around 50m. Continue north along the south ridge of **Beinn Ceann a' Mhara**, climbing rocky ground to the summit (103m), with fine views across Balephuil Bay to Carnan Mòr. Continue a short way north, crossing a stock fence. (At the north end of the ridge there are fantastic views along the west coast of Tiree, which looks very much like paradise on a sunny day.) Cross another fence, make your way over a narrow bealach and descend the northwest ridge.

Join a path at the bottom of the descent then turn right through a gate onto **Tràigh nan Gilean**. Continue north along the beach for 800 metres, then head up through dunes to join a path winding its way north above the shore. Turn left where the path intersects a pebble track and continue north across the machair for 1km to the road at **Sandaig**. Turn left along the road for 600 metres then turn left again to follow a grass track down to the shore. Cross a burn and continue along the shore or dunes at Tràigh Ghrianal, as the tide allows, to the kilometre-long beach at **Tràigh**

Thodhrasdail. Walk to Rubha Hanais at the northern end of the beach, go through the right-hand gate and continue across the neck of Rubha Chràiginis. Go through another gate and descend to **Tràigh Hough**.

Continue along the beach or the edge of the dunes as the tide allows; after 750 metres, where a rocky outcrop crosses the shore, head into the dunes to join a distinct pebble track and follow it inland for 1km.

This landscape of low-lying dunes is dotted with abandoned **bunkers, emplacements and observation posts** – long-vacant reminders of the military presence on Tiree during the Second World War.

Before reaching a cattle grid, leave the track at the foot of **Beinn Hough**'s north ridge, climbing directly south. Pass an observation post and emplacement before reaching the summit trig point (119m), which stands next to another observation post. There are fine views across the west coast and east across the island's hinterland. Continue south from the summit, descend a little then climb a short way to the communications tower on Beinn Mhurstat.

Descend the access road, turn right at the T-junction and continue southwest along the road back towards Sandaig. On the right, after 500 metres, the ruins of St Kenneth's Chapel, dating from the late-Middle Ages, stand a short way from the road. Continue for 1.5km through **Sandaig** to rejoin the track leading back to **Tràigh nan Gilean**. Retrace your steps to the gate at the southern end of the beach, then follow the path southeast, climbing for half a kilometre. Go through another gate, descend south to the dunes behind Tràigh Bhi, then retrace your outward route around to the eastern end of **Balephuil Bay**. Go through the gate and climb southwest across the grassy slope, go through another gate by a house and turn right along the road through **West Hynish**.

Dogleg past the radar station access road and continue past a couple of houses as the road becomes a track. Go through stock gates either side of the last house along the track, pass a sheepfold and go through a final gate. Climb to around 40m and continue east along the coast, soon crossing a dry stone wall and arriving above **Dùn Shiader** once more. From here retrace your outward route to (East) **Hynish**, keeping above the shore to avoid difficult terrain.

Tràigh Hough

RUM

The isle of Rum (Scottish Gaelic: *Rùm*) is by far the largest of the Small Isles (Rum, Eigg, Muck and Canna) and is the 15th largest of all the Scottish islands. It is the wettest and arguably the most mountainous island of its size in Britain. Its striking profile of jagged basalt and gabbro mountain peaks testifies to its volcanic origins. Rum occupies an area of 100 square kilometres, and is 14km north to south by 13.5km east to west at its widest points. It lies 11km south of Skye and 27km west of Mallaig. Kinloch, the island's only settlement, lies at the head of Loch Scresort and is home to the entire population of around 40 people and the marvellous Edwardian folly that is Kinloch Castle.

For much of the 19th and 20th centuries Rum was known as 'The Forbidden Island' and was used as a private sporting estate. Today, the island is owned and managed by Scottish Natural Heritage (SNH). Rum was designated a National Nature

Reserve in 1957, a Biosphere Reserve in 1976, a Site of Special Scientific Interest in 1987, and has 17 sites scheduled as nationally important ancient monuments.

↑ *Bloodstone Hill looms above Guirdil bothy (Walk 23)*

WALK 21

A Round of the Rum Cuillin

ROUTE INFORMATION

Start/Finish	Path along the Allt Slugan by Kinloch Castle (NM 402 994)
Distance	27km (17 miles); to Dibidil bothy: 18.5km (11.5 miles)
Total ascent	2025m (6645ft)
Time	9–10hrs; to Dibidil bothy: 6 –7hrs
Terrain	Rugged, rocky mountain terrain. The northernmost hills are formed largely of basalt and gabbro – a coarse-grained rock beloved of climbers and hillwalkers for its excellent grip – while the fine-grained felsite capping the southern peaks can be slippery in wet conditions. The return on the Dibidil–Kinloch path is boggy in places.
Maps	OS Explorer 397; Landranger 40; Harvey Maps, Rum, Eigg, Muck and Canna Superwalker XT25

*T*he Rum Cuillin is the finest mountaineering tour in the islands outside of Skye, yet the traverse is nowhere as difficult as Skye's Cuillin Ridge, requiring some moderate scrambling and no climbing other than a couple of short sections that are easily avoided. However, this is not an undertaking to take lightly; the route requires a substantial physical effort, involving 2025m of ascent and descent. There are several airy, exposed sections and the weather on Rum can change very quickly.

It is essential that you have a good level of fitness, good navigation skills and are properly equipped before attempting a round of the Rum Cuillin. Ensure you have plenty of daylight for completing the route and check weather forecasts before setting out: it is not a walk for very wet, windy conditions or poor visibility.

The **Rum Cuillin** is a chain of rocky volcanic mountains dominating the island's south. The northernmost hills are principally formed of peridotite basalt and gabbro, similar in construction to the Black Cuillin of Skye, while the southern peaks are of Torridonian sandstone capped with quartz felsite and Lewisian gneiss. A round of the Rum Cuillin makes for a magnificent and challenging day in the hills and usually features somewhere on the 'to-do' list of aficionados of the Scottish mountains. A complete round visits the summits of Barkeval (591m), Hallival (723m), Askival (812m), Trollaval (702m), Ainshval (781m), Sgùrr nan Goibhrean (759m) and Sgùrr nan Gillean (764m).

Climbing to the Bealach Bairc-mheall above Kinloch with the Skye Cuillin in the background

A stile with a small sign reading 'To the Rum Cuillin' crosses a fence next to the road 100 metres south of Kinloch Castle. The path follows the right bank of the Allt Slugan through woodland and past the island's generator before emerging onto open ground. (The path is distinct and easy to follow as it climbs beside the river.) Cross a couple of burns flowing into the river along the way, go through a gateway in an old deer fence and pass a small sluice dam before reaching the Coire Dubh at around 270m. Continue along the level path next to the Allt Slugan, soon arriving at a dilapidated stone dam – where the path marked on the OS Explorer map runs out. Cross the river here: 180m above the corrie to the southwest is the low point of the **Bealach Bairc-mheall** (466m) between Barkeval and Hallival. The path running directly up to the bealach isn't obvious at first, but it keeps to the left of the burn tumbling down into the corrie.

From the bealach climb northwest to the first cairn (575m) on the summit ridge of Barkeval – the actual summit is around 700 metres west along the ridge. Pass around a couple of weathered basalt outcrops and pick up a vague path to the summit cairn (591m).

The **superlative views** south and southeast onto Hallival, Askival and Trollaval, towering over the Atlantic Corrie, are reason enough to include Barkeval in the traverse. In clear conditions there are fine views southwest down Glen Harris, northwest to the rounded granite hills of Orval, Ard Nev and Fionchra and north to the Skye Cuillin.

Retrace your route to the bealach, then follow the long ridge, steadily rising southeast to **Hallival**. From below, a band of cliffs run around the summit, presenting something of an obstacle. However, a route through these cliffs can be found without difficulty by keeping to the northwest ridge.

The summit is marked by a cairn and the **views are tremendous**, particularly on to Askival's impressive north ridge. Beyond Askival, the summits of Trollaval, Ainshval, Sgùrr nan Goibhrean and Sgùrr nan Gillean are visible.

From the cairn, continue initially southwest across the summit to begin the 120m descent to the

On the bealach between Hallival and Askival with Hallival behind

Heading east from the summit of Barkeval with Hallival looming above the Atlantic Corrie

Askival (right) and Hallival seen from Ainshval

bealach. To avoid steep crags on the southeast face, descend steeply following the faint path through rocky terrain on the west side of the ridge briefly before trending southwest again to continue down to the bealach. The path climbs a little over a rocky knoll before crossing the bealach and gaining the narrow, grassy north ridge of **Askival**.

Where the ridge arrives beneath the steep crags rising up to the summit on the north and northwest faces of the mountain at around 650m, follow the path off the ridge as it skirts around Askival's east flank, contouring and rising gradually at first before climbing more steeply and sinuously through rocky terrain to the summit – its upward progress marked by a number of small cairns.

> Numerous **Manx shearwater** nest burrows perforate the grassy slopes between the rock tiers on the mountain's flanks. The summit is marked by a natural stone trig pillar with a low shelter wall. On a clear day the views over to Eigg, Ardnamurchan and Moidart are magnificent.

From the summit, descend along the vague path initially in the lee of the west ridge on its south side. As the path descends it eventually joins the ridge. The terrain is rocky in places, but the 360m descent to the **Bealach an Oir** (455m) presents no problems.

> The bealach lies at the **head of Glen Dibidil** and the view southeast along the glen to Eigg, Muck and the mainland beyond is rather fine. On its north side the bealach drops away into the immense amphitheatre of the Atlantic Corrie, with views over to Barkeval and Hallival. To the southwest, the imposing triumvirate of Ainshval, Sgùrr nan Goibhrean and Sgùrr nan Gillean form the western flank of Glen Dibidil.

From the bealach, climb directly west onto the east ridge of **Trollaval**, following a reasonably distinct path. The climb is initially straightforward, although a little easy scrambling is required through the craggy terrain encountered between 600m and the mountain's east summit (702m). The slightly higher west summit is about 50 metres beyond the east summit and a short, steep descent then ascent via a narrow ridge is required to reach it.

> There are **fine views from the summit** along the Harris Buttress and the Triangular Buttress to Harris Bay beyond. To the south, the imposing bulk of Ainshval looms above the Bealach an Fhuarain.

The route down to the Bealach an Fhuarain descends the steep south ridge of Trollaval from the east summit. The descent is awkward in

Sgurr nan Gillean looms above the Dibidil River

places; there is a vague path, but it can be difficult to find its start, especially in poor visibility. Take care to avoid descending into the craggy terrain on the mountain's southern flank. From the bealach (520m), pass beneath the buttress to the west, following a faint path. Continue on the path as it climbs to the right (west) of the buttress rising above the south side of the bealach, then crosses a rocky scree slope before gaining the northeast ridge of **Ainshval** around 670m. Continue climbing steeply southwest in the lee of the northeast ridge, following a fairly distinct path skirting above the Grey Corrie before eventually arriving at the cairn-marked summit (781m).

From the cairn, follow the path south along the whale-backed summit ridge, gradually descending around 100m to a narrow bealach before making the short ascent of Sgùrr nan Goibhrean (759m). From the summit, descend a short way before continuing southeast along the ridge, gaining just a little height to arrive at the summit of **Sgùrr nan Gillean**

(764m), which is marked with a cairn. The east ridge of Sgùrr nan Gillean drops into an area of steep crags, so the descent should be made initially via the south ridge for 300m before swinging east in a traversing descent, which is boggy and tussocky in places, to **Glen Dibidil** and **Dibidil bothy**.

> Built in 1849, **Dibidil bothy** was a ruined shepherd's cottage renovated by an MBA work party in 1970. The views up Glen Dibidil are magnificent and, directly across the Sound of Rum, Eigg lies resplendent.

To return to Kinloch, cross the Dibidil River with care and follow the pony path for 8.5km (5 miles) back to the track road running between the pier and the castle. The path is generally distinct, but pay attention to avoid losing it. There are several burns to cross en route, which can be hazardous during wet weather. On reaching the track road, turn left for Kinloch and the castle, turn right for the pier.

Kinloch to Harris Bay around the coast

ROUTE INFORMATION	
Start/Finish	Kinloch Castle (NM 401 995)
Alternative finish	Harris Bay (NM 339 957)
Distance	To Harris Bay: 18.5km (11½ miles); Kinloch return: 29km (17½ miles)
Total ascent	To Harris Bay: 945m (3100ft); Kinloch return: 1296m (4250ft)
Time	To Harris Bay: 7–8½hrs; Kinloch return 10–12hrs
Terrain	The terrain is at times rough, boggy and tussocky, but nowhere unmanageable. The mostly good path between Kinloch and Papadil can be vague in places and very wet after heavy rain. The return to Kinloch follows a metalled track.
Maps	OS Explorer 397; OS Landranger 39; Harvey Maps, Rum, Eigg, Muck and Canna Superwalker XT25
Note	During the deer stalking season – mid-August–mid-February – notify the head stalker of your intended route on 01687 462030

*T*his tough, but hugely rewarding walk takes in some of the highlights of Rum's coastline and also has a real sense of remoteness for much of the way. It should not be underestimated: the terrain is rough and navigation is difficult in places. That said, a strong, fit walker could complete the walk between Kinloch and Harris Bay and the cross-island return to Kinloch in a long day, especially if travelling light. However, it is worth taking your time to complete this magnificent walk and enjoy a bivouac or a night in Dibidil bothy along the way.

The bothy at Dibidil makes for an obvious overnight stop, although it is only a 3–3½hr walk from Kinloch. Another option is to continue on to Papadil (4½–5½hrs) or Harris Bay (7–8½hrs) and bivouac at either of these wonderful spots.

Rum boasts a wild **coastline** that is beautiful and at times spectacular, with high cliffs, rugged, rocky shores, magnificent white sand bays, remarkable geological features and abundant wildlife. Furthermore, there are superlative views of the surrounding islands and the mainland mountains.

A complete circuit of Rum's coastline – 40km (25 miles) and three days – is included in *Walking on Rum and the Small Isles*.

Alternative start from ferry slipway

From the ferry slipway, follow the track road to a junction where a signpost indicates the old stone slipway to the right and the castle and other amenities straight ahead. Take neither, but keep to the left-hand track road for a further 400 metres; just before a set of white-painted gates turn left where the Dibidil pony path begins its gradual climb south. (A sign indicates that Dibidil is 8.5km distant.)

From Kinloch Castle head southeast along the track/road, keeping straight ahead at the path junction: pass through the white-painted gates and join the Dibidil path to your right shortly after.

The path climbs steadily to 200m and, as **Loch Scresort** drops away behind you, the pyramidal summit of Hallival comes in to view to the south-west and mighty Askival soon emerges from its lee. The pony path extends to **Papadil**, and is metalled in places with large stones: other than a signpost near the beginning there are no waymarkers and it can be

River crossings are a frequent occurrence along the way

easy to lose in places – especially when distracted by the fantastic views. The path contours along, gaining and losing a little height. After 2km the Allt Mòr na h-Uamha burn is crossed followed by the Allt na h-Uamha – crossing can be tricky if the burn is in spate. Choose your crossing point carefully.

Continue contouring along, with **Hallival** and **Askival** looming over the Coire nan Grunnd above the path to the west. (The huge boulders scattered in the corrie were deposited by a glacier, which once flowed from Hallival.) As the path passes above Lochan Dubh, the view southeast to Eigg opens up magnificently – soon the entire island lies before you like a huge basalt comma – and shortly after, the tiny isle of Muck also appears. The path drops to 100m in a broad zigzag to cross the **Allt nam Bà** by way of a ford across a rock slab. If the burn is in spate, cross via some stones nearer to the rock pool beneath the narrow fissure in the rock.

Continue around the flank of **Beinn nan Stac** on the 100m contour. Eventually the view opens up across to Sgùrr nan Gileann, Sgùrr nan Goibhrean and Ainshval towering above the western side of Glen Dibidil. The path descends into **Glen Dibidil** and

the bothy soon comes into view. Follow the path down to cross the Dibidil River at a ford, although you may have to cross higher upstream when the river is in spate – do so with caution.

Built in 1849, **Dibidil bothy** was a ruined shepherd's cottage renovated by an MBA work party in 1970. The views up Glen Dibidil are magnificent and, directly across the Sound of Rum, Eigg lies resplendent.

Climb to the rear of the bothy to regain the pony path. Most of the way to Papadil the path is quite distinct, although it is vague in places and easy to lose in the complex and boggy terrain. The path climbs steadily to 200m then contours along, passing the southern tip of **Loch Dubh an Sgòir**, where it is a little indistinct. The path soon begins a gradual descent as Loch Papadil emerges below to the northwest. The path can be easy to lose as it zigzags down to the loch.

If you plan to **camp at Papadil**, turn left to skirt around the southeast shore of the loch and cross the outflow to find the best bivouac spots near the beach or above the southwest shore of the loch.

Otherwise make for the southwest corner of the small woodland: look out for a rusting iron gate and enter the woodland next to it rather than attempting to pass around the edge of the loch. Pass through the woodland, with some dense rhododendron growth, cross a burn and look out for the eerie, roofless ruins of Papadil Lodge.

Papadil Lodge was built as a shooting lodge by John Bullough, shortly after he took possession of the island in 1888. Shooting parties would be taken around to the lodge in the estate boat, the servants having already made the journey over from Kinloch by pony.

From Papadil Lodge, cross a burn and exit the woods. The path runs out here and the landscape ahead looks a formidable prospect, with the flanks of **Leac a' Chaisteil** and Ruinsival tumbling precipitously down to to the wild and rocky shore.

Cross another burn at the head of the loch and make for an iron gate, noting the view of the Papadil

Loch Papadil

Pinnacle – a jutting finger of rock standing by the shore at the southern end of the loch. Go through the gate – there is no fence – then pass through a second gate and climb steadily northeast, working your way up to 120m before contouring along. Continue into the broad gully of the Allt na Gile, contour around and cross the burn. Gain a little height and contour along at around 150m through rocky terrain.

Gradually gain height over the next kilometre, climbing to 250m – look out for a large cairn where the flank of Ruinsival is turned. This marks the start of a path that contours around the flank of **Ruinsival** before gradually descending.

> The **view opens up** along to Harris Bay and the dramatic coastline beyond, including the prow of A' Bhrìdeanach at Rum's western extremity, with Canna beyond. When free of cloud, the smooth summits of Ard Nev and Orval rise to the west of Glen Harris.

Follow the path down to cross the **Abhainn Fiachanais** – find a safe crossing point, otherwise follow the river upstream towards the outflow of Loch Fiachanais until you do. The path continues northwest, soon crossing the Abhainn Rangail on a substantial wooden bridge. Continue on the track, skirting an impressive raised beach and keeping to the right of some cairns; if the rivers are in spate, continue along the track to cross the Glen Duian River via the bridge, then follow the track to the remarkable **Bullough Mausoleum**. Otherwise, on passing some dry stone walled enclosures head diagonally (west) towards the shore – there is an excellent bivouac site in a rectangular enclosure above the beach. Cross the outflow of the Glen Duian River and climb a short way to the mausoleum – an unlikely Grecian temple perched upon the wild Hebridean shore.

From the mausoleum continue past Harris Lodge and follow the track, which soon crosses a bridge over the Glen Duian River. The track winds steeply uphill, climbing 250m before easing as it contours along the flanks of Ard Mheall and **Ard Nev**, then descending to **Malcolm's Bridge**. After a further 1.75km the Kinloch–Kilmory path junction is reached: continue straight ahead along the **Kinloch Glen** track for 3.5km to arrive back at Kinloch.

The Bullough Mausoleum at Harris Bay

WALK 23

The Guirdil Horseshoe

ROUTE INFORMATION

Start	Guirdil bothy (NG 320 014)
Distance	9km (5½ miles); Ard Nev adds 3km (2 miles). The walk in and out from Kinloch adds 10.5km (6½ miles).
Total ascent	867m (2848ft); including Ard Nev: 1087m (3568ft)
Time	4½–5½hrs; including Ard Nev: 5½–6½hrs; walking in from Kinloch takes 3–4hrs each way
Terrain	Except for the walk in, the route is mostly pathless with some rugged and boggy terrain in places. The whale-backed summits of Orval, Ard Nev and Fionchra present no difficulties. The descent into Glen Guirdil is boggy and tussocky in places.
Maps	OS Explorer 397; OS Landranger 39; Harvey Maps, Rum, Eigg, Muck and Canna Superwalker XT25
Note	During the deer stalking season – mid-August–mid-February – notify the head stalker of your intended route on 01687 462030

*T*his fine walk takes in some or all of the principle peaks of Rum's often overlooked northwest – Bloodstone Hill, Orval, Ard Nev and Fionchra. Each of these hills has splendid views across Rum and the neighbouring islands: the views of Canna from Bloodstone Hill and the Rum Cuillin from Ard Nev are particularly grand. These whale-backed granite and lava-capped hills are a less demanding proposition than their loftier cousins dominating the island's southern skyline, although the terrain is rough in places.

Unless you can get a lift or cycle along the Kinloch Glen track to Malcolm's Bridge, walking in and out from Kinloch as well as walking the horseshoe would make for a very long, arduous day. As well as making it more manageable, overnighting at Guirdil bothy – or camping nearby – really adds to the experience of walking this route.

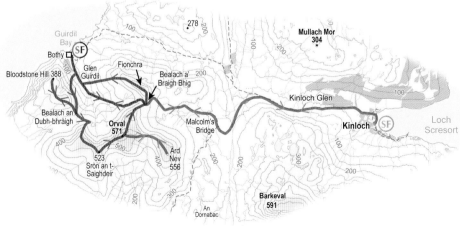

133

Contouring around the steep flank of Bloodstone Hill

THE GUIRDIL HORSESHOE

From the bothy, drop down to cross the Guirdil River where it is fordable (**do not attempt when it is in spate**). Head southeast back up the glen next to the river, initially on a track running parallel to a wooded enclosure. At the southeast corner of the enclosure begin climbing steeply up the northeast flank of Bloodstone Hill on a pathless grassy slope. Cross two shallow gullies, continue climbing, then in quick succession cross two burns flowing down gullies at obvious crossing points at around 140m. Continue climbing less steeply to about 250m, then follow traces of an old path, which contours around the hillside, to gain the **Bealach an Dubh-bhràigh**

Ard Nev, with the Cuillin beyond, seen from the summit of Orval

(260m). By a small lochan, join the old pony path that winds around the head of Glen Guirdil between the **Bealach a Bhràigh Bhig** and **Bloodstone Hill**.

Turn right (northwest) along the pony path and soon begin climbing steadily. The path drops a little to cross an area of boggy ground before climbing again to reach the lava-capped summit.

> Exercise caution as the **summit drops away** to sheer cliffs on the hill's northwest flank. The **views are spectacular**: Canna and Sanday lie supine across the Sound of Canna with Barra and South Uist beyond, while the saw-toothed profile of Skye's Black Cuillin looms to the northeast.

Retrace your steps to the bealach.

From the lochan on Bealach an Dubh-bhràigh, follow the pony path southeast for around 400 metres as it skirts around the head of the glen before leaving the track to climb just west of south along the pathless north ridge of **Sròn an t-Saighdeir**. The 275m climb on an even, steep-ish gradient on boggy, tussocky, rock-strewn terrain is not the most enjoyable of climbs, but it presents no difficulties. The broad, boulder-strewn plateau of Sròn t-Saighdeir (523m) is marked with a cairn and there are fine views along the ridge to Orval's summit and the Rum Cuillin to the

south. From the cairn, continue southeast then northeast along the grassy ridge, with a little up and down before climbing a short way to the rounded summit of **Orval**, which is marked with a cairn and a trig pillar.

Extension to Ard Nev

Across a bealach to the southeast stands Ard Nev, a lovely whale-backed hill, which has probably the best views of the Rum Cuillin to be found anywhere on the island. To include Ard Nev in your itinerary continue east from Orval's summit cairn, soon descending steadily down an even slope with steeply rising ground to your left, arriving on the bealach after 750 metres. From the bealach, climb directly along the northwest ridge of **Ard Nev** to arrive at the summit cairn (556m) after a further 750 metres. Retrace your steps to the summit of Orval; this variant adds 3km (2 miles) to the route and takes around 1hr.

From Orval's summit, continue northeast then north along the ridge. (In clear conditions there are impressive views down Glen Guirdil and along the cliffs of Orval's northwest face.) Where the ridge descends to the north it runs into craggy terrain; to avoid this, turn right (east) and descend steeply a short way before bearing northeast to descend to

Guirdil Bay and the bothy

the **Bealach a Bhràigh Bhig** (370m), which is crossed by the pony path between Malcolm's Bridge and Bloodstone Hill. If you're not returning to the bothy you can make an up-and-down ascent of Fionchra, then retrace the outward route from Kinloch.

From the bealach climb gently northeast for 200 metres before turning northwest and climbing more steeply to the distinctive cupola-shaped summit of **Fionchra** (463m); the short, straightforward climb takes around 15 minutes.

> **Fionchra** provides a good strategic outpost for views across Rum and beyond, including the towering cliffs forming the north face of Orval.

From the summit, descend northwest directly along the spine of the hill to around 350m. From here, descend more steeply west into **Glen Guirdil** to avoid the crags above Coire na Loigh. The ground is tussocky and boggy and hard going until you reach the old path contouring above the river at around 100m. Follow the path for 1km back to Guirdil bothy. A slightly easier alternative is to return to the Bealach a Bhràigh Bhig from the summit of Fionchra and follow the route description from the 'Kinloch to Guirdil...' description below. To return to Kinloch from the bothy, retrace the outward route.

Kinloch to Guirdil via the Bealach a' Bhràigh Bhig

From Kinloch Castle follow the track north for 200 metres then turn left and continue west along the south side of the Kinloch River. Follow the **Kinloch Glen** track for 3.5km, continuing left at a fork (the right-hand fork leads to Kilmory Bay). The track climbs a little, reaching **Malcolm's Bridge** after 1.75km. Don't cross the bridge, but take the footpath heading initially north along the Abhainn Monadh Mhiltich. The path soon trends west, crossing and re-crossing the burn – a boggy experience during wet weather – and begins to climb, arriving at the **Bealach a' Braigh Bhig** (370m) after 2.5km.

From the bealach, follow the old pony path as it gently descends into then contours west around the head of **Glen Guirdil**. After 500 metres or so leave the path and head directly down into the glen, following a vague path if possible. After 200 metres cross a small burn, keeping to the right-hand side of a larger burn that flows into the Guirdil River. Pass to the right of a wooded enclosure as the terrain drops more steeply towards the river. At around 100m, join the path contouring above the river; continue along the path, which can be boggy in places, for 1km to arrive at **Guirdil Bay** and the **bothy**.

Following the pony path along the Abhainn Monadh Mhiltich

EIGG

Eigg (Scottish Gaelic: *Eige*), second largest of the Small Isles, lies almost 7km southeast of Rum, 11km south of Skye, and 11.5km west of Morar on the mainland. The island is 9km (5½ miles) from north to south, 5km (3 miles) east to west and has an area of 31 square kilometres (12 square miles). The centre of the island is a moorland plateau, rising to 393m (1289ft) at An Sgùrr, Eigg's distinctive pitchstone summit. Eigg has the most varied scenery of the Small Isles and a diverse range of wildlife habitats. The Scottish Wildlife Trust manages many areas of Eigg to nurture its plants and wildlife and increase the island's biodiversity in the long-term.

Eigg has the largest population of the island group, with around 85 permanent residents. Known as the 'Jewel of the Hebrides', its fertile pastures, sheltered bays and mild climate have long marked Eigg as an attractive site for settlement, with human occupation of the island dating back 8000 years. The harbour, pier, ferry terminal and shops are situated at Galmisdale at the island's southeast corner. The main settlement is Cleadale, a fertile coastal plain on the island's northwest coast.

Looking up to the sheer face of An Sgùrr from the Grulin path

↑ *An Sgùrr seen from the bay at Galmisdale*

An Sgùrr and Grulin

Start/Finish	Galmisdale pier (NM 484 838)
Distance	11km (7 miles); shorter variant: 8km (5 miles)
Total ascent	540m (1770ft); shorter variant: 393m (1290ft)
Time	4–5hrs; shorter variant: 3–3½hrs
Terrain	The ground can be boggy in places once the track from Galmisdale is left behind. Once on the summit ridge, the volcanic pitchstone provides good grip underfoot.
Maps	OS Explorer 397; OS Landranger 39; Harvey Maps, Rum, Eigg, Muck and Canna Superwalker XT25

*A*n *unsurpassed vantage point for magnificent views of Rum, Coll, Muck, the Outer Hebrides, Skye, Ardnamurchan and the mountains of Lochaber, the towering pitchstone monolith of An Sgùrr is visible from far and wide. Climbing An Sgùrr from Galmisdale makes for a fine half-day walk – a good leg-stretcher, although not especially challenging. However, the walk along the summit ridge makes for a stimulatingly exposed sensation, as the world literally drops away on three sheer cliff-faced sides at the actual summit. Continuing on to the ruins of the cleared villages of Grulin makes for a very worthwhile extension to this walk, although route-finding can be tricky as the vague paths are hard to follow in places and some awkward terrain is traversed.*

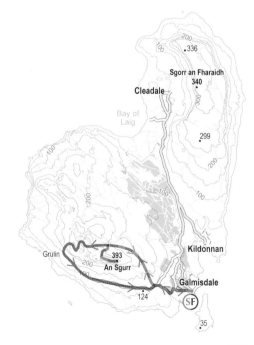

From Galmisdale pier, follow the left-hand track road, which climbs gently northwest, soon entering woodland. Keep straight on (left) where the track forks after 500 metres, following red waymarkers (the right fork leads to the village hall). A little further on, a left-hand turn leads ultimately to the Massacre Cave (a worthwhile detour on the return); keep straight on, climbing steadily before emerging from the woods through a gate – An Sgùrr now dominating the horizon. Follow the track up across the field towards a house and pass through a gate to its right-hand side. Turn left onto a track and after 80 metres join the waymarked path climbing away from the track on the right-hand side at NM 474 841.

This well-trodden path climbs steadily all the way to the summit of **An Sgùrr** and is easy to follow, although it crosses boggy ground with dense heather cover in places. The path climbs past the impressive sheer cliff forming An Sgùrr's eastern face before

Abandoned croft at Grulin, looking over to the isle of Muck

traversing beneath the northern flank of the summit ridge as the gradient slackens. The path soon turns south, climbing steeply up through a gully to a narrow grassy saddle across the spine of the ridge. From here there are great views onto the isle of Muck. Follow the red paint waymarkers east (left) up onto the exposed rock of the summit ridge and continue for 500 metres to reach the summit.

> The summit of **An Sgùrr** is marked by a trig pillar. The views are stunning and the sheer drop on three sides makes for an airy sensation.

Shorter variant
To return to Galmisdale, simply retrace your outward route.

From the summit, descend as far as the foot of the northern flank of the summit ridge beneath the gully. From here, look for a faint trodden path heading west-northwest. Follow this to the southeastern end of Loch nam Ban Móra across heathery, boggy ground. Skirt the southwestern shore of the loch on a vague path that climbs a short way from the loch edge at one point. At the western extremity of the loch turn southwest (you may be able to follow a vague path) and head over a rise to arrive above the northwestern end of a beautiful lochan tucked beneath An Sgùrr. Head northwest for 300 metres on a faint path to skirt around the north end of another fine lochan: continue northwest a short way from the lochan before beginning to descend.

The descent from here to the Grulin path can be awkward due to dense heather cover and steep rocky outcrops, but it involves no real difficulties. Pick a good line of descent from above and make a gradual traverse rather than dropping directly – the ruins of **Grulin** should soon be visible below. At the foot of the slope follow a distinct path leading southeast.

> Take time to explore the ruins of the abandoned villages of **Grulin**, which are perched above the coast with a fine outlook on to the isle of Muck. In scenes repeated in many parts of the Highlands and Islands, 14 families from Grulin were forced to emigrate in 1853 when the land was cleared for sheep farming, which became very profitable during the mid-19th century. Higher prices were offered for land empty of people, where sheep could be pastured. The ruined villages of Grulin bear witness to that dark time in Highland history.

From Grulin, follow the path, which soon becomes a track southeastwards, contouring along beneath An Sgùrr with fine views of its sheer south face. The track is easy to follow and passes the turn-off for the path to An Sgùrr after 3.3km: 80 metres further on, turn right through a gate and retrace your outward route back to Galmisdale.

CANNA

Along the cliffs on Canna's north coast

Canna (Scottish Gaelic: *Canaigh*; *Eilean Chanaigh*) is westernmost of the Small Isles, 14.5km (9 miles) southwest of Skye and 40km (25 miles) northwest of Mallaig on the mainland. It is linked to its tide-separated sister island, Sanday, by a bridge and a road at low tide. Canna is around 8km (5 miles) long and 1.5km (1 mile) wide, while Sanday is roughly 1.5km long and 0.5km wide. Canna is comprised of two plateaux, joined by a low-lying isthmus at Tarbert and rising to 210m at Carn a' Ghaill, the island's highest point. There are towering basalt cliffs along most of the north coast. A large natural harbour between Canna and Sanday is used by yachts and the CalMac ferry, MV Lochnevis, which connects Canna and the Small Isles with Mallaig.

Canna was given to the National Trust for Scotland by the Gaelic folklorist and scholar John Lorne Campbell in 1981. The islands are primarily run as a farm and conservation area, with some crofting on Sanday.

↑ *Looking on to the south coast of Canna from Sanday*

WALK 25

Around the coast of Canna

ROUTE INFORMATION

Start/Finish	A' Chill (NG 272 053)
Distance	20km (12½ miles); Eastern Canna: 10.5km (6½ miles); Western Canna: 15.25km (9½ miles)
Total ascent	750m (2460ft); eastern Canna: 422m (1385 ft); western Canna: 607m (2000ft)
Time	7–8½hrs; eastern Canna 3–3.5hrs; western Canna 4½–5½hrs
Terrain	Cliff-top moorland with a narrow trodden path along much of the way: the ground can be boggy in places. There is a track running between Tarbert and A' Chill.
Maps	OS Explorer 397; OS Landranger 39; Harvey Maps, Rum, Eigg, Muck and Canna Superwalker XT25

*T*his fine circular route around Canna's magnificent coast makes for a demanding day's walk – or alternatively it can be split into two parts. The route is exposed to the elements for much of the way along the island's high cliffs and enjoys fantastic views of Skye, Rum, Barra and South Uist. Several sites of historical interest lie close to the route and the high point of Carn a' Ghaill (210m) is near the cliff top path.

Looking on to the cliffs beneath Beinn Tighe

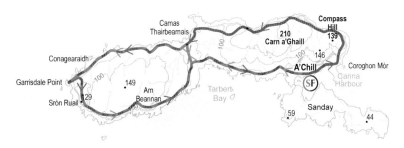

From the small, scattered settlement of A' Chill walk northeast along the road, taking the left-hand fork along a track where the road bears southeast towards the pier. Continue along the track towards the rock stack of **Coroghon Mòr**, with its crumbling stone turret. Before reaching Coroghon Mòr, pass to the rear (left) of an old stone building, go through a stock gate on the left, continue north across the field and climb a slope towards the eastern end of a woodland plantation. Go through a gate, and climb north then northeast to the summit of **Compass Hill** (139m), the high point at Canna's eastern end. (To the north and northeast the isle of Skye dominates the horizon, while the view southeast across Sanday to the western hills of Rum is magnificent.)

Head towards the cliff tops on the north coast then continue west following a narrow path winding along the cliff edge – there are sections of stock fence along the cliff tops at strategic points. Cross a stock fence via a step stile, continue along the narrow cliff top path through the low heather cover. Ignore a section of fence with a stile crossing to the cliff tops and continue inside the fence, descending a short way to cross a burn at an obvious point. Continue along the cliff top and soon cross the 200m contour on the cliffward side of **Carn a'Ghaill** (210m); a 150 metre detour south takes you to Canna's highest point, marked with a trig pillar. (Keep a lookout for white-tailed eagles.)

Continue, losing a little height, and stay on the inside of the fence where twin gullies tumble precipitously down to the shore at Sloc a' Ghallubhaich – there is a dramatic view northwest along the sea cliffs beneath Beinn Tighe. Walk on, climbing a short way to cross a fence on a step stile, then continue up and over the seaward flank of Beinn Tighe.

Cross another fence, continue contouring southwest a short way along the flank of the hill before dropping southwest along a broad gully, which is boggy in places. Descend to a dry stone wall and follow this north then northwest. Where the wall turns south head west across country for 400 metres then continue south along the cliff edge, cross a fence on a step stile then descend towards a gate in a dry stone wall. To visit the bay at **Camas Thairbearnais**, turn right and head for the shore.

Shortcut excluding western Canna

To return directly to A' Chill, turn left and go through a gate in the dry stone wall running at right angles to the wall you've just passed through (NG 238 060). Follow a track southeast across a large enclosed field to a gate at its south end. Go through and turn left to join the track that climbs a short way before descending again and running along the raised shore platform beneath the southern cliffs for 4km back to **A' Chill**.

To continue around the coast, head southwest across the field to a gate at a wall and stock fence junction (NG 237 058). Go through the gate and turn right, continuing northwest across boggy ground to regain the cliff tops. Continue along the cliff top path, soon turning south along a stock fence above the Allt na Crìche Tuatha. Cross the fence by a step stile, cross the burn and continue along the cliff top path. Cross a burn after 450 metres and on arriving at another burn after 1.2km (NG 216 056), descend a distinct path to **Conagearaidh**, a raised shore platform beneath the cliffs. It is both possible and worthwhile to continue along the shore platform as far as **Garrisdale Point**.

It is worth **exploring this undercliff domain**: the remains of sheilings, walled enclosures and the corrugations of ancient lazy beds are testament to the struggle of Canna's earlier inhabitants to eke a living from the land. A dazzling outcrop of white shell sand makes for the perfect spot to sit and admire the fine views back along the cliffs to the east.

This is a dramatic coastal landscape, not far above sea level, and the views are impressive. A short way to the south, standing clear of the cliffs, is the once-fortified rock stack of **Dùn Channa**. The lighthouse on the islet of Hyskeir – or Òigh-sgeir – is visible 10km to the southwest.

From Garrisdale Point, retrace your steps northeast for 250 metres and climb back to the cliff tops by way of the obvious grassy slopes. Continue climbing gently south to arrive at the cliff top summit of **Sròn Ruail** (129m), with its commanding views over the Sea of the Hebrides and along Canna's southern cliffs. Continue initially southeast along the cliff tops, descend a short way to cross a burn on wooden beams and carry on along the cliff top path, gaining and losing a little height along the way and crossing the occasional burn. Here the view over to Rum's northwestern hills opens up magnificently.

Cross a burn, go through a stock gate and climb to the dramatic cliff top summit of **Am Beannan**.

Descending to the raised shore platform at Conagearaidh on the north coast

The cliff top of Am Beannan with northwest Rum beyond

To the east of Am Beannan, on the raised shore platform beneath Sgorr nam Bàn Naomh ('cliff of the holy women'), are the **remains of a walled enclosure**, thought to have been an early-Christian monastic hermitage – possibly a nunnery.

From Am Beannan continue northeast along the cliffs, descend a short way, cross a burn and continue for 500 metres across a stretch of boggy ground before arriving at a stock fence. Go through the gate and descend gently, following the grass track sweeping around to the north above the coastline as it cuts in to Canna's wasp waist at **Tarbert Bay**. Contour along above Tota Tarra, making for the track beyond a long stone building.

Join the track, which soon climbs a short way before descending to the raised shore platform again and continuing its winding way for 4km back to A' Chill.

There is plenty to enjoy along the route with **great views** across Sanday to Rum and usually plenty of activity from sea birds, waders and divers. With luck or forethought, you'll arrive when the lovely Café Canna is open to enjoy a reviving beverage.

Alternative walk: Canna's western coastline
To walk just the western half of Canna's coastline, follow the track road west from A' Chill to Tarbert. At the end of the track, turn right through a gate in a dry stone walled enclosure, cross the enclosure following the grassy track to its northernmost extremity, go through a gate, turn left along the dry stone wall, cross a burn and arrive at a gate at the junction between the wall and a stock fence. Go through and follow the main route description from NG 237 058.

MUCK

Muck (Scottish Gaelic: *Eilean nam Muc*) is the smallest of the Small Isles at approximately 4km (2½ miles) east to west and 2.5km (1½ miles) north to south. It lies 4km southwest of Eigg and 13km north of Ardnamurchan on the mainland; its high point is Beinn Airein (137m). The islanders mostly live near the harbour at Port Mòr or the farm at Gallanach; most of the island is run as a single livestock farm.

Houses and farm at Gallanach

When the weather is fine there can be few British islands so idyllic. Even when the ferry delivers a batch of visitors outnumbering the island's permanent population of 30, Muck's tranquil air remains little disturbed. In high winds, however, the picture can be very different; except in its westernmost extremity, the island is low-lying and exposed to the full fury of storms blowing in off the Atlantic. However, Muck's low profile also allows for some tremendous views across to the mountainous aspects of Rum and Eigg as well as the mainland coast. The cliffs and rugged coastal terrain at the island's west have a surprisingly wild and dramatic feel, contrasting with the rest of Muck.

↑ *Port Mòr with the ridge of An Sgùrr on Eigg beyond*

WALK 26

Gallanach Bay and Beinn Airein

ROUTE INFORMATION

Start/Finish	Port Mòr (NM 422 794)
Distance	11.5km (7¼ miles)
Total ascent	442m (1450ft)
Time	4–4½hrs
Terrain	From soft, springy turf to rough and boggy ground. Single-track road between Port Mòr and Gallanach.
Maps	OS Explorer 397; OS Landranger 39; Harvey Maps, Rum, Eigg, Muck and Canna Superwalker XT25
Note	Several stock fences need to be crossed – there is livestock grazing throughout the island.

*T*his walk around much of Muck's coastline takes in some diverse terrain with constantly shifting views of the neighbouring islands and mainland mountains. The cliffs and rugged coastline of the island's west make for a remarkable contrast with the low-lying east where the coastal terrain is not especially demanding, traversing mostly soft, springy turf, with rough, boggy ground in places.

From the pier head northwest through Port Mòr village, following the island's only road, on which traffic is rare, across to Gallanach. After 1.5km the road passes near to the beach at Camas na Cairidh.

The lower part of the meadow above the shore makes a **wonderful campsite**, with fine views across to Rum. The site has a permanent yurt for hire, a composting toilet and a nearby burn for fresh water.

Continue along the road for 600 metres to arrive at **Gallanach Bay**, with its fine beach. Continue around the bay past Gallanach farm, a second, smaller beach, and further farm buildings. Where the road ends, a path leads north above the shore along the Àird nan Uan peninsula: follow the path towards a house perched above the shore. Cross a stile in front and left of the house, climb a short way, cross a wooden fence, turn right (northwest) and walk out along the peninsula following a path to the narrow, tide-separated isthmus connecting Eilean Àird nan Uan. There is a good view on to the island of **Eilean nan Each**. Retrace your steps most of the way along the peninsula before crossing above the head of the inlet on its western side. Make for the rustic-looking grass-roofed bothy standing back from the shore.

Follow a boggy path northwest along the coast for 250 metres to arrive at a beach composed of small shells. Climb a short way above the beach by a small burn and continue along the coast, soon joining a distinct path contouring above the shore beneath low craggy cliffs. Descend a little, cross a boggy area where several burns drain towards the shore. Climb again onto low cliffs and gain height as the coastline turns south. Climb steadily on a distinct path along the increasingly dramatic cliff tops, with fine views down to the rugged coastline below and across to Ardnamurchan, Mull, Coll and Tiree.

Follow the cliff top path, which descends a little before climbing again to the high cliff top above **Sròn na Teiste**. Turn northeast along the coastline towards the looming bulk of **Beinn Airein**. Descend a short way before climbing steeply diagonally up through a craggy cliff on a distinct path to an area of level ground. Climb steeply again near the cliff top to gain the summit.

The trig pillar on **Beinn Airein** (137m) makes a fine vantage point, with 360° views across Muck and over the surrounding islands and mainland.

Descend northeast on a grassy slope, avoiding rocky areas around the summit. Continue descending along the cliff top inside the stock fence. At the bottom of the descent go through a gate at a fence junction, which is hidden below a bluff. Continue across the neck of the jutting promontory at Torr nam Fitheach, then go through gateways either side of a dry stone walled sheepfold. Follow the course of the wall towards then parallel to the shore to arrive at a gate in the southeast corner of the enclosed field.

Go through the gate and follow the track for a short way before continuing south-southeast along a path following the coast. Go through a gate in a stock fence and continue along the cliff top to arrive above the rugged cliff-flanked inlet of Sloc na Dubhaich. Climb steeply a short way east to the high ground above the inlet then contour along on a path, staying above the rugged and boggy ground at the shore. Descend to cross a burn, pass through an old dry stone wall and continue around to the Bronze Age fortification known as **Caisteal an Dùin Bhàin** ('Castle of the White Fort'), which sits atop a volcanic bluff – an obvious cylindrical upthrust of rock with six metre-high vertical cliffs. From Dùin Bhàin, follow the path north above Port Mòr and, where it divides, climb a short way to follow the path along the higher ground, soon arriving at a track road. Follow the road as it winds downhill passing a house and the Port Mòr hotel before joining the Port Mòr–Gallanach road a short way from the village.

↑ *Beinn Airein seen from Fionn-aird*

SKYE

The Isle of Skye (Scottish Gaelic: *An t-Eilean Sgitheanach* or *Eilean a' Cheò*) is the largest island in the Inner Hebrides and the second-largest Scottish island after Harris and Lewis, at 77km (48 miles) long and 5–40km (3–25 miles) wide, with an area of 1656 square kilometres (639 square miles). The coastline of Skye is a series of peninsulas and bays and this is reflected in the Gaelic name, An t-Eilean Sgitheanach, which translates as 'The Winged Isle'. Skye's wing-like peninsulas radiate from a mountainous centre dominated by the Cuillin hills, which form some of the most dramatic mountain scenery in the British Isles. Skye is a relatively populous, thriving island, which has been connected to the mainland by the Skye Bridge, which replaced the ferry in 1995. Nearly half the island's resident population of around 10,000 are Gaelic speakers.

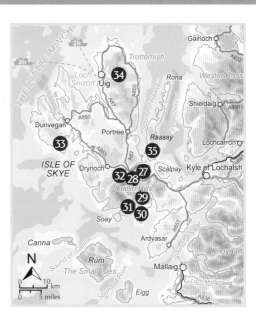

↑ *Looking south to The Storr from Baca Ruadh (Walk 34)*

Walkers climbing the northwest ridge of Bruach na Frithe (Walk 32) (photo: Brett Collins)

Skye is immensely popular with visitors from all over Britain, continental Europe and beyond. The island's magnificent landscapes are a significant part of the attraction, and its mountains are revered by hillwalkers, climbers and mountaineers. The jagged basalt and gabbro peaks of the Black Cuillin are an awesome spectacle, towering over the western side of Glen Sligachan and Loch Coruisk, with 11 Munros among their number. Across the glen, the rounded granite hills of the Red Cuillin provide an elegant counterpoint to these fearsome neighbours. Skye also has an abundance of fine hill, ridge and coastal walking beyond the Cuillin, making the island something of a walker's paradise.

A traverse of the Black Cuillin Ridge is the toughest mountain ridge traverse in the British Isles, involving considerable exposure and some grade 3 scrambling and is therefore beyond the remit of this guidebook. However, there are eight fine hill, coast and glen walks included here, taking in some of the very best walking on Skye leaving aside those routes involving more than moderate scrambling, which are beyond the means of walkers.

The Beinn Deargs

Start/Finish	Sligachan (NG 487 298)
Distance	13km (8 miles) or 11km (6¾ miles)
Total ascent	1280m (4200ft) or 933m (3061ft)
Time	5–6hrs or 4–5hrs
Terrain	The higher ground has some steep scree slopes while the lower ground can be very boggy in places. Much of the route benefits from paths of varying definition.
Maps	OS Explorer 411, OS Landranger 32, Harvey Superwalker Skye: The Cuillin
Public transport	Buses 155 from Portree and Broadford and 52 from Kyleakin – get off at Sligachan Hotel

*T*his fine route around the Red Hills – or Red Cuillin, as they're also known – takes in the summits of Beinn Dearg Mheadhonach, Beinn Dearg Mhór and Glamaig. Whereas the towering, jagged peaks of the Black Cuillin are composed mainly of basalt and gabbro, the rounded summits of the Red Hills are principally formed of granite, which lends them a reddish tinge in certain light conditions – hence the name.

Although they are smaller in scale and present none of the technical difficulties of their illustrious neighbours across Glen Sligachan, the scree-clad Red Hills should not be underestimated: a round of the Beinn Deargs and Glamaig makes for a challenging and exhilarating walk. These fine hills are endowed with splendid ridges and provide some of the grandest views on Skye – not least those on to the Black Cuillin.

Beinn Dearg Mheadonach, Beinn Dearg Mhór and Glamaig seen from the flank of Marsco   151

Descending the north ridge of Beinn Dearg Mhór towards the Bealach na Sgairde and the steep southeast flank of Glamaig

Go through a gate by the old bridge on the opposite side of the River Sligachan from the hotel. Follow the Glen Sligachan path for 250 metres, then turn left through a gate to join a smaller path continuing by the Allt Daraich gorge. Cross some boggy ground, go through another gate and follow a line of old iron fence posts. Where the posts bear left to follow the river, continue southeast on a vague path across boggy moorland: the onward path can be seen climbing the ridge ahead, and the ground becomes drier as you climb.

A brief steep section culminates at the cairn on **Sròn a' Bhealain** (429m) at the northwest end of the **Druim na Ruaige**, with Beinn Dearg Mheadhonach and Beinn Dearg Mhór looming ahead. The gradient eases and the broad, grassy ridge makes for a gentle climb before the path zig-zags more steeply up the scree-strewn slopes to a cairn. The onward route bears north-northeast, but continue southeast along the ridge for 300 metres to the summit of **Beinn Dearg Mheadhonach** (651m) and enjoy the superb views of Sgùrr nan Gillean and Am Basteir across the glen. Return to the cairn and descend the easy slopes of the north ridge to the Bealach Mosgaraidh.

From the bealach the path climbs the long, steep ridge, zig-zagging up through scree to the narrow summit of **Beinn Dearg Mhór** (731m).

From this **airy vantage point** there are expansive views east along Loch Ainort to the Inner Sound. Immediately to the north are Glamaig's main summit, Sgùrr Mhairi (775m), and its lower top, An Coileach (673m).

Descend steadily along the north ridge for around 500 metres, before bearing northwest down an extremely steep slope of scree and larger stones to the Bealach na Sgairde. (The descent requires care – walking poles are very useful here.) The daunting, steep-sided dome of Glamaig rises directly above the bealach.

Extension to Glamaig

To tackle Glamaig, climb northwest, keeping to the left of broken rocks and making your way up the very steep grass and scree slope. The tough gradient eventually eases and the summit of Sgùrr Mhairi is just a little further northwest. From the summit it is possible to descend directly west to Sligachan, but this is a punishing route down a horrendous, interminable scree slope.

Inevitably this slope is the focus of the annual (since 1987) **Glamaig hill race**, a masochistic exercise undertaken by insensible fell runners who ascend and descend the mountain in as little as 45 minutes. The race commemorates the 1899 feat of a Gurkha named Harkabir Thapa, who ran up and down Glamaig from the Sligachan Hotel in 75 minutes – in bare feet!

Discounting this option, just retrace your steps from the summit back down to the Bealach na Sgairde. From the bealach the main route descends initially southwest to pick up a path contouring around the head of the Allt Bealach na Sgàirde; gain the spur to the left of the burn, which makes for easier walking. Follow the burn down to where it meets the Allt Daraich; cross the river here and follow the left bank back to **Sligachan**.

Looking south to Beinn Dearg Mhór from Glamaig

WALK 28

Marsco

Marsco is arguably the finest of the Red Hills, which form the eastern flank of Glen Sligachan. Approached from Sligachan, Marsco is easily identifiable, standing sentinel-like in isolation with its handsome profile of elegant, sweeping lines interrupted by the craggy nose of Fiaclan Dearg, a granite outcrop on the western flank. At 736m, Marsco is neither a Munro nor a Corbett, but a Graham – those Scottish peaks between 2000 and 2500ft. Size isn't everything, however: climbing Marsco is always a worthwhile endeavour, but it is the breathtaking panorama of Skye's most iconic mountains that makes it an unforgettable one.

Marsco is usually climbed from the Glen Sligachan path as an out-and-back route along the Allt na Measarroch to the Màm a' Phobuill bealach between Marsco and Beinn Dearg Mheadhonach, then along the east edge of Coire nan Laogh to the summit ridge. This circular route is a little more demanding, but it offers variety and makes best advantage of the spectacular views this fine mountain has to offer.

Walking along the Glen Sligachan path with Marsco dominating the view ahead

On Marsco's north ridge with the Beinn Deargs behind

ROUTE INFORMATION

Start/Finish	Sligachan Hotel (NG 487 298)
Distance	13km (8 miles)
Total ascent	762m (2500ft)
Time	4½–5hrs
Terrain	Good path along Glen Sligachan; the approach to the north ridge is boggy and tussocky. The north ridge is rocky in its upper reaches. The descent along the east edge of Coire nan Laogh is steep and rocky at first. The return along the Allt na Measarroch follows a path which is boggy in places.
Maps	OS Explorer 411, OS Landranger 32, Harvey Superwalker Skye: The Cuillin
Public transport	Buses 155 from Portree and Broadford and 52 from Kyleakin – get off at Sligachan Hotel

Start at Sligachan by the old bridge on the opposite side of the river from the hotel. Go through a gate to join the Glen Sligachan path – there is a signpost for Loch Coruisk and Elgol. Keep to the main path along **Glen Sligachan**, crossing several small burns. (The views are magnificent, with the jagged summit of Sgùrr nan Gillean crowning the northern terminus of the Cuillin Ridge to the right and the Red Hills

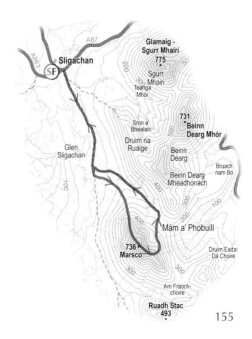

155

on the left, with the elegant countenance of Marsco directly ahead.) After 3km the path bends right then left again, passing an old iron fence just before reaching the Allt na Measarroch flowing down between Marsco and **Beinn Dearg Mheadhonach**.

Cross the river and leave the path here to your left. Follow the Allt na Measarroch eastwards for a short way, looking out for the best line to branch away over rough, boggy ground to gain the north ridge of **Marsco**. Climb initially southeast up the ridge on grassy slopes before trending south, climbing ever more steeply as the terrain becomes rockier. The gradient eventually relents and the lower northern top is reached, where there are grand views northeast to the neighbouring Red Hills, the Beinn Deargs and Glamaig. Cross a slight dip and continue on an easier gradient to the main summit.

A stone cairn is reached just before the true summit. The view across Glen Sligachan to Sgùrr nan Gillean's Pinnacle Ridge is one of Skye's finest. Continuing southeast along a vague path the ridge narrows to a steep-sided arête, which is a little airy,

although it presents no difficulties. The ridge broadens as you progress and there are terrific views straight ahead on to the saw-toothed ridges of Garbh-bheinn and its neighbour, Blà Bheinn (Blaven); to the south, Loch na Creitheach nestles in the srath (wide river valley) just north of Loch Scavaig and Camasunary.

Descend 100m to a small bealach before the minor southeast summit; follow the old iron fence north down the ill-defined ridge along the eastern edge of Coire nan Laogh. Stay parallel to the fence – there is a vague path – as it makes for the bealach at **Màm a' Phobuill**. The fence and path cross the burn flowing out of the corrie where it drops into a deep ravine – alternatively in dry conditions you can cross the burn by traversing above the head of the ravine – and soon arrives at the bealach. From the bealach, descend northwest for 2.5km along the right-hand side of the Allt na Measarroch: there is an obvious path for much of the way, although it is eroded and very boggy in its lower reaches. Rejoin the Glen Sligachan path and retrace your outward route.

Heading along the summit ridge, with Blà Bheinn (right) and Sgùrr nan Each ahead, and Camasunary and Loch Scavaig below

Blà Bheinn

*B*là Bheinn ('the blue mountain') is a fabulous mountain. An 'outlier' of the main Cuillin Ridge, it lacks none of the charisma of its illustrious neighbours. Its isolation only serves to emphasise the grandeur of this great Gothic cathedral of a mountain and bestows it with superlative views, not least of the Black Cuillin. Standing at 928m, Blà Bheinn is one of Skye's 12 Munros – the only one outwith the main Cuillin Ridge. The ascent involves none of the difficulties and exposure characteristic of the Black Cuillin, but it is a very rocky mountain nonetheless and not to be underestimated. Blà Bheinn makes for a tough but eminently satisfying climb, especially when good visibility confers magnificent vistas.

The car park at the start is along a (signposted) track on the right-hand side of the road just beyond the bridge over the Allt na Dunaiche, 3.5km beyond Torrin on the B8083 Broadford–Elgol road.

↑ *Blà Bheinn's magnificent eastern aspect*

Start/Finish	Car park on the B8083 Broadford–Elgol road (NG 561 216)
Distance	8km (5 miles)
Total ascent	990m (3248ft)
Time	5–6hrs
Terrain	Paths aid progress for much of this route but the going is tough, with lengthy sections over scree, especially higher up the mountain; near the summit a scree gully requires modest scrambling
Maps	OS Explorer 411, OS Landranger 32, Harvey Superwalker Skye: The Cuillin
Public transport	50B bus from Portree and Broadford. Get off at the car park past the bridge over the Allt na Dunaiche

Return to the road from the car park, cross the bridge and join the path on the left, which follows the Allt na Dunaiche upstream. Initially, the path is well-defined as it climbs gently across moorland, passing through a couple of gates above a steep wooded gorge through which the burn descends. Further on the route passes above a second gorge and after 1.5km the path crosses the Allt na Dunaiche. Another burn is crossed after 300 metres before the steep climb up through Coire Uaigneich begins.

From here the path deteriorates as the towering, gully-scored crags of **Clach Glas** and Blà Bheinn loom ever closer. On reaching **Fionna-choire** leave the more distinct path that continues straight ahead, bearing sharply right to begin the ascent of Blà Bheinn's eastern spur. Once the cliff edges are passed the path becomes a little indistinct for a while as it zig-zags up the steep slopes to the right.

Higher still, a faint zig-zag path eases the climb across a broad scree slope. Bear slightly left,

↑ *The Red Hills, Glen Sligachan and the distant Black Cuillin viewed from Blà Bheinn's northern summit (photo: Diana Collins)*

to the left; from here there are spectacular views of a vertical rock wall, part of the Great Prow. Continue upwards to a cairn with splendid views on to the rocky countenance of Clach Glas. As the climb continues the going becomes very rocky and the upward route continues through a narrow gully with a brief, easy scramble over rocks at its top: **Blà Bheinn**'s summit (928m), bearing a trig point, is reached soon after.

In clear conditions there are **magnificent views in all directions**, encompassing huge sweeps of mountains, sea and islands in all directions. The panorama of the Cuillin Ridge is tremendous, as is the view along Glen Sligachan, framed by Marsco to the east and Sgùrr nan Gillean to the west.

although there are tracks trending to the right, and clamber over some boulders into a narrow gully. Continue up the steep, scree gully following the path as it bears left near the top. Thereafter, the terrain improves greatly as the route approaches the edge of Blà Bheinn's eastern cliffs. Continue west up a slope

The most straightforward way to return to the start is to retrace the outward route. It is also possible to take in Blà Bheinn's slightly lower south top, but this requires a grade two scramble. From the summit descend into a pronounced gap then make the short, sharp scramble to the lower top's summit.

Blà Bheinn seen from Camasunary Bay

WALK 30

Elgol to Camasunary

*T*his fine coastal walk provides access to Camasunary, which, with the MBA bothy and plenty of good camping ground, makes a great base for climbing Blà Bheinn and Sgùrr na Stri and exploring Loch Coruisk (see Walk 31), cradled beneath the awesome Black Cuillin. It also makes an excellent out-and-back walking route in its own right. There are fine views across to the isle of Rum and the other Small Isles, as well as a magnificent view along the coast to Sgùrr na Stri with the Black Cuillin looming beyond. Golden and white-tailed eagles can sometimes be seen along the way.

The existing bothy at the western side of Camasunary Bay will close in late 2015. A new MBA bothy has been built on the eastern side of the bay, planned to open sometime in 2015.

*Walking out to Camasunary with the Black Cuillin
and Sgùrr na Stri (right) lowering across Loch Scavaig*

ROUTE INFORMATION

Start/Finish	Elgol (NG 520 139)
Alternative finish	Kirkibost (NG 545 172)
Distance	6km (3¾ miles) each way; Camasunary bothy to Kirkibost: 5km (3 miles); Camasunary bothy to Blà Bheinn (return): 7.25km (4½ miles)
Total ascent	183m (600ft) each way; Camasunary bothy to Kirkibost: 209m (685ft); Camasunary bothy to Blà Bheinn (return): 930m (3051ft)
Time	2–2½hrs each way; Camasunary bothy to Kirkibost: 1¼–1¾hrs; Camasunary bothy to Blà Bheinn (return): 3–3½hrs
Terrain	There is a trodden path for much of the way, although this is rocky in places and often wet. There are a couple of exposed cliff-top sections on the flank of Beinn Leacach
Maps	OS Explorer 411, OS Landranger 32, Harvey Superwalker Skye: The Cuillin
Public transport	55 bus from Broadford to Elgol

The path starts from the right-hand side of the B8083 in Elgol as you face the sea (NG 520 139); a green signpost indicates Camasunary 3.1 miles. Tarmac gives way to a fenced in path between houses; go through a gate and continue along the flank of **Beinn Cleat**, with a little up and down for 1.5km before dropping down to **Cladach a' Ghlinne** at the mouth of Glen Scaladal. Cross the turf to the rear of the pebble beach, step over the burn and look for the path climbing up to the cliff at the bottom of the flank of **Beinn Leacach**. (There are fine views of Eigg and Rum to the south and southwest, while to the north Sgùrr na Stri and the Black Cuillin peaks are mightily impressive.)

Climb up to the cliff top and go through a gate in a stock fence. The path continues through a tunnel of scrubby birch and alder clinging to the cliff top: there are a couple of airy sections close to the cliff edge, although these present no problems unless it is very windy. Descending to **Camasunary**, cross a stock fence on a stile and make for the bridge crossing the Abhainn nan Leac 250 metres upstream from the shore. Follow the track past the lodge and across the pasture to reach the bothy and camping ground on the west side of the bay. (A new bothy was being built in 2014–15 on the eastern side of the bay.)

To return to Elgol, retrace your steps.

Alternative return via Kirkibost

Should you wish to make this a circular walk or if the weather deteriorates, then the Am Màm path between Camasunary and Kirkibost is shorter

Low evening sunshine lights up Am Màm, flanking Camasunary Bay

(4.2km), easier and quicker (1¼–1¾hrs), although it is then a 4.5km walk along the road from Kirkibost to Elgol, unless of course with great forethought you have planned to meet the bus. To walk out to Kirkibost, return to the bridge then bear left to follow the ATV track that zig zags up and over the **Am Màm** bealach (189m) before descending at length to the B8083 just south of **Kirkibost**.

Blà Bheinn from Camasunary

It is possible – and somewhat easier than the route decribed in Walk 29 – to climb **Blà Bheinn** from Camasunary. From the footbridge over the Abhainn nan Leac (NG 518 186) near the lodge, follow the vague path along the west bank of the river for a short way before trending northeast to gain the mountain's south ridge. (The vague path soon becomes more distinct as the gradient steepens to a steady climb.) There are several rocky outcrops along the ridge and these are either turned or crossed without difficulty – small cairns mark the way. The slightly lower south top (926m) is reached first and this is separated

from the higher north top (928m) by a narrow gap. Descending into the gap requires a grade 2 scramble, which has to be re-climbed on the return. Once in the gap the north top is reached without difficulty. Retrace the outward route to return to Camasunary.

To reach **Kirkibost** from Blà Bheinn: having descended Blà Bheinn's south ridge, turn left (southeast) at the obvious path junction at around 100m (NG 521 194) and contour around for 800 metres to join the **Kirkibost** track (NG 523 189) for the remaining 3.25km (100m ascent) walk out to the B8083 at NG 545 172.

Blà Bheinn in early spring, seen from Camasunary

WALK 31

Loch Coruisk

*T*here can be few paths in the British Isles that pass through so much magnificent scenery with such relative ease as the Glen Sligachan path: to the east the elegant sweeping lines of the Red Hills, to the west the saw-toothed ridges of the Black Cuillin. This route heads south along Glen Sligachan to the Lochan Dubha, where it forks right off the main Sligachan–Elgol path to climb over Druim Hain – with magnificent views of Blà Bheinn and the Black Cuillin – before descending past Loch a' Choire Riabhaich and the eponymous river to the mountain-ringed sanctuary of Loch Coruisk. Although free of the rigours involved in scaling one of Skye's 12 Munros this is still a long, demanding walk, especially if an ascent of Sgurr na Stri is added to the equation: on a clear day this very worthwhile detour, which adds 4.5km and 225m of ascent to the walk, provides a magnificent summit panorama of the Black Cuillin – possibly the grandest vista in all of Scotland.

As an alternative, Camasunary makes a fine base for a circular route, omitting the out and return hike through Glen Sligachan and taking in Loch na Creitheach, Loch Coruisk and the infamous Bad Step, a huge, steeply pitched convex slab of rock that drops directly into Loch nan Leachd, which has to be crossed en route between Coruisk and Camasunary – there is no great difficulty involved, but it requires good nerves. An additional difficulty is the Abhainn Camas Fhionnairigh, flowing into Camasunary Bay, which can be difficult or impossible to cross at high tide or after heavy rain. The MBA bothy on the western side of the bay will close in 2015: instead a new bothy has been built on the eastern side of the bay. There are also plenty of spots for camping: it gets busy here in summer.

There is no road access to Camasunary, which can be reached from Sligachan or Elgol. The former route is a 12.5km walk that takes around 3½–4 hours each way. Walking in from Elgol to the south is shorter (6km, 2–2½hrs, see Walk 30), while the Am Màm path between Kirkibost and Camasunary is shorter (4.2km), easier and quicker (1¼–1¾hrs), but lacks the character of the coastal path.

ROUTE INFORMATION

Start/Finish	Sligachan (NG 487 298)
Alternative start/finish	Camasunary Bay (NG 516 188)
Distance	23.25km (14½ miles); from Camasunary: 19.5km (12 miles)
Total ascent	785m (2575ft); from Camasunary: 826m (2710ft)
Time	7–9hrs; from Camasunary: 5½–7hrs
Terrain	Good path through Glen Sligachan, although rocky and often wet. After heavy rain several burn crossings provide a bit of a challenge, and the path descending to Loch Coruisk is rocky and may resemble a burn at times. The path between Loch Coruisk and Camasunary is rough and boggy; the Bad Step and the tidal Abhainn Camas Fhionnairigh are serious obstacles, best avoided after heavy rain.
Maps	OS Explorer 411, OS Landranger 32, Harvey Superwalker Skye: The Cuillin
Public transport	Buses 155 from Portree and Broadford and 52 from Kyleakin – get off at Sligachan Hotel

On the opposite side of the river from the hotel, go through a gate by the old bridge to join the **Glen Sligachan** path: a signpost for Loch Coruisk and Elgol points along the glen. Keep to the main path, crossing several small burns. There are fine views of Sgùrr nan Gillean crowning the northern terminus of the Black Cuillin ridge to the right, Glamaig and Beinn Dearg Mhór to the left and, directly ahead, the elegant form of Marsco standing proud of the other Red Hills. After 3km the path bends right then left, before reaching the **Allt na Measarroch**. Cross the burn on large stones (this can be difficult when the burn is running high). Continue along the path beneath **Marsco** then, after a further 3.5km, take the right-hand fork at a large cairn at NG 502 240, just beyond the two Lochan Dubha.

The path crosses a burn and the onward route can be seen climbing up towards **Druim Hain**; to the

Climbing to the bealach between Druim Hain and Sgùrr Hain with Glen Sligachan in the background

By the Scavaig River – the outflow of Loch Coruisk

southeast Blà Bheinn dominates the view, its impressive west face presenting a daunting prospect. After a boggy section the path climbs along the right side of the valley. As height is gained the path is compromised by footfall and water erosion. The small pyramidal peak ahead is **Sgùrr Hain**, beyond which is **Sgùrr na Stri**. The gradient eases before the path reaches a large cairn atop the ridge.

> The **views are splendid** – Blà Bheinn looms to the east, Loch Scavaig and the southern end of Loch Coruisk are visible far below to the southwest, while the spires and pinnacles of the Black Cuillin dominate the skyline to the west.

The path forks by the cairn and the onward route to Loch Coruisk appears to be the path branching right: this, however, only leads to a viewpoint, so take the left hand branch (south) which leads to another cairn, where the path forks again (see Extension to Sgùrr na Stri below). Take the right hand fork, which descends at a slant south then southwest through Coire Riabhach, with Loch a' Choire Riabach to your right. The path is sketchy in places and resembles a burn during wet weather, but keep heading southwest to where **Loch Coruisk** flows out into Loch Scavaig and you won't go far wrong. To return to Sligachan, retrace your outward route.

EXPLORING LOCH CORUISK

From the shore of Loch Coruisk, the scope for further exploration is dependent on recent weather. There is a path all the way around the loch, but the route may be impassable if the Coruisk River at the head of the loch or the many burns flowing down from the hills are in spate. If attempting a circuit of the loch, it makes sense to go clockwise, so you will know at the start whether you can cross the stepping stones across the outflow of the loch without too much difficulty.

165

Heading for Sgùrr na Stri off the Loch Coruisk path, with the northern peaks of the Black Cuillin as a backdrop

Extension to Sgùrr na Stri

From the path fork at the second cairn (see above), take the left hand path contouring along the slopes below **Sgùrr Hain**. After 800 metres the rough path passes above a pyramidal monument known as **Captain Maryon's Cairn**.

> Despite its size **Captain Maryon's Cairn** can be easy to miss as it is built from the gabbro rock predominant on the mountain. The cairn stands nearly three metres high and marks the place where Captain Maryon's remains were found two years after he disappeared, having set off on a walk from Sligachan in July 1946. Maryon's friend and fellow officer, Myles Morrison, built this fine memorial – an endeavour of considerable dedication in such a remote location.

Continue along the path for 400 metres to a small burn flowing down an obvious gully. A vague trodden path climbs by the left-hand side of the burn; follow this up to the bealach below and north of **Sgùrr na Stri**'s summit. Turn right (southwest) across the head of the burn and climb a short way up a

shallow gully to gain the summit ridge. Bear south and continue climbing, crossing large gabbro slabs on the way. The cairn-marked summit is reached soon after.

> At a mere 494m the summit of **Sgùrr na Stri** ('peak of strife') is half the height of the Cuillin peaks, but the mountain's situation bestows some of the grandest views in all of Scotland. The seaward vista takes in Eigg, Rum, Coll, Ardnamurchan and Mull; to the east there is a tremendous view of Camasunary with Blà Bheinn rearing up over Loch na Creitheach. However, nothing matches the dramatic splendour of the jagged Cuillin Ridge towering above Loch Coruisk.

Retrace your outward route to return to Sligachan.

Alternative circuit from Camasunary

From the eastern side of the bay follow the path heading north by the estate lodge – an old byre is emblazoned with large white-painted letters and an arrow indicating 'Sligachan'. Follow the path around the eastern side of **Loch na Creitheach**, then on through Srath na Crèitheach, arriving at the cairn-marked left-hand turning for Loch Coruisk at NG 502 240, near the **Lochan Dubha**, after 6km. Then follow the main route description above to reach the outflow of **Loch Coruisk**.

By the stepping stones across the Scavaig River (the outflow of Loch Coruisk) follow the path southeast through the gap to emerge at the head of Loch nan Leachd. Continue along the rough path for 300 metres to reach the **Bad Step**. Descend across the slab along the obvious crack, staying low and keeping three-point contact. Once across, exhale and continue along the obvious path above the shore, enjoying fine views out to Rum, Eigg and Muck. The path is rough and boggy in places, but presents no further challenges until the Abhainn Camas Fhionnairigh, with Camasunary Bay beyond, is reached after a further 3km. Find a fordable stretch up river from the old bridge – do not attempt to cross if the river is deep or fast flowing.

Negotiating the Bad Step overhanging Loch nan Leachd

*Looking east from Bruach na Frithe towards Sgùrr a' Fionn Choire
(foreground), Sgùrr nan Gillean and Am Basteir (left)*

WALK 32

Bruach na Frithe

ROUTE INFORMATION

Start/Finish	Sligachan Hotel (NG 486 298)
Distance	14km (8¾ miles)
Total ascent	960m (3150ft)
Time	5–7hrs
Terrain	The route is well-defined to begin with, pathless in places, traversing plenty of rough and rocky terrain, including scree slopes, but any scrambling can easily be avoided.
Maps	OS Explorer 411, OS Landranger 32, Harvey Superwalker Skye: The Cuillin

*S*kye has 12 Munros, 11 on the Black Cuillin ridge (the other being the outlying summit of Blà Bheinn), and of all the Black Cuillin Munros, Bruach na Frithe ('slope of the deer forest', 958m) is the least difficult to climb: it also makes for one of the finest view points. However this is not a walk to underestimate, as the terrain is challenging at times and navigation is difficult in poor visibility. In good conditions this is an exhilarating walk that provides the most accessible introduction to the daunting delights of the Cuillin Ridge.

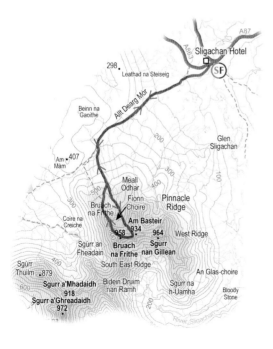

From the Sligachan Hotel, walk a short way west along the A863 and take the first path on the left-hand side. Follow the path beside the **Allt Dearg Mòr**, passing by a footbridge and continuing to a track road: turn left towards a white cottage. A sign indicates the path to the right before reaching the cottage. (This is easy to follow as it climbs across the moor beside the burn.) To the left (south), the Pinnacle Ridge of Sgùrr nan Gillean comes into view – to far greater effect than the view from Glen Sligachan.

After 4km a cairn marks the point to leave the main path and cross the burn, heading south-southeast. The path climbs the grassy lower reaches of **Fionn Choire**, with the peak of Bruach na Frithe above the head of the corrie on the right. The path is well-defined at first, but as it climbs higher and crosses a burn it becomes less distinct. If you lose the path just continue the ascent bearing southeast until reaching the rockier terrain of the upper corrie where the path becomes distinct once more, climbing across rocky ground and scree on the left side of the corrie. A steep climb over a well-trodden

The summit of Bruach na Frithe from the southeast (photo: Brett Collins)

scree slope leads to the Bealach na Lice, between **Am Basteir** and Bruach na Frithe.

> The **topography of Bealach na Lice** is complex and potentially confusing in poor visibility. To the left is the summit of Sgùrr a' Basteir, which can also be climbed without difficullty from the bealach – the magnificent view of Sgùrr nan Gillean and the Pinnacle Ridge makes it a worthwhile detour. The bealach also provides a good view of the impressive rock pinnacle known as the Basteir Tooth. To the right of the pinnacle is the rocky summit of Sgùrr a' Fionn Choire, which can be climbed by confident scramblers.

To continue on to the summit of Bruach Na Frithe, follow the path through the scree below Sgùrr a Fionn Choire, which initially stays just below the ridge to avoid some awkward going before gaining the ridge and beginning the climb to the summit. The easiest route to the top stays left of the low crags. The summit of **Bruach Na Frithe** (958m) is the only peak on the Cuillin Ridge with an OS trig point. Beyond Bruach na Frithe, the main Cuillin Ridge turns to the south and the views along the ridge in both directions make for some of the finest mountain vistas in all Scotland.

The easiest option for the return to Sligachan is simply to retrace your outward route. However, descending the northwest ridge is more entertaining. This ridge is usually considered a moderate scramble, but any difficulties it presents can be bypassed by way of a path that runs along the left side of the ridge across scree and rough ground, well below the ridge line. The path is easier to follow when descending and avoids any real scrambling. Once the steepest part of the ridge has been bypassed the path returns to the narrow crest for the final section. The ground drops away more steeply towards the end of the ridge, but the worst of the scree can be avoided by bearing right and keeping to the northern spur to descend to a more level, grassy area. From here, bear right to continue down the grassy slope to rejoin the outward route near to the stream crossing at the foot of **Fionn Choire**.

Glen Ollisdal, Idrigill Point and Macleod's Maidens

ROUTE INFORMATION

Start/Finish	Parking area at Orbost Farm, Orabost (NG 257 431)
Distance	20km (12½ miles)
Total ascent	1090m (3575ft)
Time	7–8hrs
Terrain	Trodden paths, maintained footpaths and track roads. Some rough boggy, tussocky ground as well as rocky slopes with dense heather and bracken cover
Maps	OS Explorer 407, OS Landranger 23
Public transport	The 56 bus from Portree to Glendale passes closest (3.5km) to the start: ask to get off at Orbost road end and walk
Note	If driving, leave the A863 Dunvegan–Sligachan road on the B884 Glendale road, turn left to Orabost at the first corner and continue to Orbost Farm, where there is a parking area just before Orbost House.

*T*his splendid, varied and surprisingly tough route makes a triangle out of the impressive southern end of northwestern Skye's Duirinish peninsula. Although not especially long the route tackles some rough terrain and, for a walk that doesn't take in any summits, entails a lot of climbing. The route has three distinct stages, each with its own particular terrain and degree of difficulty – starting with the most challenging and ending with the easiest.

The first part of the route from Loch Bracadale, over the Bealach Bharcasaig, on past the Ollisdal Lochs and down through Glen Ollisdal is rough going and requires competent navigation. The next section traverses the dramatic clifftops along arguably the finest stretch of Skye's coastline, to Idrigill Point and the Macleod's Maidens rock stacks. The return along the coastline above Loch Bracadale benefits from a maintained path, innovative woodland plantation and fine views on to the Cuillin – weather permitting.

By the parking area a signpost indicates the track leading down towards Loch Bracadale, which bends right to continue around the head of the loch. Follow the track above the bay and look out for a marker post immediately below power lines by a coniferous plantation. Leave the track to climb steeply right then left, following a series of way-markers up alongside a small burn to a deer fence. Follow the fence, crossing the burn and continuing around to a gate. Go through and continue, following a vague trodden path with the fence on your left. **Healabhal Bheag** looms above the Bealach Bharcasaig, your objective at the head of the glen. Where the fence descends a little, keep your height, contouring and climbing a little along sheep paths through the heather and bracken cover on the steep slopes above the forestry. This is rough, awkward going, but gradually gain height and work your way up through the rocky outcrops on the flank of An Cruachan – the eastern spur of Healabhal Bheag – until you reach a platform of level ground running around the hillside to the **Bealach Bharcasaig** (254m), where heather and bracken give way to tussocky moor grass, and a trodden path aids progress.

Cross the boggy bealach to a gate in the deer fence climbing up from Gleann Bharcasaig. Don't go through, but continue west-southwest along the fence through boggy ground to a second gate at a fence junction. Go through, turn left (south-south-west) and climb a low rise – there may be ATV tracks to follow. The Ollisdal Lochs soon come into view; pass to their left, trending southwest. Keep to the right of the burn flowing from the lochs into Coire Mòr, soon descending steeply across a grassy slope into the coire where the gradient eases. Keeping above and right of the River Ollisdal, continue southwest across tussocky ground, descending into **Glen Ollisdal**: ATV tracks may aid your progress. Make for the stone building with a corrugated metal roof that soon comes into view; this is **Ollisdal bothy**, which is maintained by the MBA – an ideal place for a lunch break.

From the bothy, follow the burn downstream to a suitable crossing point then continue above its left bank to the cliffs of Ollisdal Geo – a steep-sided inlet. Follow the trodden path southeast, climbing steadily along the cliff edge to the top of **Biod a' Mhurain** (106m).

The view opens out southeastwards across **Lorgasdal Bay**, a spectacular stretch of coastline adorned with sea stacks, caves, natural arches, towering cliffs and a magnificent water-fall – where the Lorgasdal River tumbles down to

↑ *Looking southeast along the magnificent cliffs beneath Ben Idrigill*

the shore – as well as a first view of Macleod's Maidens standing sentinel off Idrigill Point.

Follow the clifftop path around to cross the Lorgasdal River and follow a stock fence inland a little to a gate. Go through and climb steadily to the high cliffs along the flank of Ben Idrigill. From the cliff top high point of **Flossnan** (200m), with its commanding view of Macleod's Maidens, the path descends into Inbhir a' Ghàrraidh where three burns have to be crossed, the second requiring a fairly steep descent. The path becomes a bit sketchy, but it's easy to stay on track and follow the cliff top along to Rubha na Maighdeanan. The main path doesn't continue out to the viewpoint above the Maidens, but it's a straightforward and worthwhile detour. Of the three stacks comprising **Macleod's Maidens**, the largest is known as the Mother, and her two smaller companions are known as the Daughters.

Rejoin the main path, which soon leads northeast, away from the coast. The path becomes more distinct and the character of the walk changes along with the terrain. Go through a deer gate and continue through the Glac Ghealaridh, a narrow valley between low hills – Steineval to the left and **Ard Beag** to the right. As you continue above the inlet of Camas na h-Uamha, the corrugations of ancient

'lazy beds' are visible near the remains of the cleared village of **Idrigill**. Continue through a deer fence and cross the Idrigill Burn. The path climbs through a woodland plantation of birch, spruce and other native species.

> This is **Rebel's Wood**, which was established in memory of Joe Strummer, the iconic frontman of anti-establishment punk rock band The Clash, who has somewhat ironically become a posthumous national treasure.

The path descends to the Brandarsaig Burn and more abandoned crofts. The burn flows through a gully lined with rowan and aspen, which audibly shiver with a rustling of leaves in the lightest breezes. The path climbs again, passing through three deer fences in quick succession before crossing the bealach between Beinn na Boineid and **Beinn na Moine**. Descend through rocky, heathery terrain, eventually passing through a deer fence and crossing the Forse Burn. The path becomes a forestry road that passes through coniferous plantation on the slopes of **Cnoc na Pairce** before dropping down to cross the Abhainn Bharcasaig. Follow the track around the bay at the head of Loch Bharcasaig and retrace your outward route to Orbost Farm.

Macleod's Maidens – named after the drowned wife and daughters of the chieftain of Clan Macleod 173

WALK 34

The Trotternish Ridge traverse

*T*he Trotternish Ridge traverse is one of the finest ridge walks in the British Isles, yet few walkers are encountered either side of the Storr Sanctuary and the Quiraing, the tourist-magnets book-ending the steep eastern escarpment. Although it lacks the fearsome reputation, the technical difficulties and challenges of the infamous Black Cuillin traverse, the Trotternish Ridge traverse is nonetheless an exhilarating hillwalking experience through a magnificent mountain landscape with some of the finest views in Scotland.

This route joins the ridge just south of The Storr and finishes a few kilometres beyond the Quiraing at Flodigarry, making for a fantastic if demanding day on the hills. A traverse of the entire ridge from Portree to Uig is also possible, but this 47km route is a tough two-day affair requiring a bivouac along the ridge. Walking the ridge south–north keeps the prevailing southwesterly winds behind you. It is possible to get off the ridge at various points if necessary, but choose your route carefully if descending to the east to avoid crags and cliffs along the steep escarpment: the terrain to the west is gentler, but it is further to the road.

Climbing to the summit of Hartaval with The Storr in the background

Map labels

56 · Flodigarry · Poldorais · Sron Vourlinn · Sgùrr Mòr · Leac nan Fionn · 244 · Meall na Suiramach 543 · The Table Rock · Digg · Staffin Bay · The Needle Rock · Creag Loisgte · Dún Mòr · Glashvin · Maoladh Mor · Stenscholl · Brogaig · Stafainn / Staffin · Sròn an Aighe · Bioda Buidhe 466 · Druim an Ruma · Creag Cleap · Bealach Uige · Beinn Edra · 579 Beinn Mheadhonach · Druim Airigh nan Seileach · 516 · Flasvein 599 · Creag a' Lain 607 · Sgùrr a' Mhadaidh Ruaidh · Sgùrr a' Mhalaidh · An Càrn Liath · Hartaval 669 · Sròn Dubh · The Storr 719 · Needle Rock · Old Man of Storr · Loch Leathan · Bealach Mòr · Ben Dearg 552 · A855

ROUTE INFORMATION

Start	A855 – parking area by Loch Leathan NG 495 510
Finish	A855 near Flodigarry NG 464 710
Distance	27.5km (17 miles)
Total ascent	1800m (5906ft)
Time	10–11hrs (can be walked over two days with a bivouac along the ridge)
Terrain	There are stretches of path for the greater part of the route: the going underfoot is generally grassy with some heather and rocky terrain
Maps	OS Landranger 23, OS Explorer 408, Harvey Superwalker Storr and Trotternish
Public transport	57C bus from Portree – ask to be let off at the first Loch Leathan parking area

Trotternish is Skye's northernmost peninsula, its coastal strip is ringed with villages, small settlements and farms linked by single-track road. The wild hinterland rises up from the west in a series of whale-backed spurs to the mountainous ridge running the length of the peninsula, then drops suddenly away over a steep escarpment of craggy cliffs on the eastern side to an outlandish realm of rock stacks, pinnacles and lochans.

From the small parking area (NG 495 510) by **Loch Leathan**, follow a path northwest: this fades as you head across open moorland. Aim to the right of the bealach and, as you begin to climb more steeply, make for a path climbing diagonally right to left across the escarpment and follow this up to the ridge at **Bealach Mòr**. Head northeast along the edge of the escarpment, gaining height until you're above the Lochan a' Bhealaich Bhig, nestling at the foot of the cliffs. Drop a short way into the Bealach Beag, skirting above the bowl scooped out of the escarpment's edge.

175

Heading north along the ridge with the prow of Sgùrr a' Mhadaidh Ruaidh on the right

Begin the steep 260m pull northeastwards up **The Storr**'s grassy southern flank.

> Move closer to the cliff edge for fantastic views into Coire Faoin and the Storr Sanctuary with a grandstand view of the **Old Man of Storr** – a jutting 535m rock pinnacle.
>
> The summit trig point of **The Storr** is the highest point on the Trotternish Ridge, at 719m. There are fine views east across the sound to the isles of Rona and Raasay, and on a clear day, the innumerable summits of the mountainous west coast of mainland Scotland.

From the summit head northwestwards away from the north ridge and descend steadily on good ground towards the Bealach a' Chuirn (489m); the view north along the cliffs of the eastern escarpment is particularly dramatic from here. Climb northwestwards from the bealach, steeply at first then more steadily on grassy slopes to the summit of **Hartaval** at 669m. (The prow-like north ridge of The Storr is

impressive from this vantage point.) From here the ridge bends initially northwards then around to the northwest as you descend to Bealach Hartaval. The next hill on the traverse is Baca Ruadh (639m), with the lower top of **Sgùrr a' Mhalaidh** (615m) crossed just before the main summit. The promontory of **Sgùrr a' Mhadaidh Ruadh** juts northeastwards from the ridge and is reached by following the edge of the escarpment around in a big curve, first northwest then northeast. The summit (593m) gives fine views along the escarpment, particularly northwards to the distant Quiraing.

Return along the promontory, swinging northwest to continue along the ridge, then descend to a bealach before making the short, steep climb to **Creag a' Lain** (607m). There follows a short descent to the Bealach na Leacaich, which is crossed by a fence and dilapidated dry stone wall, before climbing to the whale-backed summit of **Flasvein** (599m). Drop down into Bealach Chaiplin then make the short ascent of Groba nan Each (575m). From the summit continue along the narrowing ridge close to the escarpment edge, avoiding crags on the north-western flank, and descend to the Bealach Amadal. Cross **Beinn Mheadhonach** (579m) to reach the Bealach Mhoramhain beneath **Beinn Edra**, the second highest peak on the Trotternish Ridge. The easy ascent along the ridge benefits from a path leading to the summit (611m), where you'll find an OS trig pillar with a low dry stone shelter wall.

> You can enjoy the **view back along the ridge** as far as The Storr, then look **northwards** to Bioda Bhuide and the Quiraing – the final way stations on the day's pilgrimage.

The path continues northwards, keeping close to the cliffs as you descend for over 300m to the **Bealach Uige** – arguably the best camping spot along the ridge. There are small areas of dry-ish springy grass near the escarpment edge and fresh water can be collected from a small cascade (NG 444 639) nearby. Continue northwestwards over the slight rise of Druim na Coille at 321m and follow the ridge as it dips down to the Bealach nan Coisichean at the foot of Bioda Buidhe's steep southeastern flank. Climb steeply north with the edge of the escarpment to your right then, as the gra-dient slackens, bear northeast towards the summit of **Bioda Buidhe** (466m).

From the summit follow a trodden path descending along the escarpment edge. The path follows a cliff edge northwest a short way as it angles obliquely away from the main escarpment. Descend from this low cliff to follow the main path along the escarpment edge: this leads down to a car park on the Bealach Ollasgairte (the only road crossing the Trotternish Ridge runs between Uig in the west and Staffin in the east). From the car park cross the road and join a signposted path, heading initially northeastwards, towards the Quiraing – a Tolkien-esque domain of rock stacks and pinnacles. After 1.5km the path leads between a cluster of pinnacles including the remark-able spire-like **Needle Rock** above to the left and the sinister edifice of the Prison on the right – looking very much like Castle Doom on a misty day. The path rounds a bend at an overhanging rock and continues north, passing beneath **The Table Rock**, an expanse of level, close-cropped turf sitting atop a raised rock platform. A short way beyond The Table a fork in the path is reached: turn right and soon descend past Loch Hasco. Continue on past Loch Langaig before reaching the A855 just south of Flodigarry.

Looking north along the serpentine ridge to Beinn Edra

RAASAY

It's easy to overlook Skye's next door neighbour, Raasay (Scottish Gaelic: Ratharsair), literally and metaphorically, when drawn by the siren call of the Cuillin and Skye's multifarious other attractions. But a short ferry ride across the Narrows of Raasay delivers those with the requisite curiosity to a small(ish) island with a distinctive geography, varied geology and a character all its own. The island is 23km (14 miles) north to south and 5km (3 miles) east to west at its widest point: the distinctive cockscomb summit of Dùn Caan is Raasay's

The cockscomb summit of Dùn Caan seen from Loch na Mna

highest point, at 444m. The island of Rona lies just off Raasay's north coast, and the tidal islets of Eilean Fladday and Eilean Tigh are to the northwest, while Scalpay lies 1.5km to the southeast. Raasay House sits in grounds at Clachan, overlooking Churchton Bay and the ferry pier. The island has a population of around 160 people and the main settlement is at Inverarish.

↑ *Dùn Caan, Hallaig and the east coast of Raasay*

Dùn Caan, Hallaig and the southern coast

ROUTE INFORMATION

Start/Finish	Churchton Bay pier (NG 545 362)
Distance	22km (13¾ miles) or 14km (8¾ miles)
Total ascent	823m (2700ft) or 533m (1750ft)
Time	7½–8½hrs or 4–5hrs
Terrain	Open moorland with paths, drover's tracks and minor roads, and several pathless sections
Maps	OS Landranger 24, OS Explorer 409
Access	Ferries crossing between Sconser on Skye and Churchton Bay pier take 15 minutes and are fairly frequent in summer; if walking the longer route, take an early ferry to give yourself plenty of time.

*T*his route, which describes an ellipse around the southern part of Raasay, is rather modest to start with, following minor roads and moorland paths. Once the summit of Dùn Caan is reached, however, the walk takes on an air of grandeur, with dramatic landscapes, magnificent views and the poignant vestiges of the abandoned settlement at Hallaig.

A shorter 'out-and return' route to Dùn Caan (444m), Raasay's highest point, has clear paths for most of the way and is relatively undemanding. The circular route via Hallaig is a long 22km and requires good fitness and navigational competence, as there are pathless sections. Either option takes in magnificent scenery – not least the views west to Skye's Red Cuillin and the Trotternish Ridge.

Taking in the view down to Hallaig from the summit of Dùn Caan

On the Hallaig path at North Fearns, with the Red Hills of Skye forming the horizon

From the pier follow the road to a T-junction, turn right and follow the lane to a fork. Turn left, continue past houses and bear right at a fork by a Forestry Commission sign (reading 'Raasay'). Keep straight ahead (signposted 'Fearns') along the 'Burma Road', soon climbing past vestiges of the incline railway that served the island's long-defunct iron ore mine, which was worked by German prisoners during the First World War. At the top of the road turn left through a gate (signposted 'Dùn Caan') by derelict mine buildings. Follow the track across two footbridges, at a path junction turn right (signposted 'Dùn Caan') and climb alongside the Inverarish Burn.

Go through a gate and follow the path across open moorland. The gradient is fairly gentle and the generally distinct path mostly stays close to the burn. The path eventually crosses a fence via a stile, soon reaching **Loch na Mna**, with the cockscomb ridge of Dùn Caan beyond. Ignore the path climbing onto the escarpment above the loch, instead follow a path above the shore to the inflow of the loch, which is a little rocky. A vague path leads across the Bealach Ruadh beneath the escarpment to Loch na Meilich; continue on the path heading diagonally uphill to the right of the loch. The path doubles back to the

right then zig-zags up the steep western flank of **Dùn Caan** to its rocky summit.

Marked by a trig pillar, the 444m **summit of Dùn Caan** has magnificent views, especially south-west to the Red Cuilllin and northwest to the Trotternish Ridge.

For a shorter return walk, retrace your outward route to return to the pier.

To continue to Hallaig return past Loch Mna, then leave the path through a metal gate. Head southeast across boggy moorland – with care – and pick up a vague path along the upper edge of a landslip. Follow the intermittently boggy path along to the bealach below **Beinn na' Leac** (319m) and descend by the left-hand side of Hallaig Burn. Keep left of the woodland towards the bottom of the gorge. Here you will find the ruins of the abandoned settlement of **Hallaig**, from where there are fine views of the steep cliffs rising above Raasay's eastern shores.

Cross the burn and follow a path up through a birch wood, soon joining a distinct drovers' track. The path continues beneath impressive limestone cliffs and soon reaches a memorial cairn commemorating the Raasay-born poet Sorley MacLean and his poem 'Hallaig'. Continue along the track to the road at **North Fearns**. Stay with the road for 800 metres then turn left on to an unmarked path just beyond the last white house.

Cross the burn and contour along the hillside above woodlands for 800 metres before descending obliquely through the woods to pick up a path just above the shore. Continue along the coast towards the lighthouse beacon at **Eyre Point**. Just before reaching the beacon, turn right then left along a grassy track. Go through a gate to join the road. Follow the road for 6km back to the pier, forking left downhill to pass the old pier at **East Suisinish** and turning left (signposted 'The North and Clachan') at a junction at **Inverarish**. The tramp along the road is greatly enlivened by the superb views across to Skye.

Climbing the west flank of Dùn Caan with Skye across the Sound of Raasay

BARRA

Barra (Scottish Gaelic: Barraigh, Eilean Bharraigh) has a generally rugged countenance with a hilly interior, although the west of the island has several fine white sand beaches backed by dunes and machair. The island is roughly 13km (8 miles) long and 8km (5 miles) across its widest point with an area of 60 square kilometres (23 square miles). The highest point is Sheabhal (Heaval), which rises to 383m. From the flank of Sheabhal a prominent white marble statue of the Madonna and Child, known as Our Lady of the Sea, looks out over Castlebay and the Sea of the Hebrides. The statue reflects the islanders' predominantly Catholic faith. Barra is the southernmost inhabited island of the Outer Hebrides apart from neighbouring Vatersay, which is connected by a causeway; in 2011 the population numbered 1174. In common with other islands of the Outer Hebrides, Gaelic is widely spoken on Barra. The main settlement is Castlebay (Bàgh a' Chaisteil), which takes its name from Kisimul Castle perched on a rock in the bay. Barra has a small airport at Northbay, which rather spectacularly uses the beach at Tràigh Mhòr as the landing strip.

↑ *Looking down to the dunes at Allathasdal from Dùn Chuidhir*

The Barra watershed

ROUTE INFORMATION

Start/Finish	Car park west of the high point (102m) on the road between Castlebay and Brèibhig (NL 679 987)
Alternative finish	Western end of Loch an Duin (NF 688 033)
Distance	16km (10 miles); shorter option 6km (3.75 miles)
Total ascent	1036m (3400ft); shorter option 505m (1656ft)
Time	5½–7hrs; shorter option: 2½–3hrs
Terrain	Hill and moor, with 3km along single-track road
Maps	OS Explorer 452, OS Landranger 31
Public transport	W32 circular bus route around the island

*S*tarting at the foot of Sheabhal (Heaval), this route traverses the hills forming Barra's spine, running from south to north, before descending to the road by Loch an Duin then crossing to Barra's west coast by way of the single-track road looping around the island. Heading back across country, via two remarkable Iron Age and Neolithic fortifications, Thartabhal (Hartaval) and Sheabhal are revisited on the return to the starting point. The shorter alternative ends at Loch an Dùin, requiring transport back to the start.

Our Lady of the Sea looks out over Castlebay from the flank of Sheabhal

A gate 100 metres to the east of the high point on the A888 gives access to the southeastern flank of **Sheabhal**. The ascent is fairly steep, and several paths snake their way up the grassy slopes to the marble statue of the Madonna and Child perched 100m below the summit. On a clear day the view from the statue is breathtaking: a flotilla of islands lies to the south including Vatersay, Sandray, Pabbay, Mingulay and Berneray. The onward route to the summit follows a path to the left of a rocky buttress, then turns right to arrive at the trig point (383m). To the northeast Eriskay lies across the Sound of Barra with South Uist beyond.

Continue northwest, then north, along the broad ridge to a lower, cairn-marked summit (360m). Looking west, the Borgh valley stretches out to the machair pasture and the Atlantic coast. Make your way east down to the adjacent bealach, keeping to its south side to avoid peat hags and boggy ground. From the bealach a short climb brings you to the summit of **Thartabhal**. From the summit cairn, descend gently

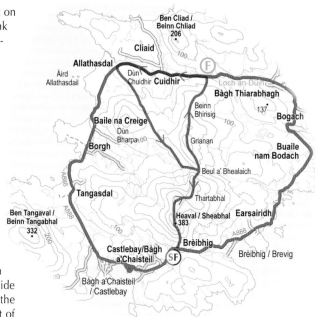

Descending to Beul a' Bhealaich with Grianan ahead

northeast a short way before turning east-northeast to descend steeply, avoiding some rocky sections. Make for a large boulder then head northwest to **Beul a' Bhealaich**, formerly used as a route between the island's east and west.

From the bealach, climb initially north before turning northwest along the summit ridge of **Grianan** – the ascent is steep at first but the gradient soon eases, and the summit is marked with a small cairn. Descend initially northeast then continue north a short way along the broad ridge, taking in Cora-bheinn, before trending northeast again to the cairn-marked summit of **Beinn Bhirisig** (198m). Descending from here can be awkward, especially in poor visibility; head west initially to avoid some low crags, then continue northeast avoiding some rocky terrain. The track running alongside **Loch an Dùin** is soon reached, where a gate gives access to the road.

Alternative finish at Loch an Dùin

The western point of **Loch an Dùin** provides an alternative finish point, which is viable if you can arrange a lift or if you're prepared to wait for the W32 bus or to hitchhike back to Castlebay, which is 11km along the road.

Follow the single-track road west for 3km to the cemetery near Dùn Chuidhir (NF 662 036). Go through a green gate a little past and across the road from the cemetery. Marker posts lead up across grazing pasture to an obvious hilltop fortification,

Dùn Chuidhir, which dates from the Iron Age. To the west the dunes by **Àird Allathasdail** look very inviting. Marker posts lead the way from the dun, southeast across pasture land and over the burn running through the Allathasdal valley.

> Further up the valley, several **ruined black houses** are passed, traces of a time before the 19th century Clearances when the valley was home to a thriving community.

Higher up the valley, pasture gives way to moorland and the waymarked route forks with one route leading to Taigh Talamhanta – the remains of an Iron Age aisled farmhouse: take the other fork and climb more steeply along the valley towards **Dùn Bharpa**.

> **Dùn Bharpa** is not in fact an Iron Age hill fort as the name suggests, but rather a 5500 year-old chambered cairn from the Neolithic period.

Continuing on, cross the stile over the fence next to the dun and contour round to the southeast across tussocky ground to arrive at another chambered cairn (NF 677 012). Contour around to the head of the valley through dense heather, passing just below **Beul a' Bhealaich**, before climbing steeply up the broad gully to the bealach (NF 681 001) between **Thartabhal** and the top (360m) to the north of **Sheabhal**'s summit, crossed earlier in the day. From here, retrace the outward route over Sheabhal to return to the start.

↑ Chambered cairn with Grianan and the Beul a' Bhealaich in the background

SOUTH UIST

South Uist (Gaelic: *Uibhist a Deas*) is the second largest of the Outer Hebrides, at 35km north to south and 11km east to west. It is connected to Eriskay in the south and Benbecula, North Uist and Berneray to the north by a series of causeways. The island's geography comprises a series of north–south strips. The west coast is fringed with an almost continuous strand of spectacular white shell sand beaches backed by expanses of machair and sand dunes. This area is festooned with flowers in late spring and summer and is a haven for wildlife, including corncrakes and otters. Further east is an area containing a vast number of small freshwater lochans and a series of small crofting settlements, bordered to the east by the A865, which runs the length of the island. East again, the terrain rises to the hills dominating the east coast of South Uist. Three sea lochs intrude from the east – Loch Skipport (Sgiopoirt), Loch Eynort (Aineort) and Loch Boisdale (Baghasdail).

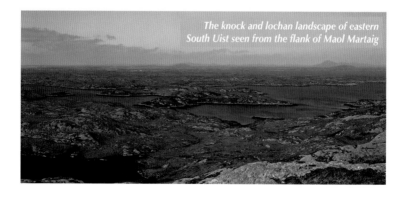

The knock and lochan landscape of eastern South Uist seen from the flank of Maol Martaig

↑ *Hecla from Beinn na Laire*

Hecla, Beinn Mhòr and South Uist's wild east coast

ROUTE INFORMATION

Start/Finish	Car park near the church (NF 756 364) at Howmore (Tobha Mòr)
Total distance	35km (21¾ miles) or 42km (26 miles)
Total ascent	1680m (5512ft) or 1985m (6513ft)
Total time	Two days
Terrain	Rough mountain and moorland terrain, boggy in places; metalled tracks and minor roads
Maps	OS Explorer 453, OS Landranger 22
Public transport	W17 bus stops on the A865 by the turn for Howmore; it is a 1km walk to the hostel

This route traverses the diverse landscapes of South Uist, crossing from the sparsely populated west of the island to a wild and entirely uninhabited mountainous area in the east. This is a challenging walk, involving some rough, pathless terrain.

The walk starts and finishes at the small, scattered crofting community of Howmore, which has one of Scotland's finest collections of thatched buildings and a remarkable collection of ruined churches. Nearby these ruins is Howmore's Gatliff Trust hostel. Herbert Gatliff, a retired senior civil servant, established the trust in 1961 to promote the hostelling and outdoor movements. Since then, the Gatliff Trust has continued to maintain its three hostels in the Outer Hebrides as well as promoting and supporting understanding of the cultural life and legacy of the people of the islands. More information about the trust and the hostels is available at www.gatliff.org.uk. In common with the Gatliff Trust's other two hostels in the Outer Hebrides, Howmore has simple, but perfectly adequate facilities and a very welcoming atmosphere.

Usinish bothy (Day 1)

DAY 1

Howmore to head of Gleann Uisinis

ROUTE INFORMATION	
Start	Car park near the church (NF 756 364) at Howmore (Tobha Mòr)
Finish	Bealach between Hecla and Beinn Choradail (NF 817 340)
Alternative finish	Usinish MBA bothy (NF 849 333)
Distance	20km (12½ miles); alt finish: 23.5km (14½ miles)
Ascent	1680m (5512ft) or 1985m (6513ft)
Time	7½–8½hrs; alt finish: 9–11hrs

*T*he route starts at Howmore on South Uist's west coast and follows a track along the machair before crossing the lochan-speckled moorland of Loch Druidibeag National Nature Reserve. A single-track road leads out to the shore of Loch Skipport and from here a path winds out towards the east coast and the long northeast ridge of Hecla. The day ends with a wild camp on the bealach between Hecla and Beinn Choradail at the head of Gleann Uisinis, or alternatively continues down through Gleann Uisinis to the MBA bothy above Uisinis Bay.

From the parking area by Howmore Church follow a track west to a path junction. Turn right along the track and follow it north for 2.3km to a path junction at the northern end of Loch Stadhlaigearraidh. Turn right and follow the track road through the scattered settlement of **Stadhlaigearraidh** (Stilligarry). Cross the A865 onto another track road, turn right past a house then left towards another house, but go through a gate on the right before reaching it.

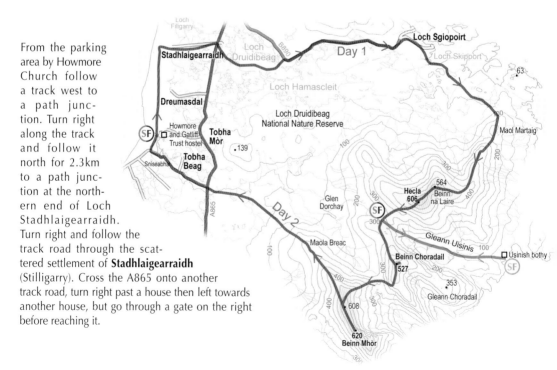

Negotiating the rough terrain alongside Loch Sgiopoirt

The **Loch Druidibeag National Nature Reserve** is an expanse of heather moorland, peat-dark lochans and mountains covering 1677 hectares (4144 acres) – a haven for the distinctive plants and birds of the Uists, including the elusive corncrake with its creaking call and the diurnal short-eared owl.

The sometimes vague path through the reserve leads across a triangular area of moorland lying in the middle of **Loch Druidibeag**, via narrow spits of land. The path is very eroded where it crosses a peat bog before passing through a gate and continuing to join the B890. Turn right to follow the single-track road eastwards, enjoying fine views across Loch Druidibeag to Hecla and Beinn Mhòr – and perhaps seeing wild ponies haunting the moorland hereabouts. Continue for 4km towards Loch Sgiopoirt, keeping right at a fork. Where a Gaelic/English signpost indicates 'Path to Caolas Mòr 2km, Footway to Hecla 5½km', follow the maintained path past some old shielings to a ruined croft house where it comes to an end after 1.2km. Thereafter an increasingly

vague and boggy path bears southeast, loosely following the coast. Keep to the seaward side of Loch Bèin, pass around its southeastern end to the flank of **Maol Martaig** and begin climbing the long ridge that culminates in the summit of Hecla.

The ascent is initially rough going over rocky bluffs, peat and heather climbing southwestwards over Maol Martaig and up the rugged knuckle of Beinn na h-Aire. Here the ridge narrows giving grand views into the deep corries on either side. At Beinn Scalabhat the ridge turns west and rough ground gives way to grassy slopes with a distinct path leading up the ridge to **Beinn na Laire** (564m). A brief descent southwest to the Bealach Gaoithe precedes a short climb to the cairn-marked summit of **Hecla** ('hooded mountain') at 606m. To the south, across the head of Gleann Uisinis stands the prow-like summit of Beinn Choradail with the whale-backed ridge of Beinn Mhòr looming beyond.

From the summit make for the broad bealach at the head of **Gleann Uisinis**. Head initially westwards along the ridge until clear of the steeper, rockier ground then descend southwards through a small

Loch Coradail in Gleann Uisinis

rocky gully. As the ground levels, gradually descend obliquely southwest towards the bealach picking a route on grassy ground between rocky slabs and outcrops. You can camp at the bealach or descend into the glen past Loch Coradail to the **Usinish MBA bothy** at the mouth of the glen.

Alternative finish at Usinish bothy
To continue to the bothy, head down the glen, keeping to the left of the main burn flowing down to the loch, then left and a little above the loch itself. (There are vague sections of path along the way.) Continue east along the outflow of the loch – the Abhainn Aon-uillt – for about 1km through rough, heathery and boggy terrain, crossing several small burns. As the view down to Bàgh Uisinis opens up, make for a large dry stone walled enclosure, the bothy sits just below to the east.

The **bothy**, which is maintained by the MBA, sits above Uisinis Bay, with views onto the Black Cuillin of Skye and the Rum Cuillin. This cosy wee bothy has 'up and down' sleeping platforms, and a new wood-burning stove was installed in 2012. There is usually plentiful driftwood down at the bay.

DAY 2

Head of Gleann Uisinis to Howmore

ROUTE INFORMATION	
Start	Bealach at head of Gleann Uisinis (NF 817 340)
Alternative start	Usinish MBA bothy (NF 849 333)
Finish	Car park near the church (NF 756 364) at Howmore (Tobha Mòr)
Distance	15km (9¼ miles) or 18.5km (11½ miles)
Ascent	652m (2140ft) or 942m (3090ft)
Time	5½–6hrs or 7–8hrs

*T*he route continues on Day 2 with ascents of Beinn Choradail and Beinn Mhòr before returning westwards across moorland then following single-track roads back to the west coast.

If you are starting from Usinish bothy, begin by retracing your outward route to the bealach at the head of Gleann Uisinis. The route description starts from the bealach.

Hecla from the northwest ridge of Beinn Choradail

191

On the summit ridge of Beinn Mhòr

From the bealach head southwards, through rocky terrain with peat hags, climbing steadily at first and passing two small lochans. The ridge rises in a series of steps towards the rocky peak of **Beinn Choradail**. As the climb steepens, skirt around on grassy slopes to the southwest of the buttress crowning the northwest face of the summit. The last 100m or so are very steep, but there are no difficulties; look for an easy way through the crags to gain the summit ridge, then head a short way northeast to the summit (527m) marked with a small stone cairn.

> There are **fantastic views** back to Hecla, down Gleann Uisinis and beyond to Skye and the Small Isles, as well as on to Beinn Mhòr – the next objective.

The northeast ridge of Beinn Mhòr is climbed from Bealach Heileasdail, but a direct descent from Beinn Choradail is steep and rocky. Head along the summit ridge for about 500 metres, initially south then trending southeast, before descending south, then west, carefully picking a route through rock bands towards the bealach. Caution is required, especially in wet conditions or poor visibility. From the bealach, climb gradually at first, keeping to its northern side and making for the grassy slope ascending the ridge between rock bands. Climb steadily for 250m to arrive at the northern end of **Beinn Mhòr**'s summit ridge.

Reaching the summit entails a superb 1km ridge walk. Heading south, a vague path becomes better defined as you approach the summit. There are fine views on to Beinn Mhòr's north face with its deep, oblique gullies. The ridge narrows to splendid effect just before the summit (620m).

> The **summit** has a trig pillar surrounded by a shelter wall. There are excellent views across South Uist and far beyond. About 300 metres further along the ridge a cairn marks its southeastern extremity.

Return to the northern end of the ridge and begin the long descent down the northwest ridge to Maola Breac. (The terrain is rocky with heather cover and peat hags.) From the stone pile cairn on **Maola Breac** make for a small group of buildings with a small coniferous plantation next to a loch 3km to the northwest, being careful not to wander into boggy ground. A metalled track (marked on OS maps) can be joined a little north of several small lochans, but be aware that these aren't all visible from Maola Breac. Follow the track for 1km to the A865. Turn right and cross a bridge over the Abhainn Ròg. Take the next left along a minor road to **Tobha Beag**, continue through the scattered hamlet and beyond Loch Ròg to a sharp left-hand bend. Turn right onto a track and follow it to a bridge over the Howmore River, turning right at a fork shortly after. Continue a short way to Howmore and journey's end.

NORTH UIST

Almost half of North Uist (Gaelic: *Uist a' Tuath*) is covered by water. On the island's largely uninhabited eastern side great swathes of this remarkable landscape are submerged under myriad freshwater lochs and lochans, while numerous serpentine sea lochs snake into the island's hinterland. The island's principal hills – the twin summits of Lì a Tuath and Lì a Deas and the distinctive wedge of Eaval – are also isolated along the eastern seaboard beyond the watery realm. All this water creates something of an obstacle for walkers, but surmounting it brings the reward of a real sense of remoteness.

The contrast with the landscapes of North Uist's western side is considerable. The Atlantic seaboard is fringed with vast stretches of white sand, backed by marram grass-crested dunes and expanses of flower-filled machair, while numerous small farms and settlements are strung out along the coast road. The routes included here reflect this contrast: an ascent of Eaval takes in the challenging terrain of the isolated loch-scattered moorland and hill country in the east, while the coastal scenery and habitats of the island's west are sampled in a fine walk around the sublimely beautiful Udal peninsula.

Tràigh Udal

↑ *Foot and paw prints in the sand on Tràigh Ear on the southeast side of Udal (Walk 39)*   193

WALK 38

Eaval

ROUTE INFORMATION

Start/Finish	Cladach Chairinis road end (NF 856 589)
Distance	12km (7½ miles)
Total ascent	475m (1558ft)
Time	4½–5½hrs
Terrain	Hill and moorland: the route crosses expanses of spongy peat bog
Maps	OS Explorer 454, OS Landranger 22
Public transport	W17 bus passes the turning for Cladach Chairinis: ask to be let off here and walk 2km to the road end
Access	The road to Cladach Chairinis branches off the A865 North Uist–Benbecula road, 2km southeast of Cairinis
Note	Take care not to block the turning area when parking at the start/finish point.

A t a modest 347m Eaval is the highest hill on North Uist, an unmistakable wedge-shape dominating the low-lying landscape. Although neither an especially long nor tough walk, this route to the summit crosses some rough, boggy ground with only vague paths to aid progress. The walk traverses a remarkable landscape and, soon after setting out, the sense of remoteness increases.

On clear days the views from the summit of Eaval are quite something, with a panaroma of North Uist's remarkable lochan-speckled landscape on all sides. Navigation is challenging in poor visibility, so it's best to choose a clear day, when you'll also have views to reward your efforts.

At the road end is a turning area by a white house. From here head southeast a short way along a track road before turning left on a track towards a thatched cottage. Continue past the left side of the cottage, initially following a path east-northeast, using the distant summit of Eaval to guide you across the moorland. The path soon disappears in the boggy and weathered terrain around some old peat cuttings – a stone pile cairn atop a small hill shows the way and a distinct path is soon regained. Descend towards the shore of Oban an Innseanaich then continue around to the northeast to cross a narrow isthmus between lochs, passing through an old rusty gate (NF 865 593) on the way.

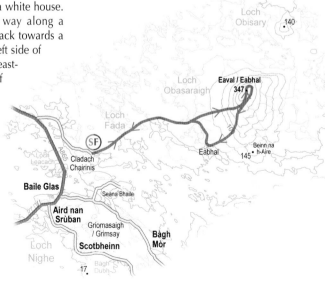

Thatched cottage at Cladach Chairinis with Eaval as a backdrop

Cross a burn on stepping-stones then continue northeast, still using the summit of Eaval as your guide. Climb a low rise, make for a small cairn across marshy ground then head for another cairn, topped by a fence post. From the second cairn descend past Ceann Airigh an Obain at the head of **Loch Fada** to a collection of ruined black houses and shielings. Pass the ruins along a path above the shoreline, which soon bears southeast. Where the path fades continue to a gate in a fence, beyond which the path reappears, and head east through heather alongside a narrow loch (NF 879 597). Aiming for Eaval once more, continue past the southern end of **Loch Obasaraigh** and go through another gate at the left-hand side of a deer fence (NF 884 597).

Follow a vague path northeast above the loch edge for 250 metres to arrive at a burn. Climb east alongside the burn steadily gaining height through dense heather cover and marshy ground, making for the bealach crossing the ridge ahead. The short, steep climb is surprisingly tough, but once the bealach is gained there are fine views across the Little Minch to the peaks of Skye and Rum. From the bealach, climb initially northwards along the summit ridge – a cairn indicates the onward route. Continue along the ridge, trending northeastwards,

195

passing to the right of a cairn-topped rocky knoll; the summit of **Eaval** lies 200 metres further on.

> The **summit** is topped with a trig point, surrounded by a shelter wall – a welcome refuge in a stiff breeze. There are fine views northwards across Loch Euphort to North Uist's other 'big' hills – Lì a Deas and Lì a Tuath.

Retrace your steps along the ridge to return to the bealach. Cross the bealach and go through the gap between two small hills to reach a beautiful lochan sitting in a hollow. Continue east a short way before descending gradually southeast through a broad gully for around 700 metres. Below to the southwest, sitting on a narrow isthmus between fresh and salt water lochs, is the abandoned settlement of **Eabhal** (NF 888 591). Trend southwards to follow a ridge down towards Eabhal – avoiding the worst of the boggy, tussocky ground at the foot of the hill.

> The **settlement at Eabhal** was formerly the home of a shepherd and his family. Although it seems a remote and isolated spot, the shepherd's children walked across the moor to school at Cladach Chairinis and back each day. The croft houses were later used as an 'outward bound' centre by an English school, but latterly the buildings have become dilapidated and are occasionally used by local crofters for shearing and dipping sheep.

Cross a burn to the rear of the buildings on small flagstones and follow a distinct path north along the eastern shore of Loch Dùn an t-Siamain for 300 metres. Continue around the loch edge to a deer fence then follow the fence across the isthmus to the gate at NF 884 597. Here you rejoin your outward route.

Hazy sky to the southeast, from the summit of Eaval

Around the Udal peninsula

*T*he northernmost peninsula of North Uist juts northeastwards towards the island of Boreray; at its northeastern extremity sits the headland of Àird a' Mhòrain. The peninsula is in fact a tombolo, a deposition landform created by a spit or sand bar gradually extending to form a bridge to an offshore island. This undemanding walk takes in beautiful white sand beaches, dunes and machair on both sides of the peninsula and also visits sites of ancient settlements. There are fine views along North Uist's northern coastline and the islands beyond.

This isn't a walk to hurry: the combination of sea air, sand and vast skies makes for a refreshing excursion. This circular route is described clockwise but it can just as well be walked anti-clockwise: whichever way you walk, try to visit the wonderful beach of Tràigh Iar at low tide.

↑ *Marram grass-thatched dunes backing the 3km strand of Tràigh Iar*

ROUTE INFORMATION

Start/Finish	Picnic site/car park by A865 at Greinetobht (NF 819 756)
Distance	11.5km (7 miles)
Total ascent	100m (328ft)
Time	4–5hrs
Terrain	Sandy beaches, machair and dunes
Maps	OS Explorer 454, OS Landranger 18
Public transport	W18 bus to Greinetobht from Lochmaddy
Note	The route is split between both sides of the OS Explorer map: therefore the Landranger may be easier to use

From the walled parking and picnic area jink left, then right, to head northwest along a track. Cross a footbridge, go through a stock gate and continue alongside a fence to a track junction. Leave the track, bearing right (north) and walk across open ground towards a long, straight stock fence. Bear left and continue towards the sand dunes forming your immediate horizon with the fence on your right. Where the fence disappears into the encroaching sand, climb a short way over the marram grass-crested dunes and descend to the breathtakingly beautiful silver sands of **Tràigh Iar**. Turn right (northeast) along the beach. The bay curves around in an immense arc to its terminus at the low-lying promontory of **Rubha Bheilis**. On reaching the neck of the promontory step up from the sands to follow a grassy track clockwise above the rocky shoreline, where the corrugations of old lazybeds are still visible.

From Rubha Bheilis descend to another fine beach fringing a small bay. Join the track climbing up from the northeast end of the bay and continue east across Udal, passing the site of the ancient settlement of Veilish. After 250 metres pass a mound on the left of the path with a fenced-off enclosure (NF 824 783).

This is is the site of a **wheelhouse** dating from the Iron Age. A large settlement with traces of at least 20 buildings was partly excavated at Udal in 1963 and 1964: the site bears evidence of continuous occupation from Neolithic times to the post-medieval period.

Continue following the track northeast to the magnificent **Tràigh Udal** beach. It's also worth crossing the small spit to the promontory of Rubha Huilis, jutting out between Tràigh Iar and Tràigh Udal, just for the views back across Tràigh Udal to the **Àird a' Mhòrain** headland. When you're ready to leave, look for a way up onto the headland from the northeastern end of the beach. Climb steeply a short way through dunes to the trig point marking the headland's high point, and soak up the expansive views along North Uist's northern coastline and northeast to the islands of Boreray, Pabbay and Berneray with the Harris Hills beyond. From the trig point descend initially northeast, then swing around to the east to join a track. Follow the track around to the southeast and where it bends southwest descend along the track to the southern shore of the peninsula.

Continue southwest, keeping above the shingle and pebble beach, until this gives way to firm sand as the tide allows. Continue along the shore for a further 1.5km until you reach **Corran Àird a' Mhòrain**, a narrow spit jutting out from the peninsula at right angles. Cross the neck of the spit to continue southwest along the sandy shore, or on the track at the upper edge of the shore, overlooking the vast sand flats of **Tràigh Ear**. After 2km a ford crosses the outflow of a burn; there are stepping-stones across the outflow, but if the tide is high, head inland a short way, go through a gate then return southeast along a track, through another gate to arrive back at the picnic area.

BERNERAY

The small island of Berneray (Gaelic: *Beàrnaraigh*) lies off the north coast of North Uist and was linked to its larger neighbour with a causeway in 1998. The ferry linking Harris and Lewis with the Uists sails between Berneray and Leverburgh on Harris. Berneray is small enough – about 5km long and 3km wide – to walk around in a relatively leisurely day, although there is much to detain visitors along the way.

Pristine sands at Rubha Bhoisnis

↑ *Looking north to the Harris Hills from Berneray's west coast*

WALK 40

Around Berneray

ROUTE INFORMATION

Start/Finish	Car park beside Berneray Community Hall (NF 909 813)
Distance	17km (10½ miles)
Total ascent	175m (574ft)
Time	5–6hrs
Terrain	Sandy beaches, machair and dunes; some walking on single-track roads
Maps	OS Explorer 454, OS Landranger 18
Public transport	W19 bus from Lochmaddy and W17 bus from Lochmaddy and points south stop at the ferry terminal and the hostel: ask to be let off at Borve
Note	When crossing croft land, avoid disturbing livestock by keeping to the edge of the fenced areas where possible.

*T*his expansive route takes in the magnificent 5km white sand dune-backed beach garlanding the island's west coast; Beinn Shleibhe – the highest point on Berneray; and several sites of historical interest. The route is described clockwise because of the prevailing southwesterly wind and the magnificent views northwards when walking along the western shore.

Walking through the dunes near Rubha Bhoisnis

Caolas
Phabaigh

Rubh a'
Chorrain

Beinn
Shleibhe
. 93

Map scale:
1:50,000

Loch
Bhrusda

Ruisigearraidh

Baile

Gatlif Trust Hostel

SF

85
.

Community
Hall

Borgh

ubha
oisnis

Loch
Bhuirgh

Sheabie

Caolas Bheàrnaraigh

Ferry terminal

From the community hall car park, go through the gate on the left and walk along the track across the machair. Shortly before the main track bends sharply right (northwest), head left (southwest) on a secondary track and follow this along to the shore of **Loch Bhuirgh**. Follow the path around the shore, soon turning southeast and passing the wreck of a large boat. Continue southeast along the springy machair turf by the shoreline to reach the small rocky headland of Cràcanais, with the causeway and the Sound of Harris ferry terminal visible to the southeast. Continue to follow the shoreline westwards, passing the remains of the old township of **Sheabie** after 1km.

> **Sheabie** was evacuated after a severe sand storm in 1697 and was likely re-occupied during the 18th century. The settlement was then evacuated during the Clearances in 1853 and remained abandoned thereafter. It is worth visiting the nearby burial ground, which is still in use.

Continue on above a fine sandy beach, with grand views on to the northern coastline of North Uist.

Head inland a short way to visit a memorial to Angus 'Giant' MacAskill.

> Also known as the Nova Scotia Giant, **Angus MacAskill** was born on Berneray in 1825 and grew to be 2.36 metres tall. He emigrated to Canada in 1831.

From the memorial head back towards the sea to cross the fence on a stile. Continue above another beach and follow the coastline around to the rocky headland of **Rubha Bhoisnis**.

> The magnificent, seemingly endless **white sand beach** forming most of the west coast of Berneray soon comes into view. Fringing azure waters and backed by marram grass-crested dunes, the beach is one of the very finest in all the Hebrides. To the west across the sound lies the small island of Boreray and Pabbay dominates the view directly to the north; the distant Harris Hills lie to the northeast.
>
> Along the shore, various waders including sanderlings, oyster catchers, turnstones, redshanks and curlews can be seen going about their business. With luck, you might spot an otter patrolling close to the shore.

Walk northeast along the incredible sweep of silver sand, rounding **Rubh a'Chorrain** until, after 5km, this remarkable beach ends at a rocky outcrop (NF 923 838). Head inland, following marker posts southeast along the course of an old fence. A short climb brings you to the summit trig point of **Beinn Shleibhe**, the highest point on Berneray. (The views now take in the east side of the island as well as a panorama of the islands all around.) From the

The Gatliff Trust hostel

summit, marker posts guide you down to the left of an old fence, through a gate beside a burial ground and then around the edge of grazing land, through another gate to the road (NF 934 826).

Drop down to the beach and follow it around for 1.5km to the two renovated thatched and white-washed blackhouses of the Gatliff Trust hostel, which sits just above the beach. Go through the gate between the two buildings and follow the track to the right then left past two houses with long garden walls to join a single-track road. Keep straight ahead, ignoring all turnings to right and left for 1km, then turn right (signposted Brusda). The road heads

away from the coast into the interior of the island. Continue straight on over a rise then down the track heading northwest and go through a gate near the head of **Loch Bhrusda**. Shortly after the loch turn left (southwest) along a track across cultivated land, initially parallel to the loch then moving nearer to the lochside. Continue along by the outflow of the loch, passing a large sheep fank then the considerably smaller Loch Beag Bhuirgh. After passing the outflow of the small loch, a short detour west leads to the Chair Stone (NF 909 815) – possibly a vestige of a Viking court – before continuing along the track to arrive back at the community hall.

HARRIS AND LEWIS

Lying 39km (24 miles) from the mainland across the Minch, Harris and Lewis (Scottish Gaelic: *Leòdhas agus na Hearadh*) is the largest Scottish island with an area of 2178 square kilometres (841 square miles). Lewis is the larger northern part of the island with Harris to the south; both are frequently referred to as if they were separate islands, and as routes in this guide are described south–north, Harris comes first. The collective name, The Long Island (Scottish Gaelic: *an t-Eilean Fada*), is sometimes used although this is normally applied to the entire Outer Hebrides. The 'border' between Harris and Lewis is formed by the mountainous boundary of the Harris Hills between Loch Rèasort on the west and the fjord-like Loch Seaforth on the east.

Most of Harris is very hilly, with more than 30 peaks above 300m (1000ft) and seven mountains qualifying as Corbetts. The island's highest point is Clisham (An Cliseam), which at 799m (2621ft) is the highest mountain in the Outer Hebrides. With its vast peat bog hinterland, Lewis is comparatively low-lying, except in the southeast, where Ben More reaches 571m (1874ft), and the Uig Hills in the southwest, where Mealaisbhal is the highest point at 575m (1885ft). Both Harris and Lewis are blessed with remarkably beautiful coastlines: the

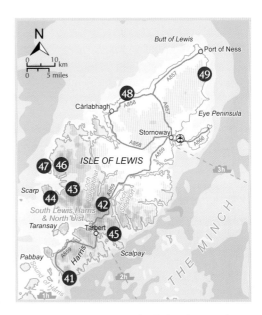

west coast of Harris is garlanded with magnificent dune-backed white sand beaches, while the rugged gneiss cliffs of Lewis are interspersed with beautiful coves and bays. Harris and Lewis is the most populous of the Scottish islands, with just over 21,000 permanent residents in 2011 – over half of whom live in Stornoway.

↑ *Looking down Glen Cravadale to Loch a' Ghlinne with Huiseabhal Mòr to the left*   203

WALK 41

Roineabhal and Rodel

A huge, barnacled whale of a mountain, the rock-strewn bulk of Roineabhal dominates the landscape at Harris' southern extremity, rising above the township of Leverburgh and the settlement of Rodel (or Roghadal). Roineabhal looms large as visitors arrive at Leverburgh from Berneray on the Sound of Harris ferry, yet paradoxically this is a hill largely overlooked by walkers drawn to the elegantly undulating ridges of the Harris Hills further north. Even on a fine summer's day, you'll likely have the summit to yourself.

Admittedly, the mountain's rocky, barren-looking countenance may have something to do with this, so too the lack of obvious paths – in Old Norse, Roineabhal means 'rough hill' and this is an entirely apposite description. However, once clear of the rougher terrain lower down the mountain's flank, the walk out along the summit ridge is quite magnificent and offers expansive views. In spring and summer numerous wild flowers, mosses and lichens adorn the mountain's rough pelt.

There are no footpaths to the summit marked on the map, but the usual ascent from Rodel follows the northern shore of Loch Thorsagearraidh, then the upper reaches of the Abhainn Thorro to the summit. The route described here climbs via the southeast ridge of Beinn na h-Àire and descends via the direct route to form a circular walk – alternatively you can simply retrace the outward route. The route starts from the medieval St Clement's Church in Rodel – make sure you allow plenty of time for a good look round this fascinating church and its graveyard.

Dating from the early 16th century and imposingly situated atop a rocky outcrop, **St Clement's Church** was the traditional burial place of the chiefs of the MacLeods of Dunvegan. The interior of the church houses a number of wall tombs and grave slabs judged the finest late-medieval sculpture surviving in the Western Isles. The intricate carvings depict various religious themes and scenes reflecting the status of those commemorated.

Of a somewhat less pious nature are the stone carvings set into the exterior of the tower depicting a man and woman exposing their genitals. They are in fact what are known as Sheela-na-gig, examples of which can be found on early churches right across Europe. Various theories suggest that they may have served to warn against immorality, or that they might in fact have been fertility symbols.

Tower of St Clement's Church, Rodel

On Beinn na h-Aire with the summit of Roineabhal across the bealach

ROUTE INFORMATION

Start/Finish	Rodel Church (NG 048 832)
Distance	8km (5 miles)
Total ascent	490m (1600ft)
Time	3–3½ hours
Terrain	Pathless, rugged terrain with expanses of bare rock and heather
Maps	OS Explorer 455, OS Landranger 18
Public transport	W10 bus to Rodel from Leverburgh or Tarbert
Note	If driving, park alongside the church wall near to the public toilets.

Head east along the A859, soon bearing left along the C79 road signposted for Fionnsbhagh (Finsbay). Follow the road, which soon turns northwards, for 2km passing a radio mast and Loch na Cachlaidh before arriving atop a small hill (NG 056 846) marked with a spot height of 63m on the OS Explorer map. Leave the road here and, keeping left of a burn, climb directly towards the lowest point in the ridge north of the cairn-marked southern summit of **Beinn na h-Àire** – 'the hill of the lookout'. The hillside can be wet in its lower reaches, but it becomes significantly drier as you gain height. As you climb, the view opens up taking in the townships of The Bays to the northeast and the mountainous profile of Skye across the Minch to the southeast.

The gradient eases as you approach the ridge, bear north and make for the higher of Beinn na h-Àire's summits (398m) with its prominent cairn (NG 048 859).

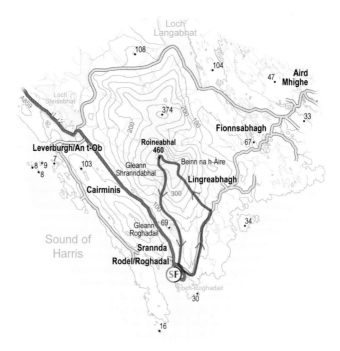

On a clear day, there are **grand views southwest** across the flotilla of islets and skerries in the Sound of Harris to Berneray and the hills of North and South Uist.

A small cairn marks the way west-northwest across the bealach at the head of the magnificent caldera of Coire Ròineabhail, forming the sheer northern flank of the mountain.

Continue west-northwest, climbing steadily up the scree and rock-strewn slope, passing a prominent cairn atop an outcrop immediately before the summit of **Roineabhal** (460m, NG 042 861), which is furnished with a trig point surrounded by a shelter wall.

Two **cairns** stand at the northern side of the summit plateau, overlooking the verdant pastures of Rodel to the south, the loch-fringed township of Leverburgh to the west and the Harris Hills to the north.

Unless you are retracing your outward route, descend initially southwards from the summit, bearing southeast to pass below the rocky slopes of Beinn na h-Àire, passing occasional small cairns marking the usual route of ascent. Resist descending too quickly and stay with the easier ground immediately below the rocks of Mullach nan Stùghadh before dropping down to the north end of Loch Thorsagearraidh. Pick up a grassy path heading southwards along the eastern shore. Keep heading south beyond the outflow of the loch, continuing through a dip fringed with gorse bushes as the church comes back into view. On meeting a dry stone wall, follow it around to the left, eventually emerging at the road opposite the church.

The Clisham Horseshoe

*A*n Cliseam (Clisham) is generally climbed from the southeast, from a parking place along the A859. This makes for a short, sharp climb of 650m over 3km which can be recommended only for the views or for those with limited time. By contrast, the Clisham Horseshoe is a fine day's walk. Approaching An Cliseam from the northwest, a long walk in on an often boggy path brings you to the foot of the ridge connecting Mullach an Langa, Mulla bho Thuath, Mulla bho Dheas and An Cliseam itself. There is some easy scrambling on the ridge and tougher sections that are easily avoided. This is an enjoyable route for those who are confident on rocky terrain with some exposure, but it's not a walk for beginners – especially not in poor visibility. On a clear day, a traverse of the ridge with An Cliseam ahead of you is a real Hebridean classic, with fine views included.

From the bridge pick up the often very boggy path (marked on the OS Explorer) heading up **Glen Scaladale** along the north side of Abhainn Scaladail. The path is fairly distinct for much of the way up to **Loch Mhisteam**, where it disappears definitively, leaving you to pick a route across rough ground to gain the east ridge of **Mullach an Langa** (NB 143 094). The ascent starts easily enough but soon steepens over rough terrain and vegetation, although the ground does become drier underfoot. This is the hardest section of the entire horseshoe, but as you gain height the view north to Loch Langabhat opens up to reward your efforts. The gradient eventually relents before a

ROUTE INFORMATION

Start/Finish	Bridge over Abhainn Scaladail (NB 183 099)
Distance	13.5km (8½ miles)
Total ascent	1065m (3450ft)
Time	6–7hrs
Terrain	Rough and rocky ridges, potentially very boggy approach and return; some bouldery sections and one exposed descent requiring caution
Maps	OS Landranger 14, OS Explorer 456
Public transport	W10 bus to Leverburgh from Tarbert or Stornoway: ask to be let off at the bridge before/after Ardvourlie
Note	There is limited parking by the bridge over the Abhainn Scaladail or 500 metres up the road towards Tarbert on the roadside verge at the start of the Harris Walkway (NB 187 096).

final steep pull up through a boulder field. From the summit (614m), marked by a small cairn, you can survey the route ahead, around the horseshoe to An Cliseam.

Continue south along the ridge with no difficulties – a rocky section between two crags is easier going than it looks – to gain the grassy ridge leading to the summit of **Mulla bho Thuath** (720m). (The view ahead onto Mulla bho Dheas is magnificent, and the sparkling white beaches of South Harris can be seen to the southwest.) Descend southwards along a path to the bealach, crossing a distinctive quartz band then follow the ridge as it turns southeast to reach the cairned summit of **Mulla bho Dheas** (743m).

The descent eastwards from Mulla bho Dheas involves some fairly tricky scrambling. This can be avoided by following a path leaving the summit immediately west of the cairn, dropping down and then traversing along the northern side of the ridge – care is required as the path is exposed and slippery. The path regains the ridge at the bealach before the subsidiary top of **An t-Isean**. A path ascends An t-Isean, bypassing some crags, then a long, grassy descent delivers you to the foot of **An Cliseam**. The climb is steep, initially grassy then rocky, although the bouldery ground can be avoided until just below the summit. A small cairn marks the northern end of the summit ridge. Continue to the summit (799m), where a trig point is enclosed by a large shelter wall.

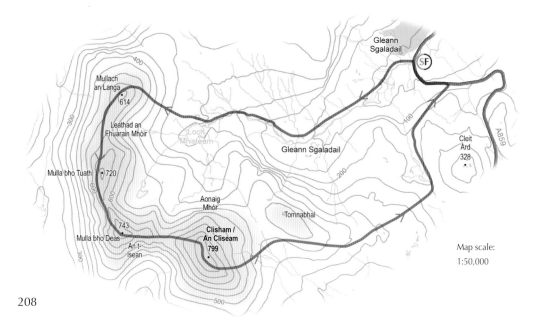

Clisham (right) and the Harris Hills seen from Bein Dhubh

climbing An Cliseam directly from the A859. (Higher up the path is dry as it winds its way through rocky terrain, but the going becomes wetter further down.) Continue down the ridge until easier ground is reached, then turn left to traverse north, then east around the headwaters of the Allt Tomnabhal. Skirt beneath the prominent rock slabs on the southeastern flank of **Tomnabhal**, keeping to the easier ground before swinging northeast across rough terrain, making for three small lochans (NB 184 083) lying directly west of **Cleit Àrd**. From the lochans, continue north along the green track of the Harris Walkway, which is boggy in places, to reach the main road after 1.5km.

Once you're done with soaking up the views (and hopefully not the weather) from the highest point in the Outer Hebrides, head southeast down the ridge following the clear path worn by those

↑ *Mulla bho Dheas (centre) with Clisham in cloud*

WALK 43

North Harris mountains and moorland wilderness backpack

ROUTE INFORMATION

Start/Finish	Small lay-by at the start of an access road east of Abhainn Suidhe Castle (NB 053 078)
Total distance	32km (20 miles)
Total ascent	2050m (6726ft)
Total time	Two days
Terrain	Mountain and moorland. Aside from the sections along the Gleann Chliostair access track, most of the route is pathless and the terrain is very rough and boggy in places.
Maps	OS Explorer 456, OS Landranger 13
Public transport	Take the W12 bus from Tarbert to Abhainn Suidhe Castle
Note	There is no longer a bridge over the Abhain Mhòr Ceann Reasoirt, therefore the river at the head of Loch Rèasort must be forded, which may be hazardous after wet weather.

*T*his challenging and rewarding route makes the most of some of the wild country at the heart of the Harris Hills. A remote bivouac at the head of Loch Rèasort punctuates a traverse of the fine mountain ridges rising either side of Gleann Chliostair and Gleann Uladail.

The route crosses complex terrain and requires competent navigation – it is not a walk for bad weather, poor visibility or inexperienced walkers. Two circular one-day options from the start point are also described here.

The trig point on Cleiseabhal with Oireabhal in the background (Day 2)

DAY 1

Abhainn Suidhe Castle to Loch Rèasort

*T*he landscapes are wild, expansive and ever-changing as you head north on the outward route through Glen Chliostair, over Tiorga Mòr and along the ridge flanking Gleann Uladail to the wilderness of Loch Rèasort.

From the layby, follow the track road northeast past Lochan Beag. Keep left at a fork, continuing along the glen past **Loch Leòsaid** and over the bridge across Abhainn Leòsaid. Continue along the track road, soon passing a small hydropower station and climbing steadily up the glen. Where the track passes beneath the pipeline (NB 069 098) from

ROUTE INFORMATION	
Start	Small lay-by, start of access road east of Abhainn Suidhe Castle (NB 053 078)
Finish	Head of Loch Rèasort
Distance	16km (10 miles); via Gleann Chliostair: 15.75km (9¼ miles); via Muladal: 18.5km (11½ miles)
Ascent	1000m (3281ft); via Gleann Chliostair: 833m (2733ft); via Muladal: 1471m (4826ft)
Time	8–9hrs; via Gleann Chliostair: 4–5hrs; via Muladal: 7–8hrs

Loch Chliostair, leave the track on the left-hand side and begin climbing northwest on rough ground, soon gaining a level area on the southeast ridge of Tiorga Mòr, just above the loch. The ridge continues climbing steeply towards the summit, passing above beautiful Loch Maolaig, nestled in the bowl of Coire Maolaig. This steepest section of the ridge is rocky and rough, but grassy gullies between the slabs aid progress. The gradient eases as the rocky ground is cleared and a vague path leads towards the rock-capped summit of **Tiorga Mòr**, with its stone-built trig point surrounded by a shelter wall.

There are **fine views all around** – to the east beyond the peaks of Ulabhal and Oireabhal a series of sinuous mountain ridges lead to An Cliseam, the highest mountain in the Outer Hebrides.

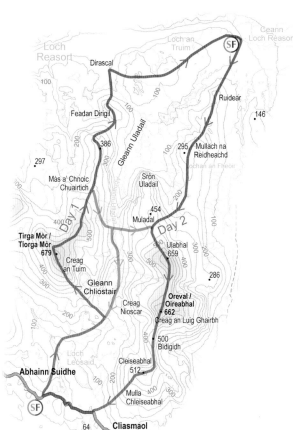

Approaching the summit of Tiorga Mòr

From the summit descend northeast, initially through rocky terrain, then continue across the grassy ridge above Lag Glas to the lower summit of Tiorga Beag (NB 062 122 – the name on the OS maps is positioned nearly 700 metres to the north of the actual summit). Continue initially north then northeast down the gentle slopes above Creagan Leathan to get a good view of the daunting buttress of **Sròn Uladail** across the glen, with Loch Uladail at its foot. Golden eagles can often be seen hunting in this area.

Alternative route via Gleann Chliostair

Descend into Gleann Chliostair by turning southeast, traversing across the headwaters of Abhainn Uladal and along the rock-strewn slopes to reach the stalkers' path at the northern end of Loch Aiseabhat. At 240m, this is the highest point of the path and there are fine views northwards to the Morsgail

Forest. From here head south down the glen, passing the dam and the power station, to return to the start.

Alternative route via Muladal

Do not head south down the glen. Instead, leave the stalkers' path and climb northeast directly to the gently rounded summit of **Muladal** (454m), a fine vantage point for views across Lewis. From the summit of Muladal continue south, following the route description given in Day 2.

Bear north again, continuing across the ridge above the rocky cliffs of Creagan Leathan. Pass by a small lochan and continue through rocky terrain to gain the summit of **Màs a' Chnoic Chuairtich** (386m), surmounted by a surprisingly substantial cairn. From the summit descend northwest through rocky terrain, keeping to the ridge for about 500 metres until it is possible to turn southeast to contour a short way beneath the crags along the steep northeast flank of Màs a' Chnoic Chuairtich. Once you are clear of the steep ground follow the easiest line of descent northeast over rough ground to the bealach between Màs a' Chnoic Chuairtich and the modest summit of Feadan Dirigil.

Climb north for 75m from the bealach to gain the summit of **Feadan Dirigil** (240m).

There are **grand views** onto Loch Rèasort and the vast, wild expanse of country beyond. Just over 1km to the north, the next objective should be visible – a collection of ruined sheilings by a small inlet at Dirascal.

Descend to the north with care, the ground underfoot is very rough and steep in places. On reaching lower ground, follow the watercourses flowing out to **Dirascal** – the ground is very rough and boggy.

From Dirascal climb south-southeast for 200 metres and at the 50m contour look for the old track climbing eastwards towards the gap between the high points of Mullach Airispridh and Mullach

an Ròin. The climb levels around 110m, where the old track – metalled with large stones for some of its length – becomes more distinct. Try to keep to the track for the next 2km as it continues east then northeast across an open expanse of peaty ground, soon passing left of a pair of lochans. The track is eroded in places, but relatively easy to follow until it passes to the left of **Loch an Truim**, where it disappears. Continue northeastwards, soon descending towards **Ceann** ('the head of') **Loch Rèasort** over rough, eroded ground making for the northwestern end of a fenced enclosure just above the shore. Pick your way around the outside of the fence by the shore to arrive at the head of the loch and the end of the day's walk.

The **old bridge** over the Abhainn Mhòr Ceann Reasoirt (NB 107 172) where it flows into the loch no longer stands, however, as long as the river isn't running high, it's worth crossing to the abandoned metal-roofed house above the old bridge on the far bank, which offers the best ground to **pitch your tent** with great views down the loch as a bonus.

Camping at the head of Loch Rèasort

DAY 2

Loch Rèasort to Abhainn Suidhe Castle

*T*he return route takes in the ridge on the eastern side of the glens, climbing over Ulabhal and Oireabhal with magnificent views in every direction.

Recross the Abhainn Mhòr Ceann Reasoirt and head southwest, initially parallel to the Abhainn Habhsaidh, across eroded peaty ground with dense heather cover. Make for the shoulder of **Ruidear** and climb up onto the ridge, where the going becomes easier. Follow the ridge crossing a series of rocky knolls marked with stone pile cairns. Cross a bealach and, trending southwest, climb a short way to the top of **Mullach na Reidheachd** at 295m, where there are grandstand views southwest on to Sròn Uladail's impressive overhanging buttress, with

ROUTE INFORMATION	
Start	Ceann Loch Rèasort
Finish	Small lay-by at the start of an access road east of Abhainn Suidhe Castle (NB 053 078)
Distance	16km (10 miles)
Ascent	1050m (3445ft)
Time	7½–8½hrs

Climbing to the summit of Ulabhal with the wild hinterland of Harris and Lewis behind

Tiorga Mòr seen from the flank of Cleiseabhal

Loch Uladail below. From Mullach na Reidheachd continue southeast a short way then descend south along the ridge through rocky and complex terrain to arrive at a lochan perched on a bealach (216m). Begin climbing again, first southwards to Gormal Mòr, then westwards across the head of a stream bed and up on to the north ridge of Ulabhal to the bealach (416m) south of **Muladal**.

Once on the ridge, climb south along the steep north ridge of **Ulabhal**, soon picking your way through and across the broken rock bands higher up to reach the cairn-marked summit at 659m.

> The **summit of Ulabhal** provides one of the finest vantage points in all of Harris, on a clear day the views take in a panorama of mountains, lochs, coastline and sea.

Continue south down the long, narrowing ridge skirting to the right of a rocky outcrop before arriving at a bealach (564m) with views eastwards into the impressive Cathadail an Ear, which drops dramatically down into Gleann Mhiabhaig. From the bealach, tackle the low crag ahead straight on then begin the easy climb southwest to the summit of **Oireabhal** at 662m.

From the summit of Oireabhal, descend steeply along the southern ridge to a bealach at 460m then climb a short way up and over the rocky knoll of **Bìdigidh** (500m). Descend south to another bealach at 425m then begin the final climb along the ridge, which swings to the west before reaching the trig point at the summit of **Cleiseabhal** (512m), which has a magnificent outlook southeast on to Taransay and along the coast of South Harris to North Uist beyond. From the summit, avoid the steeper ground to the west by descending the long southwest ridge as if aiming for the island of Sòdhaigh Mòr. Once you reach **Mulla Chleiseabhal**, swing westwards to meet the B887 road near Loch nan Caor. Turn right along the road and follow it for 1.5km back to the start.

WALK 44

Huiseabhal Mòr, Oireabhal and Huiseabhal Beag

ROUTE INFORMATION	
Start/Finish	Parking area by public conveniences at Huisinis (NA 993 121)
Distance	14km (9 miles)
Total ascent	825m (2700ft)
Time	5–6hrs
Terrain	There are paths for much of the way and the going underfoot is generally good if boggy in places
Maps	OS Landranger 14, OS Explorer 456
Public transport	W12 bus from Tarbert to Huisinis

*T*he silver sands, flower-speckled machair and magnificent coastal scenery of Huisinis makes this one of the most enchanting corners of all the Hebrides. On a fine day with sunlight sparkling on the emerald-green sea, the picture of paradise is complete. The less-visited but equally magnificent beach at Tràigh Mheilein, across a narrow sound from the isle of Scarp, is also included on this walk so allow yourself extra time to enjoy this wonderful place. The return leg along the top of the ridge presents no difficulties and gives fine views across to Scarp and, on a clear day, the Flannan Isles to the northwest and St Kilda to the southwest.

Tràigh Mheilein – Mill Beach – looking across Caolas an Scarp to the isle of Scarp

Looking across to Scarp from Huiseabhal Beag

From the parking area follow the sandy track branching right (northwest) across the machair for around 250 metres before turning right through a gate in a stock fence. Go through another gate in a dry stone wall and follow the footpath, known locally as the 'Stiamair', ultimately leading to the deserted township of Crabhadail. The path is rocky in places with steep drops at times as it climbs around the rugged coast. Shortly after the top of the

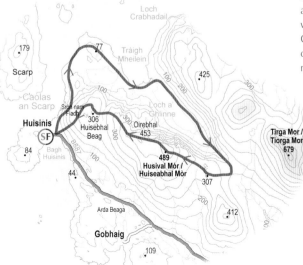

climb, branch left onto another path descending gradually towards the white sands of **Tràigh Mheilein**. Follow the path down to the shore and make your way along the marvellous beach; there are fine views across to the old settlement on the east coast of **Scarp**, with a couple of restored holiday homes dotted among the abandoned and roofless stone cottages.

From a peak of 213 in 1881 the population of **Scarp** declined until the last permanent inhabitants quit the island in 1971. In July 1934, Scarp was the site of an experiment by German inventor Gerhard Zucker in which he made two unsuccessful attempts to deliver the island's post by means of rocket mail between Scarp and Harris. Although launched successfully the rocket exploded, destroying or damaging most of its cargo. In 2007, *The Rocket Post*, a heavily fictionalised, romanticised but nonetheless very enjoyable film based on these events was actually filmed on Taransay.

Where sand gives way to pebbles at the northwestern end of the beach, head up through the dunes to skirt around the eastern flank of Meilein. Make for the narrow isthmus

217

Cairn on the summit of Huiseabhal Mòr

between the eastern end of Loch na Cleabhaig and Loch Crabhadail, then continue around past the ruined sheilings to the beach at the head of **Loch Crabhadail**. Follow the beach around to cross the outflow of **Loch a' Ghlinne**, then continue along a vague path by the eastern shore of the loch. The path becomes more defined near the head of the loch. Pass some old shielings and then climb up through Glen Cravadale, criss-crossing over the Allt a' Ghlinne on the way up. As the gradient eases a cairn is passed; at a second cairn on the more level ground at the bealach (NB 040 111), turn west, cross the remains of an old wall and continue across rock slabs to the north of Beidig (307m).

Continue northeast up the grassy slopes to reach the summit of **Huiseabhal Mòr**, marked by a small cairn. (Although less than 500m high, the summit provides remarkable 360° views.) From Huiseabhal Mòr head west across easy ground along the edge of craggy cliffs to reach the summit of **Oirebhal**. The views from the cliff edge here down to Glen Cravadale and out across Loch Crabhadail are wonderful. Descend northwest to a bealach then climb the slope directly ahead to the cluster of lochans at the summit of **Huisebhal Beag**, which is marked by a cairn. This is a good vantage point for spotting St Kilda on a clear day. From the summit descend initially southwest: bear south further down to avoid the steepest ground and aim to arrive back at the road by the public conveniences at Huisinis.

WALK 45

Circuit of Tòdun from Urgha

ROUTE INFORMATION

Start/Finish	Car park at the southern end of Lochanan Lacasdail (NB 183 004)
Distance	16.5km (10.25 miles); via Moilingeanais and Tòdun: 19km (12 miles); via Moilingeanais (excl Tòdun): 20.5km (12.75 miles)
Total ascent	968m (3175ft); via Moilingeanais and Tòdun: 1029m (3370ft); via Moilingeanais (excl Tòdun): 831m (2720ft)
Time	5–6hrs; via Moilingeanais and Tòdun: 6–7hrs; via Moilingeanais (excl Tòdun): 6–7hrs
Terrain	A mixture of good tracks, rough paths, pathless hill terrain and single-track road
Maps	OS Explorer 456, OS Landranger 14
Public transport	W14 bus from Tarbert to Urgha

This is a fine multifaceted walk with the ascent of Tòdun as its crowning glory. Much of the route follows very old footpaths, formerly the only way – other than by sea – of reaching the remote townships of Reinigeadal, Màraig and Moilingeanais from Tarbert. Consequently the route is well-trodden and easy to follow in the main – by Hebridean standards. However, there are only vague traces of path on the climb over Tòdun and, on the route extension, the path along the coast between the abandoned settlement of Moilingeanais and the head of Loch Trolamaraig is sketchy and rough going in places. The latter can be avoided by backtracking to the main Urgha–Reinigeadal path, adding 2.5km and almost an hour. The walk is enhanced by fine views out to the Shiant Islands and along the fjord-like Loch Seaforth, which separates North Harris from the wild and innaccessible Pairc region of Lewis.

From the parking area at the southern end of Lochanan Lacasadail, follow the footpath signposted for the Gatliff Trust Hostel at Reinigeadal as it climbs steadily eastwards across the moor. After 2km the path passes a cairn on the bealach (280m) between **Trolamul** and **Beinn Tharsuinn**. Continue downhill with the Gill Garbh burn to the right; the Shiant Islands can be seen 20km to the east. A smaller path forks across the stream, an extension

219

to the route that makes its way down to the abandoned village of **Moilingeanais**.

Extension to Moilingeanais

Follow the smaller path downhill, passing through a gate to join a path down to the old village sitting by the shore; another gate gives access through a boundary fence. Several of the houses are roofless shells, but in recent years, a couple have been renovated for use as holiday retreats. Please respect the privacy of anyone staying there.

> The population of **Moilingeanais** reached its peak of around forty inhabitants during the 1880s. A school was built in 1921, but in 1935 the authorities withdrew the teacher, effectively closing the school. A lodging allowance was paid for the children to attend school in Tarbert: hence they had to walk five miles to and from school each week along the 'Postman's Path', crossing the 280m bealach between Trolamul and Beinn Tharsuinn along the way. The last permanent residents left Moilingeanais in the 1960s.

Climb back up the path, but instead of going back through the gate above the village, turn right and follow the fence along to a metal gate, go through and continue northwest along a path traversing steep ground above **Loch Trolamaraig**. This path can be muddy, overgrown and tricky to negotiate in places particularly where it crosses a couple of burns, which may become serious obstacles after heavy rain (if this is all sounds a bit challenging retrace your route from Moilingeanais to rejoin the main path instead). After 1km the path rejoins the main route just before a footbridge at the head of Loch Trolamaraig.

If walking the shorter route and avoiding Moilingeanais, continue along the main path as it zigzags dramatically down the steep flank of Gleann Trolamaraig to reach a footbridge at the head of **Loch Trolamaraig**. (The extension to Moilingeanais rejoins the main route here.) Cross the bridge and continue over a second footbridge across the Abhainn Kerram. Ignore a minor path descending to the shore and continue climbing until you reach the high point of the path. To climb **Tòdun**, leave the path here and head north, making for the mountain's prominent southeast ridge.

Alternative route avoiding Tòdun

The ascent of Tòdun can be avoided by continuing along the path around the head of the loch until

Heading along the Moilingeanais path with the Shiant Islands on the horizon (right of centre)

Tòdun rises above the Reinigeadal path

it reaches the road above **Reinigeadal**. Turn north along the road and continue towards **Màraig**, passing several lochans before descending to continue alongside Loch Màraig.

Cross the gully of Allt Dubh then trend northeast to gain the ridge. Make your way northwestwards up the steep ridge – traces of trodden path weave through the rocky, heathery terrain. The ridge narrows and the gradient eases as the trig point on the summit of **Tòdun** (528m) is approached.

> There are **fine views** northwest to An Cliseam, east to the Shiant Islands and, on a clear day, the Black Cuillin of Skye to the south.

Descend initially northwest along the ridge, following a vague path for some of the way, then trend north aiming to join the Màraig–Reinigeadal road where it zigzags (NB 207 050) steeply down to run alongside **Loch Màraig**.

Follow the road westward to the head of the loch; just before a bridge over the Abhainn Mhàraig, turn left through a gate to join the path signposted for Urgha. Go through another gate and continue westwards for 500 metres; the well-maintained path then turns south, climbing steadily through Bràigh an Ruisg – a cairn marks the high point at around 130m. Descend gently into Gleann Lacasdail and continue past the larger of the **Lochannan Lacasdail**. At the southern end of the loch look out for a footbridge across the outflow into the smaller loch: cross some rough ground to reach the bridge and cross over to join a path along the opposite shore.

> This path leads along the shore of the Lochannan Lacasdail to an **eagle observatory**.

Turn right and follow the path back to the parking area.

WALK 46

The Uig Hills

*T*he Uig Hills are one of the wildest areas of west Lewis, a beautiful landscape dominated by the fine summits of Mealaisbhal ('Farmstead fell') and Cracabhal ('Crow fell'). The route is suitable for experienced walkers with good navigation skills as it traverses some rough, pathless country: although these mountains are not especially high, the terrain is rocky and complex.

The route leads into the mountains from close-by the beautiful Uig Sands. Fine mountains surround you as you head up through wild and rugged Gleann Raonasgail on a broad Landrover track. The track is left behind and a series of rocky hills are traversed – including Mealaisbhal (574m) and Cracabhal (514m) – before you drop down to cross the Gleann Raonasgail/Glen Tamnasdail track. The route then climbs to the summit of Tamnasbhal (467m) before taking in the other summits on the eastern side of the glen: Teinneasabhal (497m), Tathabhal (515m) and Tarain (410m). The route descends back to the glen alongside the Allt Uamha Mhircil and rejoins the track through the glen. The Gleann Raonasgail track provides the short cut in either direction should you want to tackle the hills either side of the glen separately.

↑ *Climbing Tathabhal with Teinneasabhal behind*

Start/Finish	Track near a quarry past the Abhainn Dearg distillery south of Càrnais on the B8011 (NB 032 314)
Distance	25km (15½ miles); shorter walk via Gleann Raonasgail and eastern hills: 21km (13 miles); western hills and Gleann Raonasgail: 20.5km (12.75miles)
Total ascent	1691m (5548ft); shorter walk via Gleann Raonasgail and eastern hills: 1044m (3425ft); western hills and Gleann Raonasgail: 1075m (3527ft)
Time	8–9hrs; shorter walk via Gleann Raonasgail and eastern hills: 6–7hrs; western hills and Gleann Raonasgail: 5½–6½hrs
Maps	OS Explorer 458, OS Landranger 13
Public transport	Post bus 242/W4: ask to be let off just beyond the Càrnais turning
Note	If driving, park just beyond the cattle grid at NB 033 313

Pass the entrance to a gravel pit on the left then turn left onto the next track. Follow it uphill then down to the bridge crossing Abhainn Stocaill and pass around a locked gate. The track bends and climbs as the view opens up along Gleann Raonasgail. The track can be seen winding up to the pass between rocky hills framing either side of the glen.

> The Uig Hills are among the most rugged in the Outer Hebrides and are prime **golden eagle territory** – keep your eyes open for suspiciously large raptors hunting along the ridges.

Shorter walk via Gleann Raonasgail and eastern hills

To walk the hills on the eastern side of the glen only, continue up through Gleann Raonasgail to arrive at the high point of the pass – Bealach Raonasgail (263m) – after 8.5km, then follow the route description from the ascent to **Braigh Buidhe.**

Pass Loch Brinneabhal to your right and continue for about 300 metres to a rise in the track, which is a good point to strike out across country – the ground is boggy in places – and gain the east ridge

On the summit of Mealaisbhal

of **Brinneabhal**. Pass some ruined shielings en route to the summit of this modest hill (213m), which provides good views of Uig Sands to the north. From the top, head southwest along a vague ridge, losing height and passing just left of a small lochan. Cross an often boggy bealach beneath the craggy northern flank of Mealaisbhal, and climb steadily around the mountain's western side for 500 metres. Turn southeast to climb steeply up the mountain's boulder-strewn flank, making for a point on the north ridge between Mula Mac Sgiathain and the rocky summit of **Mealaisbhal** (574m).

From here the direct route south to the summit involves scrambling over boulders, but this can be avoided by following a vague cairn-marked grassy path winding its way through rocky terrain to just below and east of the summit, which is marked by a large cairn. On a clear day, the views from here are marvellous, taking in the Harris Hills to the southeast, the Flannan Isles and St Kilda to the west and Uig Sands to the north.

Leave the summit and descend the southeast ridge, picking your route carefully through the rocky terrain. Make for the horseshoe-shaped Loch Dubh

Gualainn an Fhirich sitting on the bealach at 293m (NB 030 259). From here you can either climb through the steeper rock on the northern slopes of Cracabhal, which looks more difficult than it actually is, or continue southwestwards from the col, keeping right of the loch. Pass to the right of another lochan, descend a broad gully then skirt beneath crags towards Loch Clibh Cracabhal (NB 022 253). Pass to the left of the loch then climb initially south to gain Cracabhal's west ridge. Climb northeastwards to reach the summit of **Cracabhal**, marked with a pile of stones (514m). Descend southwest through rocky, lochan-dotted terrain to reach Braigh Cracabhal (400m) between Cracabhal and Laibheal a Tuath (505m). Descend southeastwards into the head of Gleann Tamnasdail, making for the highest point of the ATV track (NB 035 245): the ground is rough and heathery on the descent.

Alternative route via Gleann Raonasgail

To return to the start without including the hills on the eastern side of the glen in your itinerary, turn left (north) and continue along the track through Gleann Raonasgail for 8.5km (5¼ miles).

Descending from the summit of Mealaisbhal with Cracabhal ahead (right) and Tamnashbhal and Teinneasabhal across Gleann Raonasgail

Looking north to Uig Sands from the summit of Tarain

Cross the track and climb steeply eastwards to the hummocky bealach at **Braigh Buidhe** (NB 039 245), with Coire Dhìobadail below to the east. From the bealach ascend the northwest ridge of **Tamnasbhal** to gain the summit at 467m, with dramatic views down to Loch Dhìobadail. Retrace your steps to Braigh Buidhe, then continue north-northeast past several small lochans, climbing steadily to the summit of **Teinneasabhal** (497m), marked with a cairn of pink and grey granite rocks. Descend northeastwards across easier terrain then gradually swing northwestwards towards some lochans atop the bealach (366m). Climb steeply northwards – following a grassy gully makes the going easier – to the cairn-marked summit of **Tathabhal** (515m), the highest hill on this side of the glen. Mealaisbhal looms directly across the glen and the views south to the Harris Hills and the west coast are magnificent.

Leave the summit bearing northeast, descending easier ground before gradually swinging north to Loch Mòr Braigh an Tarain (NB 050 269). Cross the outflow of the loch where it runs into a smaller lochan immediately to the east.

Continue north, climbing a gully along the right-hand side of a small burn before bearing right and continuing up through slabby rocks to the summit of **Tarain Mòr** (NB 051 277). There are great views north to Uig Sands. From the summit head northeast towards Creag Stiogh an Fhais before dropping down to the lochans immediately south of Cleite Adhamh (243m, NB 050 281). Descend west alongside Allt Uamha Mhircil and cross the Abhainn Caslabhat with care to regain the Gleann Raonasgail track and return to the start.

Uig Hills and coast backpack

ROUTE INFORMATION	
Start/Finish	Small lay-by near Mangarstadh (NB 013 307)
Alternative start/finish	NB 032 314 if travelling by bus
Total distance	40km (24¾ miles)
Total ascent	1140m (3740ft)
Total time	13–15½hrs
Maps	OS Explorer 458, OS Landranger 13
Public transport	Post bus 242/W4: ask to be let off 500 metres beyond the Càrnais turning. For the return, the W4 has scheduled stops at Brèinis, Islibhig and Mangarstadh: check timetables at www.cne-siar.gov.uk.

*T*his splendid two-day backpacking route in this most beautiful corner of Lewis, heads south through Gleann Raonasgail on a metalled ATV track before taking to the rocky ridge forming the glen's western flank.

In case of poor weather, or to make life easier, the toughest section of the route along the ridge can be avoided by following the ATV track right the way through Gleann Raonasgail to the bealach and then continuing down through Gleann Tamnasdail.

↑ *Climbing Mealaisbhal with Tarain (left) across Gleann Raonasgail and Suaineabhal beyond*

DAY 1

Mangarstadh to Tamna Siar

A series of rugged hills – including the summits of Mealaisbhal and Cracabhal – are traversed before you drop down to rejoin the track leading through Gleann Tamnasdail to the head of Loch Tamnabhaig. After descending the glen, a rough 4km walk along a wild and beautiful stretch of coastline brings the day to a conclusion with a wild camp at the head of the west-facing inlet of Tamna Siar.

ROUTE INFORMATION	
Start	Small lay-by near Mangarstadh (NB 013 307); NB 032 314 if travelling by bus
Finish	Head of Tamna Siar
Distance	19km (11¾ miles)
Ascent	890m (2920ft)
Time	7–8½hrs

From the small lay-by, walk back along the road for 2km to the ATV track near the gravel pit (NB 033 314). Turn right onto this track and climb gradually before descending to the bridge crossing Abhainn Stocaill. The track bends left, then right again (pass around a locked gate) as the view opens up through Gleann Raonasgail. The track can be seen winding up to the pass between the ridges of rocky hills framing either side of the glen. To continue along the route via the summits of Mealaisbhal and Cracabhal, follow Walk 46 as far as the highest point of the ATV track (NB 035 245) in **Gleann Tamnasdail**.

Alternative route via Gleann Raonasgail
Continue along the track, passing Loch Brinneabhal, Loch Mòr na Clibhe and Loch Reonasgail, as you climb towards the Bealach Raonasgail, the highest point of the ATV track (NB 035 244), squeezed between the rocky flanks of **Cracabhal** and **Teinneasabhal**.

Negotiating the rough path above Loch Tamnabhaigh

From the pass, follow the rather charmless track southwards as it descends through the glen to sea level, with fine views out across Loch Cheann Chuisil and Loch Tamnabhaigh to the distant Harris Hills. At the head of **Loch Cheann Chuisil**, by some ruined sheilings, the outflow of the Abhain Cheann Chuisil can be crossed to its west side by hopping across rocks. However, the river can be difficult to cross in spate, so it may be wise to cross higher up after heavy rain. Once you're across, continue around the edge of the loch just above the shore on the rough, heathery slopes beneath **Sgaladal**. (There are vague traces of path to begin with and these become more definite – greatly aiding progress.)

There is an exposed section of path by the small stony beach at the mouth of Gleann Sgaladail and a burn must also be crossed here. Beyond the next small bay, avoid the precipitously steep section of coastline by crossing up and over the neck of Meall Arsbaig to landward. Continue above the shore to the inlet of **Tamana Sear**. There are options for camping around the headland to the south of the inlet; Rubha Garbh enjoys fine views of the isle of Scarp and northwest Harris. Otherwise, cut across the neck of the headland from Tamana Sear, following the course of an old stone wall to the west-facing inlet of **Tamna Siar** (NB 007 200). A patch of grassy ground sits above the head of the inlet and it also benefits from a fresh water spring and plenty of driftwood. However, being west-facing, it's not ideal for camping if there's a gale blowing in off the Atlantic!

DAY 2

Tamna Siar to Mangarstadh

*T*he second day provides a superb coastal walk around to Mealasta, then on around the point of
Àird Bhrèinis and back to the starting point.

ROUTE INFORMATION	
Start	Head of Tamna Siar
Finish	Small lay-by near Mangarstadh (NB 013 307)
Distance	21km (13 miles)
Ascent	250m (820ft)
Time	6–7hrs

From Tamna Siar the way along the north side of the inlet is difficult and hazardous close to the shore, so climb to around 50m keeping a lookout for a vague path, which can be followed much of the way to the road head south of Mealasta. Pick your route carefully as there are some rocky sections to negotiate and the ground is rough, boggy and heathery: the

reward is in the dramatic coastal scenery. Continue around the coast to the inlet on the south side of the rocky headlands of Àird Dhrolaigeo and Àird Ghriamanais then follow the path cutting across the low-lying neck of the headlands. Emerging on the west coast of the Uig peninsula, there are splendid views across the narrow Caolas an Eilein onto Eilean Mhèalasta, with an appealing sandy beach at its northeastern end.

Carefully follow the path along and above the shore, traversing several rocky sections and crossing several burns. (The coastal scenery here is magnificent.) Eventually you will arrive at the road head near Mèalasta. Follow the single-track road north for around 2km, passing through **Mealasta** and continuing through a gateway before arriving at **Brèinis**. Leave the road and make for the low cliff

On the west coast of Uig looking across to Eilean Mhèalasta

Uig coastline

tops, passing around the outside of stock fencing close to the cliff edge. Continue around to the beach at Camas a' Mhoil and then strike out north across country, a little inland from the shore with Loch Greabhat to landward.

Make for a prominent cairn above the shore then bear northeast, inland a little, crossing a landscape of tiny lochans and passing to landward of Loch nan Faoileag. Continue northeast above the bay at **Camas Islibhig**, cross a small bridge, go through a stock gate and head northeast across country crossing a stock fence then crossing a shallow declivity before reaching the road again around NA 998 287. From here it's a 3km plod along the road back to the starting point, unless you can arrange a lift or coincide with the bus (hitch-hiking opportunities will be very few). The dullness of walking on tarmac is, however, enlivened by the splendid landscape around you.

WALK 48

West side coastal path

ROUTE INFORMATION

Start	Na Gearrannan (Garenin) blackhouse village (NB 193 442)
Finish	Bragar School (NB 288 476)
Distance	18km (11 miles)
Total ascent	536m (1755ft)
Time	5–6hrs
Terrain	Old cliff top paths, some boggy ground and track roads
Maps	OS Explorer 460, OS Landranger 8
Public transport	The West Side Circular bus route can be used to get to and from the start and finish: check timetables at www.cne-siar.gov.uk.
Note	The A858 runs parallel to the coast a few kilometres inland passing through the west side townships at regular intervals, so the route is never far from a road end and can be easily cut short.

This recently waymarked route follows old paths for much of its length, winding along the rugged clifftop landscape of northwest Lewis, taking in magnificent white sand beaches and dramatic coastal scenery en route. The going underfoot is generally good, with some boggy sections. There are a number of barbed wire stock fences to cross, especially during the latter half of the walk, and although these are crossed by stiles they are hazardous to negotiate with a dog.

Walk down through An Gearrannan blackhouse village, pass the last house on the right (and an information panel) and turn right through a gate. Pass some ruins and continue up along the coast following the green marker posts. Cross a stile and climb to Àird Mhòr: the highest point on the headland is marked with a small cairn and has spectacular views south along the coast. Continue east following the vague path, which stays inland from the steep cliffs.

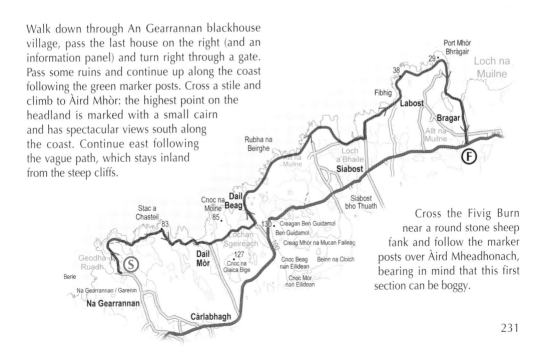

Cross the Fivig Burn near a round stone sheep fank and follow the marker posts over Àird Mheadhonach, bearing in mind that this first section can be boggy.

The path soon leads you past the impressive pinnacle-like **Stac a Chasteil** (NB 202 454) joined to the cliffs by a rocky arête.

A **blackhouse** was built on the stack between 200BC and AD200, with defensive walls protecting its approach from the clifftops.

The path now climbs a grassy slope between rocky outcrops, bearing inland slightly, following marker posts across boggy ground to a rocky knoll, from where Rubha an Trilleachain with its small natural arch can be seen to the northeast. The path descends across boggy ground to cross a stile near the cliffs then heads diagonally across the headland to cross another fence. Follow the path around the flank of Beinn Bheag, enjoying grand views of Bàgh Dhail Mòr, with the Atlantic rolling ashore and a cemetery perched above the beach. Descend grassy slopes towards the cemetery then bear right across the bridge to a parking area and toilets.

Go through a kissing gate by the cemetery and walk a short way up the road to an information board at a sharp bend. Leave the road and continue straight ahead along a boggy path between fences. Follow the marker posts up and over the high ground between **Cnoc na Moine** and Creag an Taghain before descending towards another fence with Loch Dailbheag coming into view. The path keeps to the right of the fence, climbing a little as Bàgh Dhail Beag comes into view. Where the fence turns sharply inland, don't continue through the gate straight ahead as this leads onto crofting land. Follow the fence then turn left to cross a stile. Follow the path down to a bridge over the Allt Dhaill Beag then up to the road, turn left and continue through **Dail Beag** towards the beach.

At the picnic site follow the marker posts indicating the footpath on the right – ignore the obvious path bearing left towards the coastline. Walk up the hillside to a stile, enjoying great views back across Dail Beag, the loch, beach and sea stacks. Continue across the easy ground of Tom Tolaige, Carnagil Bhàn and Druim Bratag; marker posts and red-painted stiles at regular intervals keep you on track. The coastline is impressive along this section of the

Garenin Blackhouse Village, nowadays a museum of traditional life on the isle of Lewis

Surf at Dalmore beach

route; Stac a' Phris (NB 233 472) has a large natural arch visible from the north while **Rubha na Beirghe** (NB 235 475) is a large, accessible promontory with the remains of a fortified dwelling.

Just inland of Rubha Caol (NB 243 477), the route passes over a wide arch between a deep geo on the left and an impressive blow hole on the right, which the sea funnels through at high tide. The route continues to seaward of fences enclosing croft land, following marker posts around Rubha Neidalt, along the western shore of Loch Shiaboist then across the causeway separating **Loch a' Bhaile** from the sea. Once across the causeway follow a minor road to a T-junction at Siabost bho Thuath. Turn left and head down to the end of the township road, passing through a gate and continuing northeast across a field to rejoin the coastline near a small bay. Follow the route across the easier ground to **Fibhig** (NB 268 487), then descend to cross a raised pebble bank.

Look out for marker posts along this section as the route continues back from the sea over level, boggy ground, crossing yet more stiles and a dry stone wall. The shoreline is regained where the coastline turns south towards Port Mhòr Bhràgair. Cross a stile and follow a grassy path above the shore, crossing the outflow of Loch Ordais by the shore if possible, otherwise using a wooden footbridge. Continue along a track running between the sandy bay of **Port Mhòr Bhràgair** and Loch Ordais before arriving at a picnic area by a minor road, which leads to a car park and cemetery nearby. Turn right and folllow the road to **Bragar**, keeping straight on at a crossroads in the village to reach the A858 and the bus route.

WALK 49

Tolstadh to Port Nis heritage walk

ROUTE INFORMATION

Start	Bail Ur Tholastaidh – New Tolsta (NB 532 486) or car park at NB 532 499
Finish	Eòropaidh (Europie) crossroads in Lìonal (NB 527 634)
Distance	22km (14 miles)
Total ascent	322m (1054ft)
Time	6–7hrs
Terrain	Cliff-top paths, very boggy in places
Maps	OS Explorer 460, OS Landranger 8
Public transport	The start and finish points of the walk are served by frequent bus services on weekdays and Saturdays. The W5 services to Tolsta depart from Stornoway bus station and take around forty minutes. The W1 service departs from the Europie road junction in Lìonal near Port of Ness and takes around an hour to Stornoway. For current timetables visit www.cne-siar.gov.uk.

*F*ollowing the course of an ancient route through moorland along the east coast of north Lewis, the Heritage Trail is full of historical interest and dramatic coastal scenery. However, the 'official' waymarked trail can be very boggy in places and it follows a course that often stays inland from the magnificent coastline, hence the route description given here strays from the waymarked path where safe and practical to do so.

Looking north along the coast from Lighe nan Leac

Walk to the end of the B895, cross a cattle grid and follow the road northwards with views across the sandy expanse of Traigh Mhòr towards Tolsta Head and across the Minch to the prominent summits of Assynt. As the road passes below Ben Geiraha the smaller beach of Tràigh Ghearadha comes into view. Continue northwards, crossing the 'Bridge to Nowhere' (NB 531 502) over the Abhainn Ghearadha.

Other than the track that this route follows for a while, the bridge is all that remains of **Lord Leverhulme's** scheme to push a road through to Port Nis after the First World War.

The track ends abruptly at a smaller bridge across the Abhainn na Cloich (NB 535 509), thereafter the waymarked route (green and yellow posts) is prone to bogginess. In good weather it is better to continue along the cliff tops following a well worn sheep path, which is both drier underfoot and affords better views of the coastline.

The next feature encountered is Dùn Othail (NB 543 515), a natural fortress nearly 60m high, which is separated from the clifftops by a steep ravine known as Nicolson's Leap. The route continues northeast, marker posts lead inland for around 500 metres to the west of Loch Dubh an Toa and **Lighe nan Leac**, then onwards to Loch Sgeireach na Creige Brist across the rolling moor. The path heads inland again to cross Gil an Tairbh and Gil Dibadale, which merge just before flowing into the sea at Cladach Dhìobadail. There are ruined sheilings at both **Àird Dhìobadail** and at Lower Dibadale (NB 554 546). Leaving Dhìobadail, follow the red-topped marker

posts on a short diversion from the route shown on the OS map. After 200 metres the routes converge again: from here it is probably best to stay with the main path, following the yellow-topped marker posts inland, if you want to avoid the difficult ground nearer the cliff tops beyond **Cellar Head** (Rubha an t-Selieir). However, the views are better along the clifftops if you're prepared to negotiate peat hags and tussocks and a steepish descent to cross a burn just before Filiscleitir.

Either way, the going becomes easier as **Filiscleitir** (NB 558 576) is approached.

Traditionally, people from the township of Lìonal use **Filiscleitir** for their airidhean where the women, children and cattle moved for the summer months to benefit from fresh moorland grass and relieve pressure on the croft land. The airidhean were also a popular place for courting, which resulted in many marriages between people from Ness and Tolstadh.

The main ruin on the cliff top is **Edgemoor Hall**, which was built as a place of worship by John Nicolson. He was born in Lìonal then emigrated to America where he married and joined the Plymouth Brethren. In the 1900s, Nicolson returned to Lewis with his wealthy and pious wife and they built a house on the cliff edge called Dune Tower, which was used as the chapel for the people of the airidhean. The Nicolsons conducted Sunday services here for many years and trawler crews from far and wide would land to take part: the psalm singing and the sound of the harmonium could be heard across the

Coig Peighinnean

Lìonal
Port of Ness/Port Nis
Allt Ruadh
Tàbost
Nis
Port Sgiogarstaigh
Sgiogarstaigh
107
North Minch
Cuidhsiadar
Edgemoor Hall
Filiscleitir
Cellar Head
123
Aird Dhìobadail
Loch Dubh a' Ghobha
100
Lighe nan Leac
'Bridge to nowhere'
Druim Dirìdean

Ruined chapel at Filiscleitir

moor. However, by the 1930s this era was at an end and Dune Tower lay empty.

From Filiscleitir the marker posts soon lead to a gravelled track, built by people from the townships long before Lord Leverhulme proposed his road from Ness to Tolsta; the track appears on OS maps from the middle of the 18th century. The summer shielings along the banks of the Abhainn Dubh at **Cuidhsiadar** (NB 545 562) show that local people still come out to enjoy the moor during the summer months, just like their ancestors. Continue to the road end at **Sgiogarstaigh**: if returning to Stornoway by bus, follow the road through the townships of Eòradal and **Lìonal** for 2.5km to reach the A857, turn left to arrive at the bus stop by the junction with the B8013 (signposted for Eòropaidh) after 300 metres.

Sheiling at Cuidhsiadar

ST KILDA

St Kilda is a group of small islands lying in the North Atlantic Ocean 66 kilometres (41 miles) northwest of North Uist. The islands are classified as outliers, with cultural links to the Outer Hebrides, but they are not part of the archipelago itself. Hirta (Scottish Gaelic: *Hiort*) is by far the largest island, at roughly 3.5km by 3km at its widest points, and with an area of 670 hectares. The island comprises two wide, amphitheatre-like bays, one north-facing (Glen Bay), the other south-facing (Village Bay), bounded by a serpentine ridge of hills. The highest point is Conachair, rising to 430m – its sheer northern flank is formed by the highest sea cliffs in the British Isles. There are three other islands in the archipelago: Dùn – which is separated from Hirta by a narrow channel – Soay and Boreray; as well as the immense sea stacks, Stac an Armin (196m) and Stac Lì (172m), which are the highest in the British Isles. Geologically the islands are the remnants of a long-extinct volcano, and are largely composed of Tertiary igneous granites and gabbro.

↑ *Cliffs on the north coast rising up to the summit of Conachair*

THE ST KILDA STORY

The St Kildans were an isolated community in more or less continuous occupation of their island domain for many hundreds of years, eking out a hard existence from the archipelago of remote, frequently storm-battered small islands and sea stacks that rise like jagged shards from the Atlantic Ocean. The St Kildans' life was tough, but they were a joyful people who loved to make music, sing, dance and play, while living from the land. The men abseiled barefoot down the sheer sea cliffs and climbed the vertiginous sea stacks to harvest sea birds and their eggs, which constituted a large part of the islanders' diet, while the women spun wool from the indigenous Soay sheep and tilled the sparse soil. Those who could work did so for the collective benefit of the entire population.

The undoing of the St Kildan idyll arrived on two fronts. Victorian tourism brought significant numbers of sightseers, who came to gawp at the aborigines whose heads were turned by the possibilities of commerce. They also brought diseases to which the islanders had little resistance.

Arguably more pernicious was the arrival of the Free Church of Scotland. A succession of ministers brought doctrine and the Sabbath and in return they eroded the islanders' joyfulness and took up time they could ill afford with religious observance. The St Kildans became increasingly reliant on supplies from outside and less able to meet their own needs from the land and sea, as migration, disease and high infant mortality took a grievous toll on the island population. The authorities failed to supply the regular supply ships that could have made the islanders' existence viable, and in 1930 the remaining population asked to be evacuated.

In 1957 work commenced on Hirta to establish a radar base, with barracks, roads, landing slip and other infrastructure. Since then, the island has had an itinerant population of military and civilian personnel at the base. In the same year St Kilda became a National Nature Reserve, with ownership transferred to the National Trust for Scotland. Today, there is a permanent NTS warden on Hirta and during the summer months volunteers and professionals work for the NTS, maintaining and restoring the island's built heritage. In 1987 St Kilda became a World Heritage Site for its natural history and latterly gained dual WHS status with the inclusion of its cultural heritage.

There are many theories about the origin of the name St Kilda, including cartographical error and the vagaries of pronunciation, but it is certain that the archipelago is not named after a saint bearing that name. Hirta may derive from the Gaelic for 'westland' or possibly the Old Norse for, variously, 'stag' 'herd' or 'shepherd'. Hirta was inhabited for perhaps 2000 years before it was evacuated. The physical remains of this settlement are most apparent on the south side of the island in the street of abandoned houses and the dikes, sheep fanks and *cleitan* – small, stone storage shelters unique to St Kilda, which were often used for storing harvested seabirds. By contrast, north-facing Gleann Mòr has only a scattering of *cleitan*. Although never permanently inhabited, the other islands and stacks were also used by the St Kildans for grazing the indigenous Soay sheep and for hunting seabirds.

St Kilda is a breeding ground for many important seabird species and has one of the world's largest colonies of northern gannets, numbering approximately 30,000 pairs. There are significant populations of Leach's petrels, Atlantic puffins and northern fulmars. The St Kilda wren is a subspecies of the Eurasian wren unique to the archipelago and the St Kilda field mouse is a subspecies of wood mouse found only in these islands.

WALK 50

The hills and sea cliffs of Hirta

ROUTE INFORMATION

Start/Finish	Village Bay pier (NF 102 991)
Distance	9.5km (6 miles) or 16km (10 miles)
Total ascent	720m (2362ft) or 1370m (4494ft)
Time	3½–4hrs or 5½–6hrs
Terrain	Grassy hills and rugged cliff tops, with a degree of avoidable exposure; some boggy ground
Maps	OS Explorer 460, Landranger 18

*T*he sea cliffs at Hirta's north, east and west are extremely high and steep and should be avoided in windy conditions and/or poor visibility. Avoid nesting birds: the island's great skuas or 'bonxies' will let you know if you're too near their nests by dive-bombing you with violent intent. If you have the time, energy and good weather it really is worth contemplating the longer variant route. Both can also be walked as two more leisurely excursions.

For travel to St Kilda see the 'Getting there' section in the general introduction.

Walking north to An Campar

239

From the pier, walk up the ramp and turn left along the road, passing assorted radar base buildings, then turn right and head up the grassy slope to the 'street' of houses forming the backbone of the abandoned village.

Five of the **houses** have roofs; one hosts a small museum and the others accommodate NTS volunteers.

Continue along the street until it peters out, bear right then cross the burn at the obvious point. Make for the gap in the head dike where the access road passes through.

Turn left and contour around the hillside, passing a number of cleits. Follow the faint path along the low cliffs, passing above several large dry stone walled enclosures. Make for the cliff top below the rocky outcrop on **Ruabhal** for views of the narrow channel and daunting cliffs separating Hirta from **Dùn**.

Climb to the west side of the rocky outcrop on Ruabhal to see the **Mistress Stone** – a curious rock window capped by a stone slab. There are fine views north and west along the cliff top ridge to Mullach Bi.

Continue north, soon climbing a steep grassy slope to join an access road, which passes the radar domes as the gradient eases. Pass a collection of cleits and reach a junction with the road climbing up from the village.

Overhanging rock at An Campar, looking on to the isle of Soay

Looking across Glen Bay to The Tunnel natural arch, with Boreray, Stac an Armin and Stac Lì beyond

Extension to An Campar

Turn left (west) off the road and cross the bealach at **Am Blaid** to the natural amphitheatre of **Gleann Mòr**. Follow the faint old track contouring initially westwards around the rim of the glen, passing by the rocky eminence of Claigeann Mòr where the path swings northwest to follow the cliff-top ridge. Pass a collection of cleits, which were likely used for storing harvested sea birds, and look out for a buttressed rock slab projecting out over the sheer sea cliffs.

According to tradition, the young men of Hirta performed a **ritual** on the Lover's Stone before they could marry. They would balance on their left foot on the outer edge of the rock with their right foot dangling over the abyss then bend down and make a fist over their feet. This balancing act demonstrated their agility on the rocks, proving they were able to provide for a family by climbing the cliffs to catch the birds integral to the islanders' diet.

Continue along the ridge with care; climb up through rocky ground to the high point of **Mullach Bi** (358m).

This makes for a **magnificent vantage point**: to the southeast the ridge descends in a series of rocky outcrops over the gap to Dùn with Bioda Mòr as its jagged apex, the whole resembling nothing so much as a dragon's tail. To the northeast, Conachair rises above Mullach Mòr and to the northwest the island of Soay appears beyond the An Campar headland.

Continue northwards with care, picking a route down along the rock-studded ridge. At the narrow neck of the headland, bear left to continue around the cliff-top. The view back along the cliffs is mightily impressive. Climb up to the high point of **An Campar**.

Here the **view** across to Soay and the stacks in the sound is dramatic to say the least. Looking back across An Campar, Gleann Mòr is framed to the left by Mullach Mòr and the right by Mullach Bi; 8km to the northeast lies Boreray and her twin sentinels, Stac Lì and Stac an Armin.

Continue around the headland back to the neck then contour above the western side of Glen Bay, which gives a good view of The Tunnel – an impressively proportioned rock arch through the **Gob na h-Àirde** headland framing the eastern side of the bay. Follow the cliff top above a natural amphitheatre above the bay. (This is the domain of fulmars and puffins; taking a perch to watch these birds in action is an absolute joy.) Continue contouring above the bay until you find an easy route heading southeast down into **Gleann Mòr**. Don't descend too far, but contour around at 100m making for some ruined sheilings, enclosures and cleits. Keep contouring southeastwards and cross the Abhainn a' Ghlinne Mhòir where easiest. Begin the long climb out of the glen heading southeast back towards the bealach at **Am Blaid** – a vague path runs past a line of cleits running up to the bealach. At the top of the climb, rejoin the road and turn left.

The road winds its way up to the radar station with its domes and pylons atop **Mullach Mòr**. From the northernmost tower descend a short way east to the bealach before making the stiff 100m climb to the summit of **Conachair** (430m).

The **summit** is marked by a small stone and mortar cairn – an OS trig point lies to the south, 65m below the summit. The views are astounding in every direction – should you be blessed with good visibility.

Looking down from the flank of Conachair on to Village Bay with Dùn at its southwest

Looking on to Oisebhal from Conachair; the hillside is dotted with cleits and a collection of elaborate sheep fanks sit in the hollow of An Lag

From the summit descend southeastwards.

Take great care in poor visibility, as the **north flank of Conachair** is the highest sea cliff in the British Isles. On the descent you may find the buckled propellers of a second world war Bristol Beaufighter that crashed here in 1943.

In good visibility it's worth making a detour along the narrow and steep-sided Aird Uachdarachd promontory jutting northeastwards from the north flank of Conachair. This is a great vantage point for breathtaking views onto the magnificent sea cliffs.

Follow the cliff tops around with care and continue down to **The Gap** – the low point between Conachair and the neighbouring hill, Oisebhal. Note that the east side of The Gap is a sheer drop to the sea.

Climb with care along the cliff top to the summit of **Oisebhal** (293m).

Enjoy more **incredible views** – this a great spot for a bird's eye view of the village and its collection of cleits and dikes, as well as across Village Bay to Dùn.

When you're done with the views, retrace your steps back to The Gap – descending west or southwest from the summit is very steep and awkward. From The Gap, descend southwest towards the village passing some remarkable dry stone walled sheep fanks. Follow the course of the burn down to the obvious gap in the head dike, which forms the landward perimeter of the village. Hopefully you'll have plenty of time to explore the village before you have to return to the start of the walk.

APPENDIX A

Route summary table

ROUTE	START/FINISH	DISTANCE	ASCENT	TIME	PAGE
ISLAY					
Walk 1	Bunnahabhain (NR 418 734)	20km (12½ miles)	648m (2126ft)	7–8hrs	42
Walk 2	Ballygrant (NR 396 663)	Ballygrant to An Cladach: 8km (5 miles); Beinn Bheigier circuit: 16km (10 miles)	1035m (3400ft)	Ballygrant to An Cladach 2–2½hrs; Beinn Bheigier circuit: 5–6hrs	46
Walk 3	Ardnave Loch (NR 287 728)	7.25km (4½ miles)	80m (260ft)	2½–3hrs	49
JURA					
Walk 4	Start: Ardlussa (NR 650 880) or Kinuachdrachd Harbour (NR 705 982) Finish: Tarbert (NR 607 823)	51–64km (31½–39¾ miles)	1966–1616m (6450–5302ft)	3–4 days	53
Day 1	Start: Ardlussa (NR 650 880) or Kinuachdrachd Harbour (NR 705 982)	26km (16 miles) or 13km (8 miles)	845m (2772ft) or 525m (1722ft)	8–9½hrs or 5–6hrs	54
Day 2	Start: Glengarrisdale Bothy (NR 644 969)	17.5km (10¾ miles)	663m (2175ft)	7–9hrs	57
Day 3	Start: Shian Bay (NR 531 875)	13km (8¼ miles)	294m (964ft)	5–6hrs	60
Day 4	Start: Cruib Lodge bothy (NR 567 829)	6.5km (4 miles)	172m (564ft)	2–2½hrs	63
Walk 5	A846 northeast of Three Arch Bridge (NR 550 732)	17km (11 miles)	1500m (5000ft)	8–9hrs	64
Walk 6	Ardlussa (NR 646 879)	24km (15 miles)	1050m (3444ft)	6–7hrs	67
Walk 7	A846 northeast of Three Arch Bridge (NR 550 732)	18km (11 miles)	655m (2050ft) or 525m (1722ft)	6–7hrs	70
SCARBA					
Walk 8	Poll na h-Ealaidh (NM 720 060)	9.7km (6 miles) or 10.5km (6½ miles)	589m (1932ft) or 585m (1920ft)	4–5hrs	74
COLONSAY					
Walk 9	Scalasaig (NR 395 941)	27.5km (17 miles); shortcut to Scalasaig: 23km (14¼ miles)	368m (1207ft)	6½–7½hrs	78
Walk 10	Start: Port Mòr (NR 362 948) Finish: Kiloran Bay (NR 397 977)	7.75km (4¾ miles); with Carnan Eoin: 10.75km (6½ miles)	604m (1981ft) or 744m (2440ft)	2½–3hrs or 3–3½hrs	82
THE GARVELLACHS					
Walk 11	Landing jetty at NM 669 117	5.75km 3½ miles)	256m (840ft)	2–2½hrs	87

ROUTE	START/FINISH	DISTANCE	ASCENT	TIME	PAGE
MULL					
Walk 12	Bridge over Scarisdale river (NR 517 376)	14.5km (9 miles) or 9.25km (5¾ miles)	1255m (4118ft) or 951m (3120ft)	7–8hrs or 3½–5hrs	90
Walk 13	Glen Forsa (NM 596 426)	18km (11¼ miles)	748m (2454ft)	5–6hrs	94
Walk 14	Carsaig pier (NR 545 213)	13.25km (8¼ miles)	85m (279ft)	5½–6hrs	97
Walk 15	Lane off A849 (NM 727 350)	15km (9¼ miles) or 20km (12.5miles) or 27.5km (17 miles)	843m (4300ft) or 898m (2945ft) or 1070m (3510ft)	4–5hrs or 5–6hrs or 7–8½hrs	100
ULVA					
Walk 16	The Boathouse, Ulva (NM 444 398)	11km (7 miles)	311m (1020ft)	3½–4½hrs	104
IONA					
Walk 17	Iona ferry pier (NM 286 240)	13km (8 miles) or 9km (5½ miles)	345m (1130ft) or 180m (590ft)	4–5hrs or 3½–4½hrs	108
COLL					
Walk 18	Coll RSPB Nature Reserve (NM 151 538)	14.5km (9 miles)	205m (670ft)	4–5hrs	112
TIREE					
Walk 19	Balephetrish Farm (NM 013 474)	22.5km (14 miles) or 13km (8 miles)	166m (545ft)	5½–6hrs or 3–4hrs	116
Walk 20	Hynish (NL 985 393)	30km (18¾ miles), 9.25km (5¾ miles) or 21km (13 miles)	736m (2415ft), 335m (1100ft) or 401m (1315ft)	7½–8½hrs, 3–3½hrs or 4½–5hrs	119
RUM					
Walk 21	By Kinloch Castle (NM 402 994)	27km (17 miles); to Dibidil bothy: 18.5km (11.5 miles)	2025m (6645ft)	9–10hrs: to Dibidil bothy: 6–7hrs	124
Walk 22	Start: Kinloch ferry; Finish: Harris Bay (NM 339 957) or Kinloch ferry	29km (17½ miles) or (11½ miles)	1296m (4050ft) or 945m (3100ft)	10–12hrs or 7–8½hrs	129
Walk 23	Guirdil bothy (NG 320 014)	9km (5½ miles) or 14.5km (9 miles)	867m (2848ft) or 1087m (3568ft)	4½–5½hrs or 5½–6½hrs	133
EIGG					
Walk 24	Galmisdale pier (NM 484 838)	11km (7 miles) or 8km (5 miles)	540m (1770ft) or 393m (1290ft)	4–5hrs or 3–3½hrs	139
CANNA					
Walk 25	A'Chill (NG 272 053)	20km (12½ miles), 10.5km (6½ miles) or 15.25km (9½ miles)	750m (2460ft), 422m (1385 ft)or 607m (2000 ft)	7–8½hrs, 3–3.5hrs or 4½–5½hrs	142
MUCK					
Walk 26	Port Mòr (NM 422 794)	11.5km (7¼ miles)	442m (1450ft)	4–4½hrs	147

ROUTE	START/FINISH	DISTANCE	ASCENT	TIME	PAGE
SKYE					
Walk 27	Sligachan (NG 487 298)	13km (8 miles) or 11km (6¾ miles)	1280m (4200ft) or 933m (3061ft)	5–6hrs	151
Walk 28	Sligachan (NG 487 298)	13km (8 miles)	762m (2500ft)	5hrs	154
Walk 29	Car park on the B8083 Broadford–Elgol road (NG 561 216)	8km (5 miles)	990m (3248ft)	5–6hrs	157
Walk 30	Elgol (NG 520 139)	6km (3¾ miles) each way	183m (600ft) each way	2–2½hrs each way	160
Walk 31	Sligachan (NG 487 298) or Camasunary Bay (NG 516 188)	23.25km (14½ miles), 23.75km (14¾ miles) or 12 miles	785m (2575ft), 683m (2244ft) or 826m (2710ft)	7–9hrs or 5½–7hrs	163
Walk 32	Sligachan (NG 486 298)	14km (8¾ miles)	960m (3150ft)	5–7hrs	169
Walk 33	Orbost Farm (NG 257 431)	20km (12½ miles)	1090m (3575ft)	7–8hrs	171
Walk 34	Start: A855 parking area by Loch Leathan NG 495 510 Finish: A855 near Flodigarry NG 464 710	27.5km (17 miles)	1800m (5906ft)	10–11hrs	174
RAASAY					
Walk 35	Churchton Bay pier (NG 545 362)	22km (13¾ miles) or 14km (8¾ miles)	823m (2700ft) or 533m (1750ft)	7½–8½hrs or 4–5hrs	179
BARRA					
Walk 36	Car park between Castlebay and Brèibhig (NL 679 987)	16km (10 miles) or 6km (3.75 miles)	1036m (3400ft) or 505m (1656ft)	5½–7hrs or 2½–3hrs	183
SOUTH UIST					
Walk 37	Howmore (Tobha Mòr) (NF 756 364)	35km (21¾ miles) or 42km (26 miles)	1680m (5512ft) or 1985m (6513ft)	13–14½hrs or 16–19hrs	187
Day 1	Howmore (Tobha Mòr) (NF 756 364)	20km (12½ miles) or 23.5km (14½ miles)	1680m (5512ft) or 1985m (6513ft)	7½–8½hrs or 9–11hrs	188
Day 2	Bealach above Gleann Uisinis (NF 817 340) or Usinish bothy (NF 849 333)	15km (9¼ miles) or 18.5km (11½ miles)	652m (2140ft) or 942m (3090ft)	5½–6hrs or 7–8hrs	191
NORTH UIST					
Walk 38	Cladach Chairinis road end (NF 856 589)	12km (7½ miles)	475m (1558ft)	4½–5½hrs	194
Walk 39	Car park off the A865 at Greinetobht (NF 819 756)	11.5km (7 miles)	100m (328ft)	4–5hrs	197

ROUTE	START/FINISH	DISTANCE	ASCENT	TIME	PAGE
BERNERAY					
Walk 40	Berneray Community Hall car park (NF 909 813)	17km (10½ miles)	175m (574ft)	4–5hrs	200
HARRIS					
Walk 41	Rodel church (NG 048 832)	8km (5 miles)	490m (1600ft)	3–3½hrs	204
Walk 42	Bridge over Abhainn Scaladail (NB 183 099)	13.5km (8½ miles)	1065m (3450ft)	6–7hrs	207
Walk 43	Abhainn Suidhe (NB 053 078)	32km (20 miles)	2050m (6726ft)	15½–17½hrs	210
Day 1	Start: Abhainn Suidhe (NB 053 078)	16km (10 miles)	1000m (3281ft)	8–9hrs	211
Day 2	Start: Ceann Loch Reasoirt (NB 107 172)	16km (10 miles)	1050m (3445ft)	7½–8½hrs	214
Walk 44	Huisinis (NA 993 121)	14km (9 miles)	825m (2700ft)	5–6hrs	216
Walk 45	Southern end of Lochanan Lacasdail (NB 183 004)	16.5km (10.25 miles), 19km (12 miles) or 20.25km (12.75 miles)	968m (3175ft), 1029m (3370ft) or 831m (2720ft)	5–6hrs, 6–7hrs or 6–7hrs	219
LEWIS					
Walk 46	South of Càrnais (NB 033 313)	25km (15½ miles), 21km (13 miles) or 20.5km (12.75 miles)	1691m (5548ft), 1044m (3425ft) or 1075m (3527ft)	8–9hrs, 6–7hrs or 5½–6½hrs	222
Walk 47	Lay-by near Mangarstadh (NB 013 307)	40km (24¾ miles)	1140m (3740ft)	13–15½hrs	226
Day 1	Lay-by near Mangarstadh (NB 013 307)	19km (11¾ miles)	890m (2920ft)	7–8½hrs	227
Day 2	Tamana Siar (NB 007 200)	21km (13 miles)	250m (820ft)	6–7hrs	229
Walk 48	Start: Garenin (NB 193 442) Finish: Bragar School (NB 288 476)	18km (11 miles)	536m (1755ft)	5–6hrs	231
Walk 49	Start: New Tolsta (NB 532 486) Finish: Lìonal (NB 527 634)	22km (14 miles)	322m (1054ft)	6–7hrs	234
ST KILDA					
Walk 50	Village Bay (NF 102 991)	9.5km (6 miles) or 16km (10 miles)	720m (2362ft) or 1370m (4494ft)	3½–4hrs or 5½–6hrs	239

APPENDIX B

Glossary

GAELIC	ENGLISH	GAELIC	ENGLISH
abhainn	river	*eas*	waterfall
aird	height, promontory	*eilean*	island
airidhean	pasture	*feisean*	festival
allt	burn, stream	*garbh*	rough
bàgh	bay	*geo*	steep-sided inlet
beag	small	*glas*	grey, green
bealach	pass, gorge	*gleann*	glen, valley
beinn	mountain, peak	*lagg*	hollow
bhàin	white	*lochan*	small loch
buidhe	yellow	*machair*	grassy coastal plain
caisteal	castle	*maol*	round hill
camas	bay	*mòr, mhor*	big
caolais	kyle, strait, sound	*port*	port, harbour, ferry
cladach	beach, shore, coast	*rhubha*	promontory, headland, point
cleit	small stone storage shelter	*sgurr*	peak
cnoc	round hill, knoll	*stac*	sea stack
creag	crag, rock, cliff	*taiga, tigh*	house
cruach	stack, heap	*tràigh*	beach
dearg	red	*uaimh/uamh*	cave
druim	ridge	*uisge*	water
dubh	black		
dùin, dùn	fort		

APPENDIX C

Useful contacts

General

Maps
Ordnance Survey www.ordnancesurvey.co.uk

Harvey Maps www.harveymaps.co.uk

Weather
The Mountain Weather Information Service (MWIS)
www.mwis.org.uk

Scotland Avalanche Information Service (SAIS)
www.sais.gov.uk

Bothies
Mountain Bothies Association (MBA)
www.mountainbothies.org.uk

Hostels
Gatliff Trust and hostels
(Bernery, South Uist and Harris)
www.gatliff.org.uk

Ferries
Caledonian MacBrayne (CalMac)
www.calmac.co.uk or tel 08000 665000

Airlines
British Midland www.flybmi.com
or tel 0870 6070555

Flybe www.flybe.com

Hebridean Air www.hebrideanair.com
or tel 0845 805 7465

Rail links
National Rail Enquiries www.nationalrail.co.uk

ScotRail www.scotrail.co.uk

Coach links
Citylink www.citylink.co.uk

Buses
Comhairle na Eilean Siar www.cne-siar.gov.uk/travel

Islay

Local transport
Islay Coaches tel 01496 840273

Camping
Port Mòr campsite tel 01496 850441

Kintra Farm campsite tel 01496 302051

Stalking
During the deer stalking season (1 July–15 February)
contact the Dunlossit Estate office (01496 840232)

Jura

Local transport
Argyll and Bute Council operates between
Port Askaig (Islay) and Feolin Ferry:
www.argyll-bute.gov.uk, tel 01496 840681.

A summertime Rigid Inflatable Boat (RIB) ferry runs
between Tayvallich and Craighouse:
www.jurapassengerferry.com, tel 07668 450000.

Jura Bus:
www.garelochheadcoaches.co.uk,
tel 01436 810200.

Stalking
From 1 July–15 February contact the head stalkers:

Tarbert Estate, tel 01496 820207

Ardlussa Estate, tel 01496 820323

Barnhill Estate, tel 01496 820327

Ruantallain Estate, tel 01496 820827

Scarba

Local transport
Farsain Cruises operate from Craobh Haven Marina:
contact Duncan Philips, tel 07880 714165

The Garvellachs

Local transport
Farsain Cruises operate from Craobh Haven Marina:
contact Duncan Philips, tel 07880 714165

Colonsay

Amenities
The Colonsay Hotel (accommodation and meals),
tel 01951 200316 or 200312

The Pantry Café, tel 01951 200325

Colonsay General Store, tel 01951 200265

Mull

Camping
Fidden Farm nr Fionnphort, tel 01681 700427

The Sheilings, Craignure, tel 01680 812496

Ulva

Local transport
Ferry from Ulva Ferry on demand 9am–5pm
weekdays (not Saturdays) Easter – end of September:
Sundays, June–August: tel 01688 500226
(mobile 07919 902407)

Amenities
The Boathouse licensed tea room
(from Easter – end of September)
www.isleofulva.com

Coll

Camping
Garden House, tel 01879 230374

Amenities
Island Stores, tel 01879 230484

Coll Hotel (accommodation and meals),
tel 01879 230334

Tiree

Local transport
497 dial-a-ride bus service: tel 01879 220419 –
must be booked in advance

Rum

Accommodation
Rum Bunkhouse bunkhouse@isleofrum.com,
tel 01687 460318

Stalker's Bothy,
tel 01687 462030 or 07768 249833

Camping cabins rumkabins@gmail.com

Other camping www.isleofrum.com

Stalking
From mid-August–mid-February notify the head
stalker, tel 01687 462030

Skye

Camping
Torvaig campsite, Portree, tel 01478 611849

Glen Brittle campsite, tel 01478 640404
(April to September) or 01470 521845

Staffin campsite, tel 01470 562213

Barra

Camping
Borve Camping, tel 01871 810878

Other camping www.isleofbarra.com

South Uist

Camping
Kilbride campsite, tel 01878 700568

Gleanndal campsite, tel 01878 700545

North Uist

Camping
Balranald campsite, tel 01876 510304

Moorcroft (camping and bunkhouse),
tel 01876 580305

Harris

Camping
Lickisto campsite, tel 01859 530485

Horgabost campsite, tel 01859 550386

Lewis

Camping
Ardroil campsite, tel 01851 672248

Cnip campsite, tel 07542 142750

St Kilda

Local transport
From Leverburgh, Harris:
Sea Harris www.seaharris.co.uk, tel 01859 502007

From Miavaig, Lewis:
MV Cuma (four and six-day cruises)
www.island-cruising.com, tel 01851 672381

Camping
Must be arranged in advance with the National
Trust for Scotland (NTS): tel 0844 493 2237,
www.nts.org.uk, www.kilda.org.uk

APPENDIX D

Further reading

JM Boyd and IM Boyd *The Hebrides* (Collins, 1990)

Irvine Butterfield *Dibidil: A Hebridean Adventure* (MBA, 2010)

David Caldwell *Islay, Jura and Colonsay* (Birlinn, 2002)

John L Campbell *Canna: The Story of a Hebridean Island* (Birlinn, 2002)

Roger Deakin *Waterlog* (Chatto and Windus, 1999)

Camille Dressler *Eigg: The Story of an Island* (Birlinn, 2007)

Peter Friend *Scotland* (Collins, 2012)

Mary Harman *An Isle Called Hirte* (Maclean Press, 1997)

David J Horne *The Geology of Jura* (DGB Wright, Isle of Jura)

Kathleen Jamie *Findings* (Sort Of Books, 2012)

Kathleen Jamie *Sightlines* (Sort Of Books, 2005)

Andrew Jefford *Peat Smoke and Spirit* (Headline, 2005)

John Love *Rum: A Landscape Without Figures* (Birlinn, 2002)

John Love *A Natural History of St Kilda* (Birlinn, 2009)

Angus Macdonald and Patricia Macdonald *The Hebrides: An Aerial Survey of a Culltural Landscape* (Birlinn, 2010)

Magnus Magnusson *Rum: Nature's Island* (Luath, 1997)

John Mercer *Hebridean Islands: Colonsay, Gigha, Jura* (Blackie, 1974)

Norman S Newton *Skye* (David and Charles, 2007)

Adam Nicolson *Sea Room* (HarperCollins, 2002)

Roger Redfern *Walking in the Hebrides* (Cicerone Press, 1998)

Francis Thompson *Lewis and Harris* (Pevensey, 2007)

Peter Youngson *Jura: Island of Deer* (Birlinn, 2001)

The Island of Two Harvests (Tiree and Coll Gaelic Partnership, 2008)

Spirit of Jura (Polygon, 2009)

All of the principal Hebridean isles and a number of the smaller ones are covered in greater detail by several Cicerone area walking guides:

Walking on Harris and Lewis by Richard Barrett

Walking on Jura, Islay and Colonsay by Peter Edwards

Walking on Rum and the Small Isles by Peter Edwards

The Isle of Skye by Terry Marsh

The Isle of Mull by Terry Marsh

Walking on the Uists and Barra by Mike Townsend

Heading south from Corpach Bay, west coast of Jura (Walk 4)

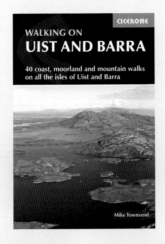
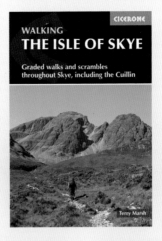

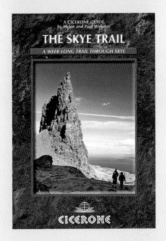
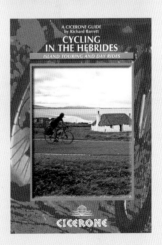

LISTING OF CICERONE GUIDES

The Danube Cycleway Vol 1
The Grand Traverse of the Massif Central
The Moselle Cycle Route
The Rhine Cycle Route
The Way of St James

AFRICA
Climbing in the Moroccan Anti-Atlas
Kilimanjaro
Mountaineering in the Moroccan High Atlas
The High Atlas
Trekking in the Atlas Mountains
Walking in the Drakensberg

ALPS – CROSS-BORDER ROUTES
100 Hut Walks in the Alps
Across the Eastern Alps: E5
Alpine Points of View
Alpine Ski Mountaineering
  1 Western Alps
  2 Central and Eastern Alps
Chamonix to Zermatt
Snowshoeing
Tour of Mont Blanc
Tour of the Matterhorn
Trekking in the Alps
Trekking in the Silvretta and Rätikon Alps
Walking in the Alps
Walks and Treks in the Maritime Alps

PYRENEES AND FRANCE/SPAIN CROSS-BORDER ROUTES
Rock Climbs in the Pyrenees
The GR10 Trail
The GR11 Trail – La Senda
The Mountains of Andorra
The Pyrenean Haute Route
The Pyrenees
The Way of St James: France & Spain
Walks and Climbs in the Pyrenees

AUSTRIA
The Adlerweg
Trekking in Austria's Hohe Tauern
Trekking in the Stubai Alps
Trekking in the Zillertal Alps
Walking in Austria

BELGIUM AND LUXEMBOURG
Walking in the Ardennes

EASTERN EUROPE
The High Tatras
The Mountains of Romania
Walking in Bulgaria's National Parks
Walking in Hungary

FRANCE
Chamonix Mountain Adventures
Ecrins National Park
Mont Blanc Walks
Mountain Adventures in the Maurienne
The Cathar Way
The GR20 Corsica
The GR5 Trail
The Robert Louis Stevenson Trail
Tour of the Oisans: The GR54
Tour of the Queyras
Tour of the Vanoise
Trekking in the Vosges and Jura
Vanoise Ski Touring
Via Ferratas of the French Alps
Walking in Corsica

Walking in Provence – East
Walking in Provence – West
Walking in the Auvergne
Walking in the Cevennes
Walking in the Dordogne
Walking in the Haute Savoie –North & South
Walking in the Languedoc
Walking in the Tarentaise and Beaufortain Alps
Walks in the Cathar Region

GERMANY
Germany's Romantic Road
Hiking and Biking in the Black Forest
Walking in the Bavarian Alps

HIMALAYA
Annapurna
Bhutan
Everest
Garhwal and Kumaon
Langtang with Gosainkund and Helambu
Manaslu
The Mount Kailash Trek
Trekking in Ladakh
Trekking in the Himalaya

ICELAND & GREENLAND
Trekking in Greenland
Walking and Trekking in Iceland

IRELAND
Irish Coastal Walks
The Irish Coast to Coast Walk
The Mountains of Ireland

ITALY
Gran Paradiso
Sibillini National Park
Shorter Walks in the Dolomites
Through the Italian Alps
Trekking in the Apennines
Trekking in the Dolomites
Via Ferratas of the Italian Dolomites: Vols 1 & 2
Walking in Abruzzo
Walking in Italy's Stelvio National Park
Walking in Sardinia
Walking in Sicily
Walking in the Central Italian Alps
Walking in the Dolomites
Walking in Tuscany
Walking in Umbria
Walking on the Amalfi Coast
Walking the Italian Lakes

MEDITERRANEAN
Jordan – Walks, Treks, Caves, Climbs
  and Canyons
The Ala Dag
The High Mountains of Crete
The Mountains of Greece
Treks and Climbs in Wadi Rum
Walking in Malta
Western Crete

NORTH AMERICA
British Columbia
The Grand Canyon
The John Muir Trail
The Pacific Crest Trail

SOUTH AMERICA
Aconcagua and the Southern Andes
Hiking and Biking Peru's Inca Trails
Torres del Paine

SCANDINAVIA
Walking in Norway

SLOVENIA, CROATIA AND MONTENEGRO
The Islands of Croatia
The Julian Alps of Slovenia
The Mountains of Montenegro
Trekking in Slovenia
Walking in Croatia
Walking in Slovenia: The Karavanke

SPAIN AND PORTUGAL
Costa Blanca: West
Mountain Walking in Southern Catalunya
The Mountains of Central Spain
The Mountains of Nerja
The Northern Caminos
Trekking through Mallorca
Walking in Madeira
Walking in Mallorca
Walking in Menorca
Walking in the Algarve
Walking in the Cordillera Cantabrica
Walking in the Sierra Nevada
Walking on Gran Canaria
Walking on La Gomera and El Hierro
Walking on La Palma
Walking on Lanzarote and Fuerteventura
Walking on Tenerife
Walking the GR7 in Andalucia
Walks and Climbs in the Picos de Europa

SWITZERLAND
Alpine Pass Route
Central Switzerland
The Bernese Alps
The Swiss Alps
Tour of the Jungfrau Region
Walking in the Valais
Walking in Ticino
Walks in the Engadine

TECHNIQUES
Geocaching in the UK
Indoor Climbing
Lightweight Camping
Map and Compass
Mountain Weather
Moveable Feasts
Outdoor Photography
Polar Exploration
Rock Climbing
Sport Climbing
The Book of the Bivvy
The Hillwalker's Guide to Mountaineering
The Hillwalker's Manual

MINI GUIDES
Alpine Flowers
Avalanche!
Navigating with a GPS
Navigation
Pocket First Aid and Wilderness Medicine
Snow

MOUNTAIN LITERATURE
8000 metres
A Walk in the Clouds
Unjustifiable Risk?

For full information on all our guides, books and eBooks, visit our website:
www.cicerone.co.uk.

Walking – Trekking – Mountaineering – Climbing – Cycling

Over 40 years, Cicerone have built up an outstanding collection of 300 guides, inspiring all sorts of amazing adventures.

Every guide comes from extensive exploration and research by our expert authors, all with a passion for their subjects. They are frequently praised, endorsed and used by clubs, instructors and outdoor organisations.

All our titles can now be bought as **e-books** and many as iPad and Kindle files and we will continue to make all our guides available for these and many other devices.

Our website shows any **new information** we've received since a book was published. Please do let us know if you find anything has changed, so that we can pass on the latest details. On our **website** you'll also find some great ideas and lots of information, including sample chapters, contents lists, reviews, articles and a photo gallery.

It's easy to keep in touch with what's going on at Cicerone, by getting our monthly **free e-newsletter**, which is full of offers, competitions, up-to-date information and topical articles. You can subscribe on our home page and also follow us on **Facebook** and **Twitter**, as well as our **blog**.

Cicerone – the very best guides for exploring the world.

CICERONE

2 Police Square Milnthorpe Cumbria LA7 7PY
Tel: 015395 62069 info@cicerone.co.uk
www.cicerone.co.uk